And the New . . .

Books by Thomas Hauser

General Non-Fiction

Missing
The Trial of Patrolman Thomas Shea
For Our Children (with Frank Macchiarola)
The Family Legal Companion
Final Warning: The Legacy of Chernobyl (with Dr. Robert Gale)
Arnold Palmer: A Personal Journey
Confronting America's Moral Crisis (with Frank Macchiarola)
Healing: A Journal of Tolerance and Understanding
Miscellaneous
With This Ring (with Frank Macchiarola)
A God To Hope For

Boxing Non-Fiction

The Black Lights: Inside the World of Professional Boxing
Muhammad Ali: His Life and Times
Muhammad Ali: Memories
Muhammad Ali: In Perspective
Muhammad Ali & Company
A Beautiful Sickness
A Year At The Fights
Brutal Artistry
The View From Ringside
Chaos, Corruption, Courage, and Glory
The Lost Legacy of Muhammad Ali
I Don't Believe It, But It's True
Knockout (with Vikki LaMotta)
The Greatest Sport of All
The Boxing Scene
An Unforgiving Sport
Boxing Is . . .
Box: The Face of Boxing
The Legend of Muhammad Ali (with Bart Barry)
Winks and Daggers
And the New . . .

Fiction

Ashworth & Palmer
Agatha's Friends
The Beethoven Conspiracy
Hanneman's War
The Fantasy
Dear Hannah
The Hawthorne Group
Mark Twain Remembers
Finding The Princess
Waiting For Carver Boyd

For Children

Martin Bear & Friends

And the New...

An Inside Look at Another Year in Boxing

Thomas Hauser

The University of Arkansas Press
Fayetteville
2012

ISBN-10: 1-55728-986-7
ISBN-13: 978-1-55728-986-5
E-ISBN: 978-1-61075-500-9

14   13   12   11   10   5   4   3   2   1

⊗ The paper used in this publication meets the minimum requirements of the
American National Standard for Permanence of Paper for Printed Library Materials
Z39.48–1984.

Library of Congress Cataloging-in-Publication Data

Hauser, Thomas.
    And the new— an inside look at another year in boxing / Thomas Hauser.
        p. cm.
    Includes bibliographical references.
    ISBN 978-1-55728-986-5 (pbk. : alk. paper)
    1. Boxing. I. Title.
    GV1133.H33 2012
    796.83—dc23

                                                                            2012014026

For Ruby Chapman

welcome to the world

Contents

Author's Note

And the New . . . contains the articles about professional boxing that I authored in 2011. The articles I wrote about the sweet science prior to that date have been published in *Muhammad Ali & Company; A Beautiful Sickness; A Year at the Fights; The View From Ringside; Chaos, Corruption, Courage, and Glory; The Lost Legacy of Muhammad Ali; I Don't Believe It, But It's True; The Greatest Sport of All; The Boxing Scene; An Unforgiving Sport; Boxing Is;* and *Winks and Daggers.*

Fights and Fighters

In recent years, some commentators have compared Manny Pacquiao's accomplishments to those of Henry Armstrong. So it made sense to look back at the man who many consider to be boxing's alltime #2 pound-for-pound fighter behind Sugar Ray Robinson.

Henry Armstrong Revisited

Henry Armstrong is largely forgotten today; overshadowed by memories of Joe Louis and Sugar Ray Robinson. Some boxing fans have seen bits and pieces of him on film; a barrel-chested fire-plug of a man, 5 feet 5-½ inches tall, with an irrepressible smile; always moving, like a kid in a playground with a seemingly inexhaustible supply of energy.

Boxing fans also know that Armstrong won multiple titles. But in recent decades, the concept of a "world champion" has been watered down. So let's put what he did in perspective.

Armstrong fought twenty-seven fights in 1937 and won all of them, twenty-six by knockout. He captured the featherweight crown that year by knocking out Petey Sarron. Then, over the next nine months, he added the welterweight championship with a lopsided decision over Barney Ross and annexed the lightweight title with a victory over Lew Ambers. For good measure, he fought twelve title fights in 1939 and won eleven of them.

Armstrong held three world championships simultaneously at a time when boxing had eight weight divisions and one champion in each division. He was "pound-for-pound" before the phrase was invented for Sugar Ray Robinson. His accomplishments were almost beyond comprehension.

The details of Armstrong's early life are shrouded in uncertainty. He gave different versions of events to different people. The *Ring Record Book* says that he was born in Columbus, Mississippi, on December 12, 1912. That conforms with his public statements. But British writer Bob Mee (who studied the census rolls in Lowndes County) argues persuasively that his actual date of birth was December 12, 1909.

Armstrong was the eleventh of fifteen children born to Henry and America Jackson. His mother was an Iroquois Indian. His father was black with some Indian and Irish blood mixed in. At birth, he was given his father's name; Henry Jackson Jr.

The Jacksons were a sharecropping family. They grew cotton. Then boll weevils descended on the cotton fields, and Henry Sr went north to St. Louis with his two oldest sons (Oilus and Oscar). They found factory jobs, and when they'd saved enough money, the rest of the family joined them in a three-room house on the rough-and-tumble south side of the city.

America Jackson died young. "My mother was strong," Henry recalled years later. "But having all those kids; you're just human. She'd have a kid today and start working almost tomorrow. She just worked herself down and caught what you call consumption of the lungs."

Henry's paternal grandmother took his mother's place in the life of the family. At her urging, he continued his education and graduated from Vashon High School. Then he took a job as a laborer for the Missouri Pacific Railroad at a salary of twenty dollars a week. After six months, he was laid off. He later claimed that, while working for the railroad, he read in a St. Louis newspaper that Kid Chocolate (then undefeated in forty-two professional fights) had beaten Al Singer at the Polo Grounds in New York and been paid a purse of $75,000.

Jackson was impressed with Kid Chocolate's earning power. In due course, he landed another job; this one at the Universal Hat Shop, where he cleaned and blocked hats and made deliveries. He also decided to try his hand at boxing and learned some fundamentals at the "colored" YMCA on Pine Street in St. Louis. At the YMCA, he met an older fighter named Harry Armstrong, who watched him spar and offered the opinion, "You're a good fighter, but no boxer. You can't be good just by being willing to hit and be hit. A boxer doesn't take hits. He slips them and the other guy gets hit."

With guidance from Armstrong, Henry Jackson had three amateur fights in St. Louis and won them all by knockout. Then they journeyed to Pittsburgh to try their hand in the professional ranks. At that point, Armstrong decided that Henry needed a catchier name and dubbed him "Melody Jackson."

On July 27, 1931, Jackson made his professional debut against Al Iovino in North Braddock, Pennsylvania. His purse was thirty-five dollars. The next day's edition of the *Pittsburgh Post-Gazette* told the tale.

"Al Iovino, Swissvale, 123 pounds, knocked out Melody Jackson, recent importation from the South, in the third round with two minutes and 27 seconds of the session gone. Jackson started out trading wallops and kept it up until he grew tired with both lads slugging toe-to-toe. Iovino got Melody in bad condition as round three progressed, the southern lad showing extreme dislike for body blows. When Al clipped him with a long overhand left that found its target, Jackson went face down upon the canvas."

Four days later, Jackson had his second pro fight and won a six-round decision in Millville, Pennsylvania. But the fight was tougher and the purse was smaller than he and Armstrong had thought they would be. They returned to St. Louis. Then, in pursuit of more lucrative opportunities, they rode on the underside of trains to California, stopping in hobo camps for rest and food along the way. The trip took eleven days.

Jackson and Armstrong spent their first few nights in California with other drifters and homeless people at the Midnight Mission in Los Angeles. Eventually, they rented a partitioned area with a single bed between the laundry room and backyard of a house for a dollar a week.

At that time, amateur boxing in California was a semiprofessional sport. Jackson soon signed a contract to fight as an amateur under the guidance of a manager named Tom Cox. But there was a problem. He'd fought twice professionally in Pennsylvania.

At Harry Armstrong's suggestion, Henry Jackson became Harry's little brother, Henry Armstrong. That was the name on the contract that he signed with Cox. The fighter later claimed that, during his first year as an amateur in Los Angeles, he had between eighty-five and ninety fights and won all of them. A more plausible accounting is that he won fifty-eight of sixty-two amateur fights, earning a few dollars on the side for each fight. He shined shoes to make ends meet.

In summer 1932, "Henry Armstrong" competed for a spot on the United States Olympic Team but was eliminated in the trials. At that point, Cox sold his contract to Wirt Ross, a manger with connections in the pro game. Armstrong approved the assignment and extended the terms of the contract so that it would last for five years. That bit of business taken care of, he turned pro with Harry Armstrong as his trainer and lost four-round decisions in his next two fights. Each time, he was overmatched. Basically, he was exciting cannon fodder. But he made fifty dollars for each fight.

Henry Armstrong now had one win and three losses in four pro fights. But he was learning how to harness his natural physical gifts; strength, quickness, stamina, and the ability to take a punch. In the two years after his first four fights, he fought thirty times and lost only once. At one point during that stretch, he had five draws in six fights; a testament to judging that was biased against him. But he was fighting in an era when blemishes were an expected part a fighter's record and didn't doom his future.

In November 1934, Wirt Ross sent Armstrong to Mexico City to fight Mexican native Baby Arizmendi (a world-class featherweight) for a purse of $1,500. Years later, in an autobiography entitled *Gloves, Glory, and God,* Henry maintained that, just before the fight, Ross told him, "Don't get too ambitious, son. You're not supposed to win this fight."

Armstrong responded, "I thought I'm supposed to win all my fights," and Ross explained the facts of life to him.

"You're a good boy, but there's a lot you've got to learn about the fight game. I want you to take it easy in this fight. I gave my word that we'd fight this one the way Arizmendi's manager wanted it. It was the only way I could get you signed. Just fight to go the full ten rounds."

Arizmendi won a unanimous decision. Afterward, Ross told Armstrong that he wouldn't be paid because the gate receipts had been stolen.

In 1936, Ross sold Armstrong's contract to Eddie Mead for $10,000. Hollywood stars Al Jolson and George Raft were partners in the purchase. Later that year, Henry moved up to lightweight. By autumn 1937, he had 72 victories on his ring record.

On October 29, 1937, Armstrong returned to the featherweight division and challenged Petey Sarron for the 126-pound crown at Madison Square Garden. Making weight was a struggle; but on the morning of the fight, he weighed in at 124 pounds. Later that day, relaxing in bed, he drew parallels in his mind between what he hoped to accomplish in boxing and the exploits of George Dixon, Joe Gans, and Kid Chocolate; three great black champions who had come before him.

In the dressing room before the fight, Eddie Mead told Armstrong, "Sarron isn't such a hot puncher. Just walk in, throwing punches hard till you give him the punch it takes to put him out."

Harry Armstrong (who was Henry's chief second) later recalled that both fighters "fought savagely" that night and "threw caution to the winds."

Joseph Nichols summed up the bout for the *New York Times*, writing, "Sarron clearly won the first four rounds of the sizzling battle by eagerly inviting Armstrong's attack and cleanly beating the Negro in counters. Neither fighter paid heed to the so-called finer points of boxing. They merely rushed at each other time and again, both arms swinging, and the encounter was one long succession of thrilling exchanges to the head and body. When the sixth round started, Armstrong sprang at his adversary and drove both hands to the body. One punch, a heavy right, apparently robbed Sarron of all his strength, for he was able to do nothing except cover up while Armstrong belabored relentlessly with lefts and rights to the midsection. Recovering somewhat, Sarron jumped at Armstrong and traded willingly with him until the latter, releasing his long right, crashed it squarely against Sarron's jaw. Sarron slumped to his knees and elbows and slowly lifted himself."

But the beaten champion was in no condition to continue. Referee Arthur Donovan stopped the battle at 2:36 of the sixth round.

That night, there was a victory party at the Cotton Club in Harlem. Armstrong said later that he felt like "a giant firefly in a blackout" and recalled that celebrities who wouldn't have given him a glance in passing a few days earlier greeted him "like a long-lost relative."

There hadn't been many African American champions before Armstrong. Joe Gans, Jack Johnson, Tiger Flowers, and Joe Louis (who preceded Armstrong by four months) were the most notable. Major League Baseball and the National Football League were still all-white institutions. "Boxing," W. C. Heinz later noted, "gave the black man a better break than he received in any other sport because it needed him. But it only gave him what it had to."

That said; Armstrong fought in a manner that demanded attention.

"I look at films of the oldtime fighters a lot," says Emanuel Steward. "Henry Armstrong is the first boxer I ever saw who was like a machine. It wasn't combinations as much as it was punches coming all the time. Nobody could throw that many punches, but he did. He had incredible stamina and was absolutely non-stop. He was a perpetual-motion punching machine. When the bell rang, he got in your face and started throwing punches from every angle. He was like a machine gun. It wasn't bang! It was bang-bang-bang-bang-bang-bang! Nothing stopped him. He just kept coming and coming and punching like a windmill in a hurricane.

He was born with natural gifts that allowed him to fight the way he did. There was no way to get away from him and no way to tie him up. When you fought Henry Armstrong, you were fighting for your life every second of the fight. A lot of his defense was in his offense. He never slowed down. But if you look at the films closely, you see all the subtle things he did. He could take a punch, but he also kept his chin close to his chest, so you couldn't hit him cleanly. He had a way of getting his elbows back against his body so, when he got inside, the opponent couldn't tie him up. His arms never got out to where you could clinch with him. That's what enabled him to be perpetual motion and grind people down with that relentless suffocating attack of his for fifteen rounds."

"There had never been a fighter like him before," adds Don Turner. "In the ring, he was pressure pressure pressure. Perpetual motion, throwing punches all the time from all angles; bobbing and weaving so the other guy couldn't land a good shot. He never took a step back. You had to fight his fight because he gave you no choice. And you had to punch with him because he never stopped punching. He just wanted to fight. He overwhelmed his opponents. In boxing, very often, the mind carries the body. Henry Armstrong made every sacrifice that a fighter has to make to be great. His will to win superseded everything."

Armstrong fought seven times in the twelve weeks after he defeated Sarron; all of them knockout victories in non-title fights. Then, in late January 1938, while driving home to California, he suffered what he referred to in his autobiography as "a nervous breakdown." He was taken to a "ranch" in Fontana, California, where he recuperated for a week.

Two days after his release, Armstrong was back in the ring. He fought four times in February 1938 and three times in March; each time as a lightweight, winning all seven fights. The seven men he defeated (Chalky Wright and Baby Arizmendi among them) had 445 victories at the time he fought them. He'd now won 37 consecutive fights, 35 of them by knockout, and was referred to in the nation's press as "Hammering Hank . . . Homicide Hank . . . Hurricane Hank . . . The Human Buzz-Saw . . . The Human Dynamo."

Then Armstrong attempted the unthinkable.

"Joe Louis had just won the heavyweight championship," Armstrong later recalled. "He was going to take all the popularity, everything, away from all the [black] fighters because everyone was saving their money to see Joe Louis. I had three managers; George Raft, Al Jolson, and Eddie Mead. They came up with the idea that I had to get super-popular, colossal. They said, 'We want you to win three championships. We worked this out because we were trying to make more money. They said, 'If you can win three championships, you'll have the flamboyance of a heavyweight. These guys were the thinkers. I said, 'It sounds pretty good to me. Okay; get 'em together.'"

Only one man prior to Armstrong (Bob Fitzsimmons) had won championships in three weight divisions. And Fitzsimmons accomplished the feat over the course of twelve years. Armstrong had something far more audacious in mind. He hoped to hold the featherweight, lightweight, and welterweight titles at the same time.

Armstrong's management team wanted him to fight lightweight champion Lew Ambers after beating Sarron and then go after welterweight champion Barney Ross. But Al Weill (who managed Ambers) was resistant to the idea, so Armstrong challenged Ross first.

Ross (named Beryl David Rosofsky at birth) was from New York and was known as "The Pride of the Ghetto." He'd won the lightweight title by beating Tony Canzoneri in 1933 and seized the welterweight crown from Jimmy McLarnin two years later.

Ross-Armstrong was scheduled for May 26, 1938, at the outdoor Madison Square Garden Bowl in Long Island City. It would be the first time in boxing history that a reigning featherweight champion had challenged for the welterweight crown.

Rain caused a five-day postponement.

Despite the 147-pound division limit, Ross weighed in at 142 pounds; Armstrong, at 133 ½.

Ross was a 2-to-1 favorite. But he was well past his prime. He won the first few rounds by outboxing Armstrong and controlling the fight with his jab. Then he faltered. Cornerman Art Winch (also Ross's co-manager) asked his fighter, "You started so nice. What's wrong, Barney?" Soon, everything was wrong.

Ross, in his own autobiography, later described the pivotal middle rounds as follows.

Round six: "Something happened to my legs. I couldn't seem to move on them. My arms felt as if they had lead weights on them. It was all I could do to get them up to protect my face, let alone fight back."

Round seven: "I was puffing badly, starting to wheeze. I fought for breath. I was lucky to get out of the round alive."

Round eight: "He rained left hooks on my mouth and blood gushed out. He hit me in the eye and it closed tight. Another punch cut my lip open. Another crashed into my nose, starting another flow of blood. Blood was dribbling into my good eye, so I was practically blind. I was taking such a beating to the stomach, I wanted to throw up right in the middle of the ring."

Writing for the *New York Times,* James P. Dawson called the fight "fifteen rounds of vicious savage fighting that was so one-sided as to render the result a foregone conclusion midway in the battle."

"Like a human tornado," Dawson recounted, "Armstrong cut down Ross. There was no resisting force. Henry just pounded the gallant Ross tirelessly, pitilessly, through every one of the fifteen rounds. Armstrong demonstrated almost from the opening bell that his style, his strength, his inexhaustible supply of stamina, perseverance, his grim determination, in short, his singular fighting stock in trade were too much for Ross."

Ross never went down. He made it to the final bell, barely, on courage alone. His eyes were slits. He was bleeding from the nose and mouth. He was beaten to a pulp but refused to quit, begging his corner and referee Arthur Donovan for the right to continue until the very end.

"A champ's got the right to choose the way he goes out," Ross said when the carnage was done.

Armstrong later claimed that he carried Ross the final three rounds out of respect for the champion. Maybe he did; maybe he didn't. There's no corroborating evidence to support or rebut that claim. Either way; he won a lopsided unanimous decision.

"This is your night," Ross told his conqueror at the final bell. "I've had mine."

In his dressing room after the fight, the beaten champion told reporters, "He's a great fighter, who never rests and never gives you a chance to rest. I can't say he's a hard one-punch hitter, but he certainly can wear you down. I wish I could have fought him five years ago. I was at my peak then. There was something missing in me tonight." Then Ross said wistfully, "That was my last fight. I wasn't going to go out lying down."

Unlike many beaten fighters, Ross was true to his word. He never fought again.

Twenty-two days after Armstrong beat Barney Ross, Joe Louis fought Max Schmeling at Yankee Stadium and annihilated his German foe in one round. The Brown Bomber was now America's hero. Nothing that Armstrong did could match the exploits of his fellow champion. But there was still a third championship to pursue.

On August 17, 1938, Armstrong challenged Lew Ambers at Madison Square Garden for the lightweight crown. It was one of the bloodiest, most brutal slugfests of modern times. James P. Dawson called the action "fifteen rounds of fighting as fast, furious, and savage as has ever been seen."

In round three, Ambers opened a cut on the inside of Armstrong's lower lip that bled profusely for twelve rounds. Then Ambers was knocked down and badly hurt in the fifth and sixth rounds.

As the fight progressed, Armstrong took control on a primitive level. But another factor was at work.

Armstrong wasn't a dirty fighter, but he was a physical fighter. With his perpetual motion style, he threw punches from all angles and some of them went low. Coming straight forward, he also led with his head from time to time.

Referee Bill Cavanagh took four rounds away from Armstrong for low blows.

By the late rounds, Armstrong was severely cut around both eyes and blood was streaming from his mouth. Cavanagh warned that the blood was making the canvas slippery and that he was on the verge of stopping the fight.

"Don't stop it, Mr. Cavanagh," Armstrong begged. "I'm leading on points."

"The ring is full of blood," the referee countered. "And it's your blood."

"Then I'll stop bleeding."

After the twelfth round, Armstrong told his corner, "Don't give me no mouthpiece. Just let me go."

He fought the last three rounds swallowing his own blood so Cavanaugh wouldn't stop the bout. Twelve stitches were needed to close the cut on the inside of his mouth.

Factoring the four penalized rounds into the scoring, one judge scored the bout 8 rounds to 7 in favor of Ambers. The other two scorecards read

8–6–1 and 7–6–2 for the new lightweight champion and first-ever simultaneous triple champion of the world.

After Armstrong beat Ambers, he relinquished his featherweight crown. He knew that he would be unable to make 126 pounds again. Over the next nine months, he successfully defended the welterweight title six times and had one non-title bout. On August 22, 1939, he put his lightweight championship on the line in a rematch against Ambers at Yankee Stadium.

Again, it was a thrilling fight. Armstrong suffered a terrible cut above his right eye that obscured his vision. And again, he was severely penalized for low blows.

Afterward, James P. Dawson wrote, "Applying the law more severely than ever before and certainly more painfully than it ever has been applied in a championship bout, referee Arthur Donovan penalized Armstrong five rounds [two, five, seven, nine, and eleven] for low blows."

Ambers won a unanimous 8–7, 8–7, 11–3–1 decision.

"The title," Dawson noted, "was not won on competition alone, but on fighting rules and ethics. Four of these [penalized] rounds, Armstrong won on competition without a doubt. On this observer's scoresheet, Armstrong was the victim of an injustice."

The loss broke a string of forty-six consecutive victories for Armstrong.

In October 1939, two months after his loss to Ambers, Armstrong defended his welterweight championship five times in twenty-one days. That's not a typographical error. Three more successful defenses followed.

Then, on March 1, 1940, weighing 142 pounds, he moved up in weight yet again and challenged Ceferino Garcia for the middleweight title. The consensus at ringside was that Armstrong deserved the decision. The bout was declared a draw.

Returning to welterweight, Armstrong scored knockouts in five more title defenses over a five-month period. On October 4, 1940, he put his championship on the line against Fritzie Zivic at Madison Square Garden.

Zivic was a dirty fighter, adept at thumbing opponents in the eye and doing whatever else he could get away with outside the rules. "I'd give 'em the head, choke 'em, hit 'em in the balls." he said when his career was over. "You're fighting. You're not playing the piano."

It's now believed that Armstrong was virtually blind in his left eye before he fought Zivic. By the middle rounds, his right eye was swollen to the point where he could hardly see at all. The bout was even on two of three scorecards going into the fifteenth round. Zivic dominated the final stanza.

Joseph Nichols wrote in the *New York Times,* "Fritzie Zivic did what the rank and file of boxing followers deemed impossible at Madison Square Garden last night. He crushed the heretofore invincible Henry Armstrong into decisive defeat in a savage fifteen-round struggle. Pacing himself splendidly and standing up under Armstrong's hardest punches, the durable Zivic made his way to the championship by exhibiting a willingness to trade with his foe when expedient and to stay away and stab effectively with a long left hand when that course appeared the better one to pursue. The steady impact of the clever Zivic's sharp left to the face gradually caused a swelling about Armstrong's eyes. The tenth round was the one in which every spectator in the house went delirious. The boxers stood toe to toe and each fired his heaviest artillery. In the eleventh round, the defending titleholder was blind to all intents and purposes. Zivic, aware of his foe's plight, kept the battle at long range and ripped both hands to the head at every opportunity. The pitifully handicapped Armstrong had trouble even locating his tormentor. As he returned to his corner at the end of each round, he would murmur prayerfully, 'If I could only see.' In going down to defeat, Armstrong exhibited a brand of courage that will cause him to be long remembered even if he had not in the past held the featherweight, lightweight, and welterweight championships of the world simultaneously."

The last of Armstrong's three championships was gone.

On January 17, 1941, Armstrong and Zivic fought again. A standing-room-only crowd of 23,190 (the largest in the history of Madison Square Garden) witnessed the battle. Five thousand more fans were turned away.

Zivic dominated from beginning to end, beating Armstrong as brutally as Armstrong had beaten Barney Ross.

James P. Dawson wrote, "Armstrong was pelted from all angles and with every blow known to boxing. Zivic handled him as he willed, spearing and cutting him at long range, battering the daylights out of him at close quarters. By the sixth round, Armstrong was uncertain of his footing as he shuffled forward. His eyes, swollen from the fourth on, were ripped open in the eighth. In the ninth and tenth, Armstrong was pounded almost beyond recognition."

After round ten, referee Arthur Donovan told the badly battered Armstrong that he would give him one more round.

"Armstrong," Dawson recounted, "responded to this warning with a flash of the fighting demon of old. Through the eleventh round, he pulled the crowd to its feet in as glorious a rally as this observer has seen in twenty-five years of attendance at these ring battles. The former champion hammered Zivic all over the ring. He pelted the titleholder with lefts and rights to the body, plied him with savage thrusts of the left and wicked right smashes to the head and face, blows with which he hoped to turn the tide of crushing defeat that was engulfing him. For two minutes, Armstrong went berserk. He was a fighting maniac, the Hammering Henry of old. It was glorious spectacle while it lasted. Then Zivic stepped to the attack. Through the last minute of the eleventh round, he hammered Armstrong mercilessly with short chopping stinging lefts and rights that ripped open old wounds and started a flow of blood."

Donovan stopped the fight in the twelfth round. Afterward, Dr. Alexander Schiff of the New York State Athletic Commission warned Armstrong that he risked going blind if he fought again.

After the second Zivic fight, Armstrong said that he was done with boxing. His championship days were gone and he had no desire to fight again. Then a predictable problem surfaced: money.

Armstrong had made over a million dollars in purses. But management had taken a generous share. He'd lost money on several business ventures, including a Chinese restaurant in Hollywood and the Henry Armstrong Melody Room in Harlem. He'd partied with a lot of women and thought of himself as "a rich playboy, flashing around town in a yellow convertible." He was a soft touch for handouts.

"Too many night clubs," he acknowledged in his autobiography. "Too many $1,000-dollar bills. Too many fine cars, fine clothes, fine parties. The money was rolling in. But the money was also rolling out."

On June 1, 1942 (sixteen months after being knocked out by Zivic), Armstrong returned to the ring in San Jose, California, against a club fighter named Johnny Taylor.

"I was there that night," promoter Don Chargin remembers. "I was a kid; I didn't know much then. But I was amazed. Armstrong was on a downward slide, but he still had an aura about him and he was still perpetual motion. All the way from his dressing room, up the aisle into the ring, he was throwing punches. While he was waiting to be introduced, he was throwing punches. Then the bell rang, and he kept throwing punches. He knocked Taylor out in the fourth round. Three months later, they fought again and Armstrong knocked him out in three rounds. Years later, I asked Taylor, 'You took such a beating the first time; why did you fight him again?' And Taylor told me, 'It was an honor being beaten by him.'"

Armstrong fought fourteen times in 1942, winning all but once. Ten victories in twelve fights during the first eight months of 1943 followed. "Every fighter tries a comeback," he said. "It's hard to quit the only job you know. There's always some money to be made, even on the other side of the hill."

But as Barney Ross noted from his own personal experience, "When you start to slide in this racket, nobody can stop it. There's only one way to go. Down."

On August 27, 1943, Armstrong fought Sugar Ray Robinson at Madison Square Garden. Robinson had a 44-and-1 record with 30 knockouts and was twenty-two years old. His boyhood idol had been Henry Armstrong. After a storied amateur career, Sugar Ray had made his professional debut with a second-round knockout of Joe Echevarria at Madison Square Garden on October 4, 1940; the same night that Armstrong lost his welterweight championship to Fritzie Zivic.

Robinson carried Armstrong for ten rounds, and everyone in the arena knew it.

Joseph Nichols wrote of the fight, "Ray Robinson enjoyed a brisk workout at the expense of veteran Henry Armstrong in the star bout of ten rounds at Madison Square Garden last night. Robinson enjoyed it, but nobody else in the Garden got any satisfaction from the spectacle, which was as tame as a gymnasium workout between father and son. Going along quite as he pleased, Robinson handled the one-time triple champion exactly as he was, a has-been whose best days were far behind him. Robinson, with the speed and agility that go with his 22 years, merely pecked away at his opponent, riddling him with a ceaseless spray of long lefts to the head. On infrequent occasions, the New Yorker essayed a right-hand punch to the head. Some of these blows landed, albeit with little force. Most of them missed, and by such wide margins that several critics were moved to observe that Ray was of no mind to punish the ex-champion. Each of the ten rounds was a repetition of the other nine."

"I'd hit him enough to get him in a little trouble," Robinson said years later. "But whenever I felt him sagging, I'd clinch and hold him up. I didn't want him to be embarrassed by a knockdown."

"I know it looked bad," Armstrong admitted to reporters after the fight.

But he kept fighting. Nineteen fights in 1944.

When his career was done, Armstrong would observe, "When you're champ, you have to keep going to stay on top. You have only a few years to make your money. After that, you're just another has-been. When you're through, you're through. When you're old, you don't get young again."

On January 14, 1945, Armstrong fought to a draw against Chester Slider in Oakland, California. They fought again on Valentine's Day, and Slider won a ten-round decision. That was it. The ring career of boxing's perpetual motion machine had come to an end.

After Armstrong's boxing days were over, life came at him with the same merciless pounding that he'd dealt out to others in the ring. His management team had kept him fighting regularly, so their end of the purses would keep coming in. That had also limited his drinking, which was a problem at times; although there's a school of thought that fighting as often as he did was one of the factors that drove him to drink.

With no fights to train for, there were fewer and fewer days when Armstrong was sober. On a January morning in 1949, he woke up in the drunk tank at a police station in Los Angeles. He'd jumped the curb while driving drunk the night before and crashed his car into a lamppost.

Later that morning, the judge at his arraignment gave him a tongue lashing, admonishing him that he was "letting a million boys down."

The following night, Armstrong went out and got drunk again. Then, driving home, he heard what he called the voice of God speaking to him. In that moment, he surrendered to Christ, put his life in God's hands, and vowed to never drink again. Eventually, he became an ordained minister in the Morning Star Baptist Church, where he was known as "God's ball of fire."

"I became friendly with Henry late in his life," Don Chargin recalls. "He'd given up drinking by then. He was very likable, very talkative, constantly quoting from the Bible. He talked a lot about how his drinking days and carousing days were behind him; that he hadn't been a very good husband or father when he was young, but that he was a much better person and much happier now that he'd found the Lord. I think he was sincere. He seemed to have peace of mind."

"I met him in the 1980s," Don Turner reminisces. "They brought him to Cincinnati to work with Aaron Pryor for a couple of days. Pryor fought like Armstrong used to fight, and his management team thought that maybe Pryor could learn something from him, plus it would be good publicity. It was the sort of thing where you go over to someone you admire and introduce yourself. We talked in the gym for about fifteen minutes, small talk. And it was wonderful. He was a very nice humble man."

Jerry Izenberg met Armstrong when the fighter testified before a New York State legislative committee that was considering legislation to ban boxing.

"He was talking about the good that boxing can do in a man's life," Izenberg recounts. "And the lawyer for the committee was giving him a hard time. Armstrong was blind in one eye, and the lawyer asked him in a very condescending way, 'How did that happen, Mr. Armstrong?' Armstrong told him, 'I was a boxer. It happened as a result of boxing. I was a good boxer. I'm not ashamed of that.'"

But life was hard. In Armstrong's later years, he lived in poverty and suffered from cataracts, persistent pneumonia, malnutrition, and dementia. He died on October 23, 1988. The cause of death was listed as heart failure.

It's difficult to take a fighter out of one era and know with certainty how he would have performed in another. But the prevailing view is that Armstrong would have been a champion in any era.

He's remembered today primarily because he held the featherweight, lightweight, and welterweight titles simultaneously. Putting that accomplishment in a larger perspective, the most credible accounting of his fights lists him as having 149 wins (including 101 knockouts) against 21 losses and 10 draws. In the forty-six months prior to his losing the welterweight title to Fritzie Zivic, Armstrong's record was 59–1–1. During his reign as champion, he won 21 title fights. He was knocked out only twice in his career; in his first pro fight by Al Iovino and in the 131st by Zivic. There was a time when he could beat any fighter in the world from 126 to 147 pounds. And that was during the "golden age" of boxing, when there were a lot of very good fighters.

"Sugar Ray Robinson told me that Henry Armstrong was an alltime great," Don Elbaum recalls. "Rocky Marciano told me that Henry Armstrong was an alltime great. Willie Pep told me that Henry Armstrong was an alltime great. That tells me all I need to know."

"I never saw a better small man than Henry Armstrong, and I don't expect to," Jack Dempsey said late in life. "They don't make them like that anymore."

"If Sergio gets much better," promoter Lou DiBella said after Martinez-Dzinziruk, "he won't have to learn how to speak English. The rest of us will have to learn how to speak Spanish."

Martinez-Dzinziruk: "Maravilla" Was Marvelous

At 9:15 on the night of March 12, 2011, Sergio Martinez entered his dressing room at the MGM Grand Theater at Foxwoods Resort Casino in Mashantucket, Connecticut.

A gray Formica star with a Plexiglas slot designed to accommodate a nameplate was attached to the door. The slot was empty. A sheet of paper with the instructions, "Red Corner—Sergio Martinez—Ready by 10:50," was taped above the star.

The room was long and narrow with beige carpeting and cream-colored walls. Its most distinguishing feature was an L-shaped Formica counter that stretched the length of two adjacent walls. Ten vanity mirrors were set above the counter. Each one was bordered by thirteen lights and matched with a black swivel chair and had its own make-up drawer. Ten boxes of tissues offered further proof that, on gentler nights, this was a chorus girls' dressing room. A sign by the door warned, "The lighting of candles in the dressing room is strictly prohibited. We appreciate your cooperation."

The room was a reminder that, for thousands of years, women have sold their bodies for the entertainment of others. When Jimmy Cannon called boxing "the red light district of professional sports," he was referring to the unsavory business aspects of the fight game. Boxing at its core is the sale of a fighter's body for entertainment, a particularly brutal form of skin trade.

Martinez is one of boxing's most talented practitioners. He was born into poverty in Argentina. "Life sometimes takes you through a path where the lighter thing is boxing," he said not long ago.

That says all one needs to know about the circumstances of Sergio's life when he was young. He began boxing in 1995 at age twenty. Two years later, he turned pro. In the fourteen years since then, he has lost twice in fifty-one fights.

The first loss came in 2000 at the hands of Antonio Margarito. "I was trained but I was not prepared," Martinez has said of that fight. "I started well, but it was impossible for me to win that night. He was a professional boxer, a great champion. And at that moment, I was a boxer who, three or four years before, was working on roofs. I was playing soccer with my friends when Margarito had already been a professional boxer for six or seven years. What had to happen happened. In terms of spirits, I never was down after that defeat."

The second loss was a majority-decision verdict in a bout against Paul Williams in 2009. Martinez rebounded from that setback by dethroning middleweight champion Kelly Pavlik on April 17, 2010, and knocking Williams unconscious with a single punch in the second round of their November 20, 2010, rematch. Those victories earned him recognition from the Boxing Writers Association of America as its 2010 "Fighter of the Year."

March 12th at Foxwoods was the next test for Martinez. As is often the case in boxing, considerable backroom maneuvering accompanied the making of the fight.

Martinez (the WBC middleweight champion) had hoped to face the sanctioning body's mandatory challenger (Sebastian Zbik). But HBO demanded that he face Sergiy Dzinziruk (the WBO 154-pound belt-holder) instead.

That didn't sit well with Team Martinez. The Ukrainian-born Dzinziruk had a 37-and-0 record and is nicknamed "Razor" because of his cutting jab. Worse, he was considered all but impossible to "look good" against because of his cautious counterpunching style.

Also, failing to fight Zbik meant that Martinez would be stripped of his belt, since WBC president Jose Sulaiman was believed to be anxious to install a less formidable champion in the hope of giving Julio Cesar Chavez Jr (one of his favorite fighters) a realistic chance of winning the title.

In the end, Team Martinez opted for HBO's dollars (a $2,600,000 license fee less $850,000 for the Dzinziruk camp). The WBC happily relieved Sergio of his title and declared that it was elevating Zbik from "interim" to "undisputed" middleweight champion. Then, proving once again that he has a lesser sense of shame than one might expect in a noble public servant, Sulaiman announced that Martinez had been designated the WBC "middleweight champion emeritus."

The dictionary defines "emeritus" as "retired or honorably discharged from active professional duty, but retaining the title of one's office or position." That's a poor fit with Sergio's active status.

Undeterred, Sulaiman then announced that Martinez-Dzinziruk would be contested for the WBC's "diamond belt." That allowed him to charge a sanctioning fee for the fight plus $45,000 for the belt itself. On casual inspection of the bauble, $45,000 appeared to be a mark-up of astronomical proportions.

In his dressing room on fight night, Sergio made himself comfortable in one of the swivel chairs and read text messages from friends. Abraham Lopez and David Sanchez were with him. Martinez and Sanchez became friendly after Sergio moved from Argentina to Spain in 2002. Lopez joined Sergio's circle when the fighter relocated in Oxnard, California, several years ago.

One person conspicuous by his absence was trainer Gabriel Sarmiento. Two days earlier, it had been announced that, for "personal reasons," Gabriel wouldn't attend the fight. Pablo Sarmiento (a member of Martinez's training staff, who has worked Sergio's corner in recent outings) would be the chief second in his brother's absence.

"It's private, so there's not much I can say about it," Lou DiBella (Martinez's promoter) told the media at the final pre-fight press conference. "Gabriel was with Sergio in training camp all the way, so they've worked on everything together. We're comfortable with Pablo."

Still, this was the first time in eight years that Gabriel (who, in fact, was having difficulty with the criminal justice system in Spain) wouldn't be in Sergio's corner.

When he finished texting, Sergio turned his attention to a flat-screen television monitor mounted high on the wall in a corner of the room. Javier Fortuna vs. Derrick Wilson (the fifth fight of the evening) was about to begin.

Martinez and Fortuna are stablemates. That was a problem. Pablo Sarmiento and the rest of Sergio's cornermen were at ringside with Javier. The HBO telecast was slated to begin at 10:30 with a bout between Andy Lee and Craig McEwan. If Lee-McEwan ended in the first round, Sergio would be expected to walk at 10:50. But if Fortuna-Wilson went the distance, Martinez's cornermen wouldn't be back in the dressing room until 10:25. That wouldn't leave enough time for Sergio to have his hands wrapped, warm up, and be ready to fight.

At 9:55, Buddy McGirt (who was working Dzinziruk's corner) came in.

"We're going to wrap now," McGirt said. "Are you sending someone over to watch?"

Neither Lopez or Sanchez had the requisite expertise. Lopez went down to ringside to see if he could pull Adam Flores out of Fortuna's corner to do the job.

Ten o'clock came and went. The inspector assigned to Martinez's dressing room was getting edgy.

"We're on the clock here, guys. You've got to start getting ready."

"I'm sorry," Sergio told him. "My corner is not here yet."

Fortuna stopped Wilson on an eighth-round knockout. At 10:07, Sarmiento, Ricardo Sanchez-Atocha (who co-manages Martinez with Sampson Lewkowicz), and cornerman Cecilio Flores (Adam's brother) entered the dressing room.

Martinez put on his trunks, laced up his shoes, and did some light stretching exercises.

At 10:18, Sanchez-Atocha began wrapping Sergio's hands, left hand first. Eighteen minutes later, the job was done.

Lee-McEwan began at 10:40. HBO production coordinator Tami Cotel entered the room and announced to all concerned, "You have ten minutes from the end of this fight."

Martinez needed at least twenty-five minutes to get ready. He hadn't gloved up, warmed up, or done any padwork.

"Don't worry," he was told. "Whatever happens, you don't go to the ring until you're ready. They can't start the fight without you."

Cecilio Flores began stretching Sergio's legs . . . Sanchez-Atocha gloved him up . . . Sergio began shadow-boxing in three-minute segments . . . Sanchez-Atocha greased him down.

At 11:01, Martinez began hitting the pads with Sarmiento. Pablo is quieter and less demonstrative than his brother. He gave instructions in a soft voice that everyone in the room except Sergio strained to hear.

Ten minutes later, the time crisis was over. Martinez had broken a sweat and was sharp. Lee-McEwen was only in the eighth round. Whatever Sergio did from this point on would be designed simply to maintain his readiness.

There was more stretching and another round of padwork. Then it was time.

Sergio put on his robe and hugged everyone in the room. There was joy in his eyes. "This is a night of celebration," he said.

Martinez was a 5-to-1 betting favorite. Each fighter had weighed in a day earlier at 158.8 pounds. Both men were southpaws. At 6 feet even, Dzinziruk was two inches taller and had a clear reach advantage.

Eight rounds of intense fighting at a high skill level followed.

The first two rounds belonged to Martinez. Dzinziruk has a punishing jab. But he doesn't double up on it and he doesn't move his head enough. A good jab is about timing. In the early going, Sergio got off first, nullifying Sergiy's jab with single and double jabs of his own. When Martinez let his hands go, Dzinziruk didn't. When Sergio paused, Sergiy was quick to fire.

In round three, the action evened out a bit. Martinez seemed to be expending more energy than his opponent. Whenever Sergio stopped moving, Dzinziruk popped him with a sharp stinging jab of his own.

Eighteen seconds into round four, Martinez landed a glancing overhand left to the top of the head and Dzinziruk went down to the extent that his knee touched the canvas. It was the first time in his career that a knockdown had been scored against him. Later in the stanza, Sergiy landed some good straight lefts that got Sergio's attention. But the knockdown made it a 10–8 round.

Round five belonged to Dzinziruk until the two-minute-fifty-one-second mark when another left (again, to the top of the head) put him on the canvas for the second time.

After five rounds, Martinez was seven points ahead on each of the judges' scorecards.

But round six, which could have been scored either way, was cause for concern. Sergio's face was puffing up, particularly around his eyes, and he appeared to be tiring.

Round seven was the second round in a row in which Dzinziruk had a statistical edge in the number of punches landed. Martinez was digging deep to keep the fight on even terms and eating more leather than he would have liked. Worse; he was having trouble seeing out of his left eye (which had a slice on the eyelid) and overreaching a bit with his left hand.

Sarmiento was slow to leave the ring at the end of the one-minute break following round seven. And Martinez was slow leaving his corner. He was starting to look his age.

Not to worry.

Sixty-five seconds into round eight, Martinez landed a straight left flush on the jaw over a Dzinziruk jab. The first two knockdowns of the fight had scored points but neither blow had done much damage. This one did damage. Dzinziruk went down and was wobbly when he rose. Two more knockdowns (numbers four and five for the fight) followed. Referee Arthur Mercante Jr halted the action at the 1:43 mark of the round.

Over the course of the fight, Martinez outlanded Dzinziruk 226 to 161. To the surprise of many, he also outjabbed the jabber. He rose to the occasion, dug deep, and did what he had to do to win. He outfought Dzinziruk; he outthought Dzinziruk. He fought creatively and was mentally strong as well.

How good is Martinez?

Let's start with the fact that he's a superb athlete and a complete fighter. He has good footwork and good balance. Quickness and speed are two different things. Martinez has fast hands and he pulls the trigger quickly. Put him in against a style that's different from what he has seen before and he deals with it. Becoming a world champion seems to have made him a more confident fighter. He can whack and he's setting down on his punches more now than he did before.

Sergio is thought of as a "small" middleweight. But his body is solid and his torso is remarkably thick for someone who moves with as much grace as he does. There's nothing fragile about him. In the ring, for all his personal charm, he's a tough SOB.

One of the most remarkable things about Martinez is that, almost without exception, fighters with the best "natural instincts" started young. Sergio didn't take up boxing until age twenty. Sixteen years of hard work and discipline have made him the fighter he is today. But he also has the instincts of a fighter. There are times when he seems to be playing chess in the ring against his opponent.

It's rare for a fighter to improve in his mid-thirties. But Martinez is doing just that. And he does things with speed and timing that a thirty-six-year-old man isn't supposed to possess.

As for what comes next; the middleweight division is short on credible challengers. And not many "name" fighters at 154 or 160 pounds appear anxious to step into the ring with "Maravilla." Sergio said recently, "I'm not thinking of going up to 168 because I'd be too small physically. I would give up too much of an advantage to 168-pounders."

Thus, it will be hard to find a big-money super-fight for him.

Meanwhile, let it be said that Martinez brings elegance and grace to a brutal trade. He has a high level of self-respect and the vanity of a great performer. But as Bart Barry notes, "There are no silly press-conference antics; no vitriolic conference calls; no made-for-infomercial hand-pad tricks; no ring entrance on a swing; no posse of buffoons wrestling Michael Buffer for the camera during introductions. Just a good-looking athlete wearing championship belts and bowing to those gathered in his name, followed by an artistry of motion rarely seen in boxing."

Four years ago, when Martinez was fighting club-fight opponents in out-of-the-spotlight venues for a few thousand dollars, he told an interviewer, "I believe I was born to be a champion. It is a road that is already made. I only have to walk it."

He is at his destination now.

This was the first in a series of articles about Manny Pacquiao vs. Shane Mosley.

Shane Mosley's Odyssey

There was as time when Shane Mosley was viewed by those in the know as the future of boxing. To paraphrase Cassius Marcellus Clay Jr, he was young, handsome, fast, and couldn't be beat.

Mosley won his first 38 fights; 35 of them by knockout. He defeated Philip Holiday to win the lightweight championship in 1997 and dominated the division with eight successful title defenses. Then he moved to welterweight and dethroned Oscar De La Hoya to claim the 147-pound crown.

Shane and Roy Jones Jr were the top two fighters on virtually every pound-for-pound list. No less an authority than legendary trainer Eddie Futch said that Mosley would have been competitive against Sugar Ray Robinson in his prime.

On January 26, 2002, everything changed. Mosley and Vernon Forrest entered the ring at Madison Square Garden as the two best welterweights in the world. Shane was an overwhelming favorite. But he had the habit of pulling straight back when moving away from a foe.

When a fighter pulls straight back against a taller athletically gifted opponent, he gets hit.

Against Forrest, Shane absorbed a hellacious beating in the early rounds. "When you get hit with a big shot," he said afterward, "your equilibrium goes, your timing goes with it, and you get hit with more shots. It takes a few rounds for you to get your charge back."

Showing incredible courage, Shane fought his way back into the fight. Then, in the late rounds, Forrest put more of a beating on him en route to a unanimous decision triumph.

Time goes by. Mosley isn't one of boxing's young guns anymore. He'll be forty years old in September.

There was a time when Shane's greatest assets were youth, speed, and power. As he moved up in weight (fighting eight of his last fourteen bouts in the junior-middleweight division), he slowed a bit and his power failed to increase in tandem with his size.

Just as significantly, Shane acknowledges, "When I started my rise, my thing was, 'I can't lose. I have to make a living from this and no one can beat me.' Then you're on top and you cross over a barrier where you're not working out as much as you should because you're only fighting twice a year and the fire goes out a bit."

Mosley is popular within the boxing community. He's a warrior and has always been willing to go in tough. He really will fight anyone. He has a lot of pride. He's stubborn, good-natured, and a nice guy. His smile is genuine. People like him. Outside the ring, there's no meanness in him.

The greatest knock against Shane is that he sometimes makes unwise choices. He beat Oscar De La Hoya twice, turned down a third fight, and wound up losing to Winky Wright for a fraction of what he would have made against Oscar. Testimony before a grand jury that investigated BALCO (including Mosley's own testimony), confirmed that he used banned performance enhancing drugs in 2003. Shane has claimed that he took the drugs unknowingly. Circumstances suggest otherwise.

Now Shane is readying for what might be the last big fight of his ring career. On May 7, 2011, he'll do battle with Manny Pacquiao at the MGM Grand Hotel and Casino in Las Vegas.

The choice of Mosley as Pacquiao's opponent disappointed those who believe that Shane was once an elite fighter but is now little more than an elite name. He hasn't won a fight since January 2009 and, over the past fifty months, has two wins against two losses and a draw.

There are whispers . . . "Shane Mosley is an aging fighter. It shows in his face; you can hear it in his voice. His reflexes have slowed; his legs are gone. He's running on fumes."

Speed has always been one of Mosley's biggest advantages. When he was decisioned by Floyd Mayweather Jr last year, Floyd's speed seemed to befuddle, perhaps even intimidate, him a bit.

Thus, Freddie Roach (Pacquiao's trainer) says, "I feel very confident about this fight. The longer it goes, the better for us. We're going to fight at a fast pace and make sure that Shane fights three minutes of every round. Footwork will be key; lateral movement, going in-and-out. I think we can break him down and take him out in the late rounds. Since nobody has ever stopped Shane before, it would be icing on the cake if we can stop him."

The odds opened with Pacquiao as a heavy favorite. There's a degree of distortion in the betting line because Manny has such a fervent constituency. Still, Shane is a decided underdog for a reason.

That said; a Mosley victory isn't out of the question.

The bar might rise as a fighter gets older. But at any given time, there's one weight that's best for a fighter. Shane is back at 147 pounds, which is where he belongs.

Mosley is 5 feet 9 inches. Over the years, taller fighters have given him trouble. Vernon Forrest (6 feet), Winky Wright (5 feet 10 inches), and Sergio Mora (6 feet) accounted for five of the seven blemishes on his record. Pacquiao is two-and-a-half inches shorter than Shane.

Then there's the matter of the common opponents that Pacquiao and Mosley have fought. Manny scored impressive knockout victories over Oscar De La Hoya and Miguel Cotto, while Shane won two narrow decisions over De La Hoya and lost to Cotto.

But (and this is a big "but") Mosley destroyed Antonio Margarito en route to a brutal ninth-round knockout. Pacquiao dominated Margarito and won a lopsided decision. But in the sixth round, Antonio hurt Manny, badly.

One can argue that Margarito was there for Mosley to hit. Antonio is slow and stood right in front of Shane all night long. But Antonio was just as slow and just as stationary against Pacquiao. The difference might have been that Shane is naturally bigger and a naturally bigger puncher than Manny and takes a better punch.

Either way, it should be remembered that Mosley was widely viewed as over-the-hill and a heavy underdog before he fought Margarito.

Don Turner trained Evander Holyfield for his monumental upset of Mike Tyson in 1996. "Like most people, I think Pacquiao will win," Turner posits. "But fighters are the most unpredictable of all athletes. Both guys have a lot of heart. Shane can still punch. Pacquiao is willing to take a punch to land one, and that could get him in trouble. Pacquiao can be hurt; he isn't invulnerable. Joshua Clottey didn't throw many punches, but the ones that landed showed on Pacquiao's face after the fight. Margarito did a lot of damage with one shot to the body. Shane isn't what he used to be; we know that. But Shane still has skills. He takes a good punch. He hits hard enough to break Pacquiao's nose and open a cut around Pacquiao's eye. Let's say some of Shane's punches land just right."

"We'd be fools to underestimate Shane and think that he's shot," acknowledges Freddie Roach. "He still has speed, a right hand, and good power. We can't just walk in to him, because he's a good counterpuncher. We can't stand in front of him, because he'll land the right hand and the hook. Early in the fight is when he's going to be most dangerous. He whacked Mayweather with a pretty good right hand that had Floyd holding on early. I'd rather that Manny not get hit with a punch like that."

And Naazim Richardson (Mosley's trainer) adds, "I understand why people are picking Pacquiao to win. If you look at recent fights, his performances lead you in that direction and Shane's performances lead you in the opposite direction. But Shane can win this fight."

"Pacquiao hasn't had much trouble with the bigger guys he's fought so far," Richardson elaborates. "His opponents at the lower weights were more competitive against him, and the reason for that is speed. The big guys that Pacquiao has fought were too slow to deal with him. Shane is faster than any of those guys. Also, Pacquiao will fly at you like Superman. But when he does that, he's open if you can time him. The reason he had so much trouble with [Juan Manuel] Marquez is that Marquez is a technician. After Marquez adjusted to Pacquiao's speed, he was able to time him. Shane can do that too."

"Manny Pacquiao is a phenomenal fighter, one of the best in history," Richardson continues. "And he's there to fight. He'll jump on your ass and take everything you hit him with to get his own punches in. But don't count Shane out. Any man that Shane hits at 147 pounds, he can hurt him. All the people who are saying that this will be a walk in the park for Pacquiao don't know what they're talking about."

So how will it end?

"You have two guys who fight their heart out," says Don Turner. "Right now, one guy has equal boxing skill and is superior physically to the other. You can't take Shane back to the way he was because he's thirty-nine. But he'll fight hard enough that he'll make some noise early."

Given that reality, Mosley's best chance of winning would seem to lie in making this a Hagler-Hearns type of fight. If he does that, chances are that Pacquiao will oblige him and fans will get a firefight that's well worth their money. After that, what happens happens.

One unknown is whether Shane is still mentally tough enough to fight that kind of fight. He showed that toughness in the first loss of his career against Vernon Forrest. That was in keeping with the maxim that great fighters have great tolerance for pain and will walk through fire during the prime years of their career.

But as fighters age, they reach a point where their tolerance for pain diminishes. They're often less willing (and less able) to walk through fire to win.

Mosley has taken a lot of punishment over the years; in fights and in the gym. In some ways, he fights "like a Mexican fighter." But against Mayweather, Shane's will to fight through the rough spots seemed to waver. As that bout moved into the late rounds, he looked like a man who was trying to survive rather than win.

The most likely scenario for Pacquiao-Mosley is that both fighters will engage and Shane will have his moments. But at night's end, his body will come to the conclusion that enough is enough.

Still, a word of caution—The odds on Pacquiao-Mosley opened with Shane a 6-to-1 underdog. Vernon Forrest was a 6-to-1 underdog the night that he turned Shane Mosley's world upside down.

In recent years, Manny Pacquiao has grown increasingly important to the sweet science.

Manny Pacquiao: The Face of Boxing

Throughout its history as a mainstream sport, boxing has been inextricably linked in the public mind to the heavyweight champion of the world.

There were times when he wasn't even the best fighter in the division. James Braddock was overshadowed by Joe Louis. Sonny Liston lurked ominously during Floyd Patterson's reign. And in the 1980s, Sugar Ray Leonard, Marvin Hagler, Thomas Hearns, and Roberto Duran shared the spotlight with the heavyweights.

But for most of boxing's history, from the early English pugilists through Mike Tyson and Lennox Lewis (who engaged in the last heavyweight title fight that truly mattered), the heavyweight champion has been The Man. Everyone, not just sports fans, knew his name.

Manny Pacquiao is now more important to boxing than the heavyweight champion. He has become the face of boxing.

A Pacquiao fight is an EVENT, like a rock concert by an iconic performer. He's a standard-bearer for the Filipino people. And their idolatry has rippled around the globe, transforming into crossover appeal insofar as the American public is concerned.

Pacquiao now has international star power. And his fame keeps growing.

The kick-off press tour for the May 7, 2011, fight between Pacquiao and Shane Mosley told the tale. Manny was escorted from place to place like a head of state. The number of media members present at each stop was overwhelming. Tim Smith of the *New York Daily News* summed up what happened when the tour touched down in New York.

"A day with Pacquiao," Smith wrote, "is an exhausting marathon of fighting through clamoring fans, listening to the same questions over and over, and jumping in and out of a caravan of fast-moving black SUVs. As he left the venue, Pacquiao and his group made their way through a kitchen and were set to walk out of a back entrance. But as security opened the door, they were met with a pack of fans clamoring for auto-graphs. They had to have the fighter wait inside until they could clear a path to his waiting car. Once he got into the car, fans surrounded it, screaming for Pacquiao. Everywhere he goes, people want a piece of him. They want to touch him, take a picture with him, have him sign some-thing. Pacquiao takes it all in stride. 'It's all part of being famous,' he said."

The following day, February 15th, was styled as *Mr. Pacquiao Goes to Washington*. Manny was escorted to the floor of the United States Senate by Senate Minority Leader Harry Reid. Then Manny and his wife, Jinkee, journeyed to the White House, where they met with Barack Obama in the Oval Office.

"I'm stunned by what has happened," Bob Arum (Pacquiao's pro-moter) said afterward. "I knew that Manny could become big, but this has gone beyond my wildest expectations."

There's a difference between a fighter being good and a fighter being marketable. Pacquiao is both.

Why is he so special in the public mind?

One reason is the way in which Arum has promoted him. But Pacquiao's personal qualities are the key.

Ten years ago, I wrote, "To be marketable, a fighter has to appeal, not just to boxing fans, but also to the general public. He has to find his way into the 'people' and 'celebrity' sections of the newspaper. He needs cer-tain personal intangibles and he has to be willing to work at the commer-cial aspects of the game. Marketing expert Leigh Steinberg states the criteria as follows: 'How can the public identify this figure? What distin-guishes him from any other person on the face of the earth? The chal-lenge is to clearly and distinctly create a persona for this individual as opposed to any other person in the world.'"

Pacquiao combines an endearing personality with good looks.

He's generous with his time and wealth.

He sings.

"How good is Manny's singing?" Arum is asked.

"He sings better than Oscar," the promoter answers.

But most notably, Pacquiao has dedicated himself to improving the lives of the Filipino people. Last year, he was elected to Congress; an event that CNN listed as one of "twenty stories that changed Asia" in 2010.

It's too early to know with certainty what Pacquiao's impact in the political arena will be. But with his high profile, he offers hope for raising international awareness and action on such issues as the crusade against slave trafficking.

"People expect a lot from me," Manny says. "I try not to disappoint them."

"If anyone doesn't like Manny Pacquiao, then he must have done something to them personally," says Naazim Richardson (Shane Mosley's trainer). "Because it's impossible to not like Manny Pacquiao."

Then there's Pacquiao, the fighter.

"For me, boxing isn't about hurting each other," Manny says. "Boxing is entertainment and making people happy."

But a fighter has to hurt his opponents to win. And Pacquiao is very good at it.

Manny has won titles in eight weight divisions. That's a remarkable accomplishment. But as Emanuel Steward notes, "It isn't all about Pacquiao moving up in weight. Part of it is that he's just not coming down as far. He hasn't had to starve himself and weaken himself to make weight like so many fighters do today."

Pacquiao has beaten some of the best fighters of his time. Erik Morales, Marco Antonio Barrera, Juan Manuel Marquez, Oscar De La Hoya, Ricky Hatton, Miguel Cotto, and Antonio Margarito are among his victims.

And he's an exciting fighter. Much of his defense is in his offense. In recent years, he has been so dominant in the ring that his excellence is often taken for granted. That's a disservice to Manny's work ethic and the contributions made by Freddie Roach.

Roach began training Pacquiao in 2001, when Manny came to the United States to challenge Lehlohonolo Ledwaba for the IBF 122-pound crown.

Freddie is a teacher. "You teach every fighter differently," he says. "That's because they all learn differently and have different natural ability."

The word from inside Team Pacquiao is that, after less-than-ideal training camps for Manny's fights against Miguel Cotto, Joshua Clottey, and Antonio Margarito, Pacquiao's focus has returned to the level that it was at prior to his fighting Ricky Hatton.

That's bad news for Mosley.

Also, as Naazim Richardson notes, "Things are at a point now where, when you fight Pacquiao, you're fighting the man and you're also fighting the perception of how great he is. People are so busy watching Pacquiao that they don't see what the other guy does. It's like Joe Frazier said about fighting Ali. When Joe hit Ali, they talked about how great Ali's jaw was. When Ali hit Joe, it was, 'Look how fast Ali's hands are.'"

Pacquiao is now the consensus choice among knowledgeable boxing people as the best pound-for-pound fighter in the world. The most compelling argument in favor of his supremacy is the fact that Floyd Mayweather Jr won't fight him.

"I think that Mayweather might be a little scared," Marvelous Marvin Hagler said last year. "If you're going to fight, let's fight. Do you want to fight the guy? Yes or no? Pacquiao is saying, 'Come on! Let's do it today.'"

"Floyd is scared of Pacquiao for some reason," Roy Jones adds. "If they told Ali that he had to fight George Foreman with one hand tied behind his back, he would have done it. And Floyd found a reason to not take the fight."

Pacquiao says simply, "People know that Mayweather is not ready to fight me."

Meanwhile, tickets for Pacquiao-Mosley have completely sold out. A thousand tickets went unsold when Mayweather fought Mosley last year.

Put it all together and it's clear that Manny Pacquiao is now The Man. In recent years, boxing has been on the ropes. Pacquiao is in the vanguard of those fighting to give new relevance to the sport and bring it back.

In the end, Pacquiao-Mosley was a Manny Pacquiao fight. Nothing more, nothing less.

Pacquiao-Mosley: The Event

There was no catchy title like "Gory Glory" or "The Brawl for it All." The May 7, 2011, fight between Manny Pacquiao and Shane Mosley was for the WBO welterweight crown, but that was a footnote. The event was marketed simply as Pacquiao-Mosley, although PACQUIAO-Mosley might have been more appropriate. It was a Manny Pacquiao fight. That was what mattered.

In recent years, Pacquiao has taken on a Superman-like persona. The ability to fight for survival was ingrained in him as a child. In the ring, he attacks with savage fury. He has achieved greatness as a fighter. But unlike many superstars who rise from poverty to glorious heights, Pacquiao is appreciative of those who helped him along the way and truly grateful for what he has now.

People hang on Manny's every word. He uplifts them with his presence and treats them like he wants to be treated: The Golden Rule. He goes to great lengths to avoid disappointing anyone. There's no macho swaggering. Each day, he seems enchanted by the wonder of the road he has traveled.

Unlike Mike Tyson (whose fights were "events" with an ugly undercurrent), Pacquiao brings an aura of good will to the proceedings. The mood on site at the MGM Grand in Las Vegas was upbeat throughout fight week. Bob Arum hosted the proceedings, telling the assembled media that Tecate (a fight sponsor) is "a terrific beer" and Pacquiao is "the greatest superstar in boxing since Muhammad Ali."

There were five hundred applications for media credentials; many of them from what Top Rank director of publicity Lee Samuels called "premier press." Tickets went on sale on January 31st and sold out soon after. Pacquiao was guaranteed a $20,000,000 minimum purse; Mosley, $5,000,000.

The respective trainers—Freddie Roach (Pacquiao) and Naazim Richardson (Mosley)—were part of the story line. Each is respected and popular in the boxing community.

"Pacquiao fights like [Floyd] Mayweather talks," Richardson told the media. "Believe me; we understand that Pacquiao is a problem. I could tell you all these things that Pacquiao has and praise him to the sky, but it's easier if I tell you this. The only attribute in boxing that Manny Pacquiao doesn't have is height and range. Everything else, man, he's got it all. He's got great ring generalship. He's got movement, speed, power, one-punch power, combination punching."

When asked if Mosley's sparring partners offered a reasonable facsimile of Pacquiao, Naazim responded, "The last fighter I saw who fought like Pacquiao was Aaron Pryor. If anyone was fighting like Pacquiao, they'd be off somewhere defending their own title. They wouldn't have time to come to our camp."

Meanwhile, Roach praised his opposite number, saying, "Naazim is a very good trainer. He's experienced. He knows how to get to his fighters. He brings out the best in people. It's a great challenge for me to come up with a better game plan than he does."

Richardson and Roach share the bond of having battled through physical disabilities.

Richardson has recovered from a stroke suffered three years ago.

Roach has Parkinson's disease. He takes medication three times a day and receives Botox injections in his neck every three months to control the symptoms. "The progression has been slow," he says. "I know how to handle it. I don't let it get in my way."

Despite his illness, Freddie is far from frail. Constant gym-work has given him biceps that Popeye would envy.

Like most fighters, Roach comes from a hard place. "My father was a mean guy," he says. "He taught us killer instinct. If you're in a fight, you're in it to win. If you hurt somebody, finish him off. That's the way he ran the household. There was fear when you were around him."

One day before Pacquiao-Mosley, Freddie was honored by the Boxing Writers Association of America for the fifth time as its "Trainer of the Year."

Pacquiao calls Roach "master" and "my big brother."

Julio Cesar Chavez Jr (who Freddie also trains) refers to Bob Arum as "the Freddie Roach of promoters."

"I have a lot of Eddie in me," Roach says, referring to the legendary Eddie Futch (who trained Freddie as a fighter and took him on as an apprentice when his ring career was done). "I know how to train a fighter. But when the bell rings, I sit down and Manny is the one who fights. It's about Manny, not me. I have the best job in the world, if you want to call this a job. I have the best life in the world. I ask myself sometimes, "Is this really happening to me?"

Mosley could have been forgiven for asking himself the same question. Once again, despite a career highlighted by two victories over Oscar De La Hoya, he was the B-side in a super-fight, the other guy, the opponent.

"Shane Mosley is pretty much the forgotten man in this media circus," Rick Folstad wrote shortly before Pacquiao-Mosley. "After all, this is the Manny Pacquiao Hour; a one-man act that doesn't have room for a sidekick. Mosley is just a little trimming, extra frosting, a guy left out in the cold, peering through a greasy window at the celebration he never got invited to. It almost feels like he's an afterthought in this fight, someone who was needed to fill an empty chair when they started snapping photos for the history books."

Pacquiao treated Mosley with respect. "He knocked [Antonio] Margarito out," Manny said at the final pre-fight press conference. "I fought Margarito and we finished twelve rounds; so advantage to him for that."

Naazim Richardson addressed the matter of Shane's age (thirty-nine), saying, "There's a difference between a legendary fighter who has age and an old boxer. When special gets old, you can still be extraordinary."

And Mosley noted, "Margarito landed the most punches ever on Manny Pacquiao. If Margarito is fast enough to land punches on Manny Pacquiao, then I know I'm fast enough to land punches on Manny Pacquiao. My thing right now is to get the win. We can talk about my being the underdog afterward."

But Shane was a heavy underdog for a reason.

Several reasons, actually. Pacquiao is a great fighter. And the prevailing view during fight week was that Mosley looked older than he had before his previous two outings (a loss to Mayweather and a draw against Sergio Mora).

"I think I can still do all the things in the ring that I could do five years ago," Shane said three days before Pacquiao-Mosley.

Not many people believed him. The question of the week was not who would win, but whether or not Pacquiao would knock Mosley out.

"The biggest mistake a trainer can make is to think that his fighter can't be beaten," Roach cautioned. "If you just walk into Shane and attack him, he'll counterpunch the hell out of you, and he has knockout power."

"I lay in bed last night, trying to fall asleep," Freddie acknowledged on Thursday morning. "I was asking myself, 'Is he going to try to box us? Bang with us? Will he go to the ropes and try to sucker us in? I ran through every scenario that might happen. And when I'd gone through them all, I fell asleep."

But Roach was confident. "I don't think Shane can handle the pace that Manny will set for him," Freddie said. "Shane is a tough guy, a very durable guy. But like most fighters, Shane is at his best when he's faster than the other guy. He wasn't against Mayweather and he won't be against Manny. I've never seen a fighter with the combination of speed and power that Manny has. It's like an explosion when he hits you. I think Manny will knock him out."

Expectations run high for Pacquiao each time he steps into the ring. It's an article of faith among the faithful that he can't lose.

Meanwhile, the Pacquiao Circus, Manny's Magic Mystery Tour—call it what you will—rolled on.

Early in the promotion, while Shane was at ESPN headquarters in Bristol, Connecticut, Pacquiao and his wife were meeting with Barack Obama at the White House in the Oval Office.

"I told him, 'Mr. President; I heard you like basketball,'" Manny later recounted. "And President Obama told me, 'I like boxing too.' I invited him to this fight, but he said he cannot come."

Most superstar fighters isolate themselves during fight week. Except for contractually mandated promotional appearances, they shut out the outside world.

Pacquiao took an opposite tack. Sporting a Justin Bieber hair-style (he prefers to think of as evocative of Bruce Lee), he was remarkably accessible in Las Vegas.

"I never worry about Manny once he gets to work," Roach said.

"It's the 'getting him to work' part I worry about. There's always distractions. There are days where I get fed up with all the craziness. Fortunately, Manny is such a hard worker that, once we get going, everything is fine."

Pacquiao, in turn, says of his many outside-the-ring activities, "They are only distractions if you allow them to distract you."

Manny spent several hours on Wednesday night rehearsing for a planned post-fight concert and took advantage of every opportunity during the week to plug his new musical release: *Sometimes When We Touch*, recorded with Dan Hill.

"I feel happy every time I hear music," he said.

Roach was less pleased.

"I went to Manny's room at eleven o'clock last night," the trainer groused on Thursday morning. "There were guys in there filming a TV show. I wasn't happy about it. I said, 'Manny; you have to go to bed.' Don't these people understand that he's fighting in two nights in the biggest fight of the year?"

Pacquiao-Mosley was Showtime's biggest fight since Holyfield-Tyson II in 1997 (not counting Lewis-Tyson, which was a joint venture with HBO). Thus, Pacquiao was shadowed for much of the week by a *Fight Camp 360* film crew whose members wore black T-shirts with red lettering on the back that read, "Waiting for Manny." That was a reference to the phenomenon known as "Pacquiao time" (chronic lateness caused by stopping to pose for photographs and sign autographs for fans).

The *Fight Camp 360* crew was in attendance on Thursday at 1:00 PM, when Pacquiao began a nine-interview satellite-TV tour. Sitting in dressing room #1 at the MGM Grand Garden Arena (which had been turned into a darkened television studio), Manny patiently answered questions and repeated familiar themes.

"I do my best to give a good fight to the people . . . I'm always motivated to do my best for the fans . . . It is never personal between me and my opponent. We are just doing our job."

"Why haven't we seen a Pacquiao-Mayweather fight?"

"Something is wrong with him. For some reason, he doesn't want the fight. I don't know why."

"How do you see your place in boxing history?"

"I'm satisfied with what I've achieved in boxing. I don't have to compare myself with anyone else."

"What do you think about mixed martial arts?"

"For me, MMA is too brutal. I don't want to hurt anyone's feelings, but I think boxing is the best."

"Tell us about the new Manny Pacquiao cologne."

"The cologne is good," Manny said with a twinkle in his eye. "You can smell like Manny Pacquiao."

Then Pacquiao moved down the corridor to meet with the Showtime and Top Rank announcing teams. Al Bernstein, Gus Johnson, Antonio Tarver, Jim Gray, James Brown, Barry Tompkins, Rich Marotta, and Steve Farhood were there.

How would he feel if he lost on Saturday night?

"Losing sucks. It has happened to me, so I know. And it would be worse now because so many people are hoping for me. I don't want to disappoint them."

"Do you think you're a great fighter?"

"That's what people say."

"Can you get better?"

"I think so."

Then came the all-but-mandatory question about Floyd Mayweather Jr.

"I'm happy with what I have done in boxing," Pacquiao answered. "If that fight happens, good. If that fight does not happen, I'm okay with that."

"Is there anything more you can do to get Mayweather to fight you?"

A smile crossed Manny's face.

"I could pick up the phone and call him and say, 'Floyd; I'm tired of people asking me when are we going to fight. Let's do it.'"

"Have you thought about doing that?"

"That's my promoter's job to do."

The weigh-in on Friday was open to the public. Fans began lining up at five o'clock in the morning. By the time Pacquiao and Mosley stepped on the scales shortly after 3:00 PM, all six thousand seats were taken.

One wondered if there might come a time when all of the hopes, dreams, expectations, and demands that have been placed on Pacquiao's shoulders become an unsupportable burden.

★　★　★

On Saturday night, Freddie Roach arrived at dressing room #2 at 5:20 PM. He and assistant Billy Keane moved a table from mid-room to a far corner. Then the trainer emptied out his carry bag, arranging the tools of his trade on the table. Gauze, tape, scissors, warm-up mitts . . .

At 5:30, Roach fashioned six "ligaments" (strips of tape rolled vertically so they resemble sticks of incense) that would be placed between Manny's fingers when the fighter's hands were wrapped.

"I know I'm wasting my time," Freddie said. "Naazim will make me re-roll them, but I feel like doing it now. I told Manny this afternoon, no matter how your hands are wrapped, Naazim will make a fuss. He does it every time. He'll complain to the inspector. He'll ask for the head of the commission to come in and make a ruling. All he wants is to get the two of us excited. Don't let it bother you."

Roach smiled.

"Manny told me, 'Don't worry; I don't get excited.' That's true. I don't see how he handles everything, but he does. I went to Manny's room last night. The corridor outside the room was jammed. I asked the hotel security guys, 'What the fuck are you doing?' They told me that Manny said the people outside the room could stay. Then I went inside his room, and it was more crowded than the corridor."

"It doesn't stop," Freddie continued. "This afternoon, I was in Manny's room. He had a seating chart of the arena and a pile of tickets on his bed. Five hours before the fight, and he's worrying about who's sitting where."

Keane went to Mosley's dressing room to watch Naazim Richardson tape Shane's hands.

Manny arrived at 6:35. There were fewer entourage members with him than is usually the case when he fights. Security at the MGM Grand was more stringent than at previous Pacquiao outings. But space in the dressing room was tight because of the presence of three camera crews representing Showtime, the Manny Pacquiao website, and an independent documentary production.

Manny went into the bathroom. Jim Gray entered to conduct a pre-fight interview.

"Manny is in the bathroom," a cameraman informed the Showtime production team in the truck. "I just heard the toilet flush . . . I hear water running. I think he's washing his hands."

Pacquiao returned. Jim Gray conducted the interview. A cameraman whacked his camera against Manny's shoulder. Roach winced.

At 6:50, a Nevada State Athletic Commission inspector asked for a urine sample.

"I just peed," Pacquiao told him.

Manny looked toward his physical conditioner, Alex Ariza, for help.

"I'm not in charge of peeing," Ariza said.

"Right now, I cannot pee," Manny advised the inspector.

"Not a problem," the inspector responded. "Let us know when you're ready."

There was another interview; this one for Top Rank's international television feed.

Pacquiao took off his shirt and pants. As he disrobed, he seemed to grow larger.

Three cameras were within arm's reach with a boom microphone overhead. Manny is used to thirty friends inhabiting every nook and cranny of his dressing room. This was different. The television lights were on constantly. The room was hot; the area around him, claustrophobic.

He put on his trunks, socks, and boxing shoes.

At 7:00 o'clock, Michael Koncz (Pacquiao's lead adviser) came into the room with Harry Reid (the senior United States senator from Nevada) and Sig Rogich (a political power broker).

"How are you, Congressman?" Reid inquired.

Brief pleasantries followed.

Five minutes later, Naazim Richardson entered and Pacquiao (as is his custom) began wrapping his own hands. When an extra hand was needed, cornerman Miguel Diaz assisted in the process.

Richardson was uncharacteristically unintrusive.

After Diaz applied the first ligament, Naazim pointed to the second one. "Can I look at that, please."

Roach handled the ligament to Richardson, who flexed it back and forth.

"Okay," he offered.

At 7:38, the taping was done.

"Thank you, gentleman," Richardson said.

There had been no gamesmanship. Perhaps that was out of respect for

Pacquiao and the fact that Manny had done most of the wrapping himself. Or maybe Richardson simply felt that everything had been done in compliance with the rules.

Referee Kenny Bayless entered and gave Pacquiao his pre-fight instructions . . . There were stretching exercises . . . Shadow-boxing . . . Padwork . . . A prayer . . . Then the fight.

16,412 fans had gathered inside the arena. The atmosphere was electric when the bell for round one rang.

The electricity was soon short-circuited.

Mosley tried to survive rather than win the fight. He started cautiously, keeping his distance, making Pacquiao come to him. Initially, one had the impression that he was looking to land a big counter off a Pacquiao mistake. That ran contrary to the prevailing view that Shane's best chance to win was to force a firefight, land something big, and outmuscle Manny on the inside.

But as the rounds passed, it became clear that Shane had something else in mind.

"I'm going to fight hard," he'd said before the fight. "Everybody knows that."

He didn't.

More than most fighters, Pacquiao tests his opponent's resolve. How do you fight a hurricane?

Before long, it was apparent that Mosley wanted a sparring session, not a memorable fight. According to the Sports Media Technology statistics, he threw only five "power punches" per round and a mere five combinations during the entire bout.

The pattern was the same throughout. Pacquiao stalking. Shane on his bike. There were few highlights. A straight left hand put Mosley on the canvas in round three. In round ten, referee Kenny Bayless mistakenly ruled that a trip to the canvas caused by the entanglement of feet was a knockdown in Shane's favor (he later apologized to Pacquiao for the mistake).

In sum, it was a disappointing effort on Mosley's part. He fought a safety-first fight. Also, safety second, third, fourth, fifth, sixth, and on through the end of round twelve. As David Greisman wrote, "Shane struck out looking instead of going down swinging." Or phrased differently, he mailed it in and put insufficient postage on the envelope.

The judges differed in their treatment of the tenth round (when Pacquiao visited the canvas). That accounted for the 120–107, 120–108, and 119–108 variation in scoring.

"I feel bad for the people," Manny said afterward. "The people want a good fight, exchanging a lot of punches. That's what I want. Mosley was always running. Every time I want to throw a lot of punches, he goes away. I was expecting him to fight me at least five rounds of the twelve [translation: I was hoping for a fifth-round knockout]. I want him to go toe-to-toe with me, so we can give a good fight. But he feel my power and did not want to go toe-to-toe. What could I do?"

Roach was more blunt.

"One guy tried to win the fight and one guy didn't," Freddie offered. "Mosley just tried to survive. When you get to that point in boxing, it's time to call it a day. If you go into a fight, especially a fight as big as this one, and don't try to win, you're done."

Mosley's admirers will say that Shane has enjoyed an illustrious career and has nothing left prove.

That's good, because he's not likely to prove much anymore. Once an elite fighter accepts being an opponent, the good part of his career is over.

As for the future; the world wants to see Pacquiao-Mayweather. But Floyd has studiously avoided that fight and, presumably, will continue to do so in the months ahead. Boxing's former pound-for-pound king has been reduced to "tweeting" his followers, offering them YouTube links to Pacquiao's three losses, and advising them that he spent the night of May 7th watching a Lady Gaga concert on HBO.

Thus, Pacquiao's next opponent will most likely be Juan Manuel Marquez.

And after that?

"Manny is transitioning more and more into politics," Roach says. "He wants to be as successful in politics as he has been in boxing. I think you're looking at two more years, two fights a year, and then he's gone. If he continues doing things the way he has been, that shouldn't be a problem. Manny lives a healthy lifestyle in between fights. His work ethic is incredible. He works even harder now than he did when he first came to my gym. I just don't want him to fight too long."

Recently, Pacquiao asked Roach, "When I slow down, will you tell me that it's time to stop?"

"I will," Freddie promised.

At some point, the magic carpet ride will end. Let's hope it ends well.

Micky Ward was never a world champion, but he's a boxing success story.

Micky Ward: "The Fighter"

Eight years ago, *Irish America* honored Micky Ward as one of "The Irish 100." Ward received his tribute at the magazine's annual awards banquet at the Plaza Hotel in New York.

"I don't know why I'm being honored," Micky said that night. Then he turned toward fellow honoree, Robert Morris, leader of the New York City Fire Department's "Rescue One" unit. "I go in the ring two, maybe three, times a year, and it's for myself. Guys like Captain Morris are the real heroes. They put their life on the line every day to keep the rest of us safe."

That's Micky Ward. Unpretentious, soft-spoken, a bit shy, more of a listener than a talker. Now, seven years after the end of his ring career, he has been catapulted into the spotlight with the release of the feature film, *The Fighter.*

The Fighter stars Mark Wahlberg as Ward and centers on the relationship between Micky and his half-brother, Dickie Eklund. Sterling performances by Christian Bale (as Eklund), Amy Adams (as Micky's girlfriend, Charlene), and Melissa Leo (as Alice Ward, the conniving matriarch of the dysfunctional Ward clan) give it extra impact. Dickie's addiction to crack and the havoc it wreaks on those around him is a key plot element. The film won two Oscars and two Golden Globe awards.

Ward was born in Lowell, Massachusetts, on October 4, 1965. He turned pro at age nineteen and won his first fourteen fights before dropping a split decision to Edwin Curet. He rebounded with four wins; then went through a stretch that saw him lose six of nine bouts leading to a thirty-two-month hiatus from boxing. He returned to the ring in 1994 and won nine straight to land a world title fight against Vince Phillips.

Micky was stopped on cuts by Phillips (the only "KO by" of his career). He retired from boxing in 2003 with a 38-and-13 record and 27 knockouts to his credit.

The key to Ward's legacy as a fighter lies in his last three fights; a brutal trilogy against Arturo Gatti. The first of these encounters is widely regarded as one of the most dramatic slugfests of all time. Micky won.

"It was a tough fight," Ward said afterward. "Two guys with a lot of heart; two guys with the will to win. I was very drained, as tired as I've ever been. The night after the fight, I sat down and watched the tape. That's when I knew it was something special. That's also when I said to myself, 'These two guys are nuts.'"

Ward versus Gatti captured the imagination of fight fans across the nation. For their rematch, each man was paid the remarkable sum of $1,200,000. That led Micky to note, "If someone had told me ten years ago when I lost all those fights and retired from boxing that someday I'd make a million bucks from one fight, I'd have thought they were crazy."

Gatti prevailed in their second encounter and also the third. "Micky is a great guy," he said when the fighting was done. "I can't say anything bad about him. Even if I wanted to, I couldn't find anything bad to say."

Ward responded in kind, offering, "It's not about who's tougher. We're both tough guys. It's about respect. In the ring, we tried to kill each other. But I have a lot of respect for Arturo. I like him; he's a nice person. I'd never say anything bad about him and I think that he feels the same way about me. I wanted to beat him more than anything in the world. But outside the ring, he's a beautiful guy."

Gatti died in Brazil in 2009. Initially, the authorities ruled that he'd passed out or been knocked unconscious after a night of hard drinking and been strangled to death. His wife (an exotic dancer named Amanda Rodrigues) was charged with first-degree murder. Then investigators did a suspicious about-face, claiming that Arturo had committed suicide by hanging himself with the strap from his wife's purse.

"Arturo's death really shook me up," Micky says. "It was a terrible tragedy. I wasn't there, so I can't tell you what happened. But it's hard for me to believe that he killed himself."

That brings us to *The Fighter,* the Hollywood version of Ward's life. Purists don't like the movie. Its factual distortions and other departures from reality bother them.

George Kimball, longtime boxing writer for the *Boston Herald,* covered Ward from his days as an amateur through Micky's final professional fight.

"I have problems with the movie," Kimball says. "It depicts Micky's family in a way that's bound to humiliate them. I can live with that because some of them were pretty bad. But the boxing career that's shown in the film isn't Micky's and that bothers me. Chronologically, the storyline is way off. There are fights in the film that bear no relationship to what actually happened. And the make-believe world championship fight at the end is ridiculous. Micky never won a world title. When he beat Shae Neary in London (the climactic scene in *The Fighter*), it was for a belt given out by a silly alphabet-soup organization called the World Boxing Union. That belt meant so little to Micky that he gave it up rather than defend it. The great thing about Micky Ward is that he's appreciated and respected by people who know boxing even though he never won a world title. Why construct a nonsense storyline and pretend that fiction is history?"

The best way to enjoy *The Fighter* is to forget about the details of Micky's life, treat it like fiction, and enjoy the show.

That might be hard for some members of Ward's family to do. As Kimball notes, "Micky's mother is presented as such a selfish venal matriarch, she could be Fagin in drag. Alice presides over a flock of daughters; big-haired, gum-chewing, chain-smoking, foul-mouthed, small-town bimbos. This gaggle of slovenly crones serves the approximate function of the witches in Macbeth."

"Some of the people in my family don't like the movie," Micky acknowledges. "I understand how they feel. But I like it; I think it's great. The one thing I'm sorry about is that they ended the movie before my three fights with Arturo. They wanted the film to focus on me and Dickie and Dickie's problems with drugs. But Arturo was such a great guy. We shared so much. He had his issues; he lived like he fought. But he deserved to be in the movie."

Dickie Eklund has had problems with drugs and the law in the years since the happy ending portrayed in *The Fighter*.

Micky has enjoyed smoother sailing and is content with his life today. He and Charlene were married in 2005. He has one child, a twenty-one-year-old daughter named Kasie, from a previous relationship, and is a member of Teamsters Union, Local 25, in Boston.

"I shuttle people around to movie sets when there's work in town," he explains. "When I'm not doing that, I'm busy with other things."

Those other things include part ownership of an outdoor hockey rink in Chelmsford, Massachusetts, and teaching youngsters to box on the second floor of a nearby Gold's Gym.

"I loved boxing," Ward says, looking back on his years in the ring. "The one-on-one, the competition. Being a fighter is about sacrificing your body and doing everything you can within the rules to win. I gave boxing everything that was in me. I never cut corners in training or in a fight. I started my career at 140 pounds and I finished my career at 140 pounds, which tells you how hard I worked to stay in shape. I still follow boxing. But the fighting part of my life is over now. I'm forty-five years old. To be honest with you, I don't miss it."

It has been suggested that *The Fighter* will boost Ward's profile the same way that *Raging Bull* elevated Jake LaMotta to iconic status. In truth, that's unlikely to happen. LaMotta was a hall-of-fame fighter. Micky was a courageous warrior, but his skills weren't at that level.

And just as significantly, Ward shuns the limelight. "Some people like a lot of attention," he says. "I don't. I'm happy being in the background, so the movie won't change my life. I'm just a regular guy, the same old me. Don't worry; I won't go Hollywood on you."

I hadn't planned on writing when I went to the fights on July 15, 2011.
But Delvin Rodriguez vs. Pawel Wolak demanded attention.

Rodriguez–Wolak: A Great Fight

Pawel Wolak sat on a chair in a small dressing room on the second floor of Roseland Ballroom in New York. The entire right side of his face from his mouth to his hairline was grotesquely misshapen and swollen. His right eye was completely shut and looked like Sylvester Stallone's after Rocky Balboa's first fight against Apollo Creed. It was as though someone had shoved a tennis ball beneath the skin and painted the entire area purple.

"I wasn't hurt," Wolak said. "I just couldn't see out of my eye. I don't let people hit me on purpose. But this is boxing, so you're gonna get hit. The doctor asked me a couple of times if I could see. How could I see? But I'm a fighter, so I said yes."

"Have you seen your face yet?" Wolak was asked.

"Not yet. I imagine it looks pretty bad."

We live in an era when the fundamental assumptions that underlie boxing are sorely tested. The "do-or-die" attitude that once illuminated the sport often seems like fantasy. David Haye punked out against Wladimir Klitschko because (he says) he hurt his little toe three weeks before the fight. Shane Mosley and Devon Alexander disappointed in multi-million-dollar outings.

Wolak had just fought Delvin Rodriguez with each man receiving a purse of $15,000. In an era of overhyped, overpaid, manufactured-story line encounters, they'd reminded people of what boxing is about.

Rodriguez–Wolak was a crossroads fight for both men. Rodriguez is a boxer-puncher, who came into the bout with a 25–5–2 ledger, but had gone 2–3–2 in his last seven fights. The prevailing view was that he'd been jobbed by the judges several times. But he was perilously close to becoming an opponent.

Wolak is a brawler with a good chin and the ability to absorb punishment. Prior to facing Rodriguez, he'd compiled a 29-and-1 record against mostly club-fight-level opposition and was moving toward a title shot. Pawel's way of dealing with an adversary's punches is to walk through them. He's a pressure fighter who unloads like a non-stop threshing machine and beats opponents down with his forearms, shoulders, and every other available body part. But he's not a power puncher and is too squared up when he fights, which makes him a large target.

One day after Rodriguez-Wolak, write-ups would describe the fight as "awesome . . . incredible . . . breathtaking . . . thrilling . . . ."

It was all of that. Everyone who was at Roseland Ballroom on July 15th will remember the battle.

There was no feeling-out process. Rodriguez started well, staying in the pocket, predicating his defense on getting off first rather than moving in and out of range with his legs. He landed the sharper harder punches in the early going, doing damage with a stream of left hooks and upper-cuts. There were virtually no jabs from either man.

By the end of round three, Wolak's right eye was starting to swell. But after four rounds, Rodriguez appeared to be tiring. He was the naturally smaller man, having moved up from 147 to 154 pounds to face Pawel. And he was being worn down by the rough-house trench-warfare pace.

At the midway point, the fight was dead even. Then Wolak started to tire. Getting whacked in the head again and again will do that to a fighter. Rodriguez said, "I'm still here," with his punches. And by the end of round seven, Pawel's right eye was useless. The only function it served was to make his head a bigger target for Delvin and add to the drama of the moment.

The last three rounds, everyone in attendance understood that they were watching a time-capsule fight. Wolak was fighting for every second of every round and Rodriguez engaged him. The action was non-stop and brutal.

Wolak was getting hit by left hooks on his damaged right eye that everybody in the arena except Pawel could see coming. His left eye was closing too. But he refused to surrender, fighting by the maxim, "If this guy is close enough to hit me, then he's close enough for me to hit him back."

When it was over, most observers at ringside (including this writer) gave Rodriguez a slight edge. Virtually no one thought that Wolak had won. Tom Schreck scored the bout 97–93 for Delvin. But he was over-ruled by Julie Lederman and Steve Weisfeld, who called the fight a draw.

Rodriguez was relaxed and happy in his dressing room after the fight. There was some moderate swelling and bruising on his face, but he had the aura of a winner about him.

"I knew it was going to be a tough fight," Delvin said. "That's the way Wolak is. He doesn't hit that hard. But whatever you do, he keeps coming."

"How do you feel about the decision?"

"A draw is discouraging," Delvin answered. "But it's better than a loss, which is what I've gotten in some fights that I know I won. And I'd rather have my face tomorrow morning than his."

That was in keeping with the overall sentiment that, yes, Rodriguez deserved the win; but Wolak had fought with such courage and the fight was so thrilling that it was hard to begrudge Pawel the draw.

The larger question is whether the fight should have been allowed to continue. The damage to Wolak's eye gave the bout incredible drama, but it also endangered Pawel's long-term physical well-being.

Wolak came into the fight with a lot of scar tissue above his right eye. He'd been cut there in six previous outings. A more serious problem might be permanent damage to the soft tissue underneath the skin.

Danny Milano (one of the foremost cutmen in boxing) worked Rodriguez's corner. He had a good view of the carnage as Rodriguez-Wolak unfolded.

"The way it swelled up, it looked to me like the eye socket might have been damaged," Milano said after the fight. "I wasn't in Pawel's corner. There were people who had a closer look at the eye than I did. But I think they should have stopped it. Pawel was still in the fight and he's a warrior. But he took a horrible pounding on that eye. He might never be the same after tonight."

There's a chance that, from now on, every time Wolak enters the ring, he will be an impaired fighter.

Meanwhile, let it be said that, in an age of phony championships and incompetent corrupt power brokers, Pawel Wolak and Delvin Rodriguez dignified boxing. They showed why many people, myself included, believe that boxing at its best is the greatest sport of all.

AFTERWARD: DECEMBER 3, 2011

The rematch between Delvin Rodriguez and Pawel Wolak lacked the drama of their first encounter because Pawel had two eyes this time instead of one left eye paired with a balloon on the right side of his face. Also, Rodriguez clearly won the second time around (although the fight was closer than the 100–90, 98–92, 98–91 scoring of the judges indicated).

Wolak is relentless. At times, he seems to regard getting punched in the face as nothing more than an inconvenience that momentarily slows his forward progress. He has a great chin but not a great punch.

In their first fight, Rodriguez stayed in the pocket and relied on getting off first as his primary defense. This time, he used his legs and distance to defensive advantage. Wolak, as he usually does, went to the body throughout the fight. Delvin successfully countered with uppercuts. The last round saw Pawel reeling around the ring, all but out on his feet.

Four days after the fight, Wolak announced his retirement from boxing. Over the course of a seven-year career, he compiled a 29–2–1 record as a courageous honest fighter who brought honor to himself and the sport of boxing. I hope he's honest with himself and stays retired.

"Boxing," Hugh McIlvanney has written, "carries a far higher risk of recurring injustice than any other sport."

A Note on the Refereeing in Agbeko–Mares

Anyone who cares about boxing has to be appalled by referee Russell Mora's conduct of the August 13, 2011, fight between Joseph Agbeko and Abner Mares.

Agbeko was defending his IBF bantamweight title against Mares at the Hard Rock Hotel and Casino in Las Vegas. Agbeko is promoted by Don King Productions. Mares is promoted by Golden Boy.

Mora is thought of in some circles as a "Golden-Boy-friendly" referee. Alan Hopper (vice president of public relations for DKP) says that, several days before the fight, King complained to Keith Kizer (executive director of the Nevada State Athletic Commission) about the choice of Mora as the referee. But King's influence has waned in recent years. Mora remained in place.

Once the fight began, Mares went low from the opening bell. By any objective standard, Mora should have deducted a point for low blows as early as the second round. By this writer's count (after watching a tape of the bout), Mares landed FIFTY-FIVE punches below the belt. And they weren't pity-pat punches or borderline shots. Many were hard blatant flagrant fouls.

For those who think that legal body shots hurt, consider the debilitating effect of a low blow. When a fighter's protective cup is jammed into his groin again and again, it takes a toll. Moreover, Agbeko was wearing his trunks low and his belly-button was fully exposed, which made the fouls even more flagrant. Yet absurdly, Mora kept warning Agbeko for pushing Mares's head down (which he wasn't doing) instead of insisting that Mares fight within the rules.

Mora also blew two knockdown calls. In round one, an off-balance Agbeko tumbled to the canvas when his left foot became entangled with

Mares's left foot. The referee called it a knockdown. That mistake was understandable. A referee's eyes can't be everywhere all the time.

The second knockdown was a different matter. Two minutes into round eleven, Mares landed yet another flagrant low blow. Agbeko crumpled to the canvas in pain. Mora was in perfect position to see the foul, yet he called the occurrence a knockdown.

Agbeko controlled round eleven apart from the "knockdown." But as a consequence of the miscall, the stanza was scored 10–8 for Mares. If Mora had called the low blow and deducted a point from Mares (as he should have), it would have been a 10–8 round in favor of Agbeko (a four-point swing that would have changed the outcome of the fight).

As it was, C. J. Ross scored the bout even. She was overruled by Oren Shellenberger and Adalaide Byrd, each of whom favored Mares by a 115–111 margin.

Agbeko vs. Mares is now known as "Agbeko vs. Mares + Mora."

"The referee is not supposed to decide the champion," Agbeko said afterward. "The referee's job is to make sure it is a fair fight, not steal the title for one fighter."

Kudos to the Showtime announcing team for recognizing the problem early and calling it like it was throughout the fight.

Al Bernstein took the lead: "(round one) Another low blow by Mares. He better watch it. There's a low blow again . . . (round two) Abner Mares has landed at least five low blows. There's another one. Russell Mora's got to take a point away pretty soon . . . (round three) Another low blow . . . (round four) Another low blow by Mares . . . (round five) You've got to take a point away at some point. I'm loath to criticize referees. I hate to do it. But in this instance, you have to take a point away. Mares again goes low. You better take a point away or he won't keep [his punches] up . . . (round six) That's low blow number twenty-eight in this fight by Abner Mares [actually, by this writer's count, it was number thirty-three] . . . (round seven) Russell Mora is not even bothering to look anymore. I hate to do this; I hate criticizing officials. That was a left hand in the worst spot. How can you not take a point away? I'm sorry to be a broken record on this. But come on . . . (round eight) Again; he goes low . . . (round nine) There he goes again. I'm not trying to lean on Russell Mora. I'm not trying to be unfair. But when you don't take a point away from a guy for landing twenty low blows, it doesn't look good . . . (round ten) Oh, my. Oh my goodness. If he doesn't take a point away. This is outrageous. It's an outrage. Good God!"

Then came the second "knockdown." Forgive the hyperbole; but Stevie Wonder could have seen that it was a low blow. And incredibly, Mora started counting.

"Oh, my God!" Bernstein proclaimed. "Russell Mora had a good look at that. He's in perfect position. That's so low; you can't miss that. How could you not see that? This is the most disgraceful performance by a referee I've seen in the last fifteen years."

Showtime's blow-by-blow commentator Gus Johnson chimed in from time to time: "Oh, man! Another low blow by Mares . . . The left hook continues to fall well below the beltline . . . Joseph Abeko has been hit low repeatedly, but the referee is refusing to take a point. If Abner Mares wins this fight, it will be a tainted win."

And Antonio Tarver had his say: "That's another low blow . . . He [Mora] is the man in charge in that ring. He should be seeing these low blows . . . That low blow is almost to the knee . . . He's been getting hit with these low blows since round one . . . Those punches have to be taking a toll on Joseph Agbeko. All night long; it's totally unfair . . . That was a low blow. This referee has failed in this fight totally . . . This referee has stolen a good fight from us because he's not doing the job he was paid to do."

After the fight, Jim Gray conducted an on-air interview with Mora. At that point, as Michael Woods later wrote, the referee's "non-existent credibility went into the sewer from the gutter."

"You just raised the arm of Abner Mares," Gray began. "The question is, 'Would he have won without your help?'"

"I don't help the fighters," Mora responded. "I enforce the rules. Those punches were on the beltline. They're fair punches. I have to call them fair."

Gray then showed Mora the knockdown on a television monitor and asked, "Tell us right now if you feel this is below the belt."

Faced with clear unambiguous evidence of his wrongdoing, Mora offered an inane excuse: "It has a different viewpoint, looking at it here in slow-motion. When I saw it live, I saw it was a fair punch on the beltline."

Fight fans might recall that Mora was also the referee who allowed Nonito Donaire vs. Fernando Montiel to continue after Donaire nearly decapitated Montiel in the second round of their fight in February. I often disagree with Jose Sulaiman. But in this instance, the WBC president is worth quoting.

"It was a criminal act," Sulaiman said. "Montiel was in a poor state. And after telling him to walk and he does not, and after asking him to raise his arms and he does not; [the referee] still allows him to continue. We will object to this referee whenever we can."

Donaire later added his thoughts to the dialogue, branding Mora "a horrible referee."

Boxing has seen too many fights lately where the referee and ring judges seem to have their own agenda. Mora's problem in Agbeko-Mares wasn't one blown call. It was a consistent failure to enforce the most fundamental rules of boxing.

"Incompetence is usually the answer for most of the riddles in boxing," Carlos Acevedo wrote of Mora's conduct. "But Russell Mora was a quantum leap removed from mere ineptitude. Mora was clearly biased in favor of Mares and, worse than that, seemed to enter the ring with a predetermined notion of what he was going to do. Mares had carte blanche to whack Agbeko below the belt as often as he wanted."

The boxing community will remember Mora's performance in Agbeko-Mares for a long time. It should also look closely at how the Nevada State Athletic Commission handles the matter. The NSAC has a policy of refusing to acknowledge that its officials make mistakes. That policy breeds suspect officiating and is one of the reasons for what happened in Agbeko-Mares.

Meanwhile, if Russell Mora looks at a tape of Agbeko-Mares and still thinks that he did his job properly, he shouldn't referee fights anymore.

Floyd Mayweather Jr vs. Victor Ortiz was another showcase event that fell short of expectations.

Mayweather-Ortiz: Sucker Punch

Bart Barry wrote last year that the marketing plan for Floyd Mayweather Jr's fights has become, "How can we fool the public again?"

With that in mind, there came a time about a month ago when I tuned out Mayweather vs. Victor Ortiz. I didn't read the conference-call transcripts. I didn't go to Las Vegas for the fight. I didn't buy the pay-per-view. On fight night, I was curious enough to follow the action via short texts posted at brief intervals on ESPN.com. On Sunday morning, I watched the now-infamous fourth round and its aftermath on YouTube.

Mayweather is a superbly talented fighter. "Anything my mouth says, my hands can back it up," he states. "Once you put me in that squared circle, I'm home."

Floyd also has a penchant for anti-social behavior, having been criminally convicted twice for beating up women. He is currently under indictment for assaulting the mother of three of his children (in addition to physically threatening two of the children). He has engaged in racist homophobic rants; burns hundred-dollar bills in nightclubs to flaunt his wealth; and demeans opponents as a matter of course.

"I've been in a lot of fights," Arturo Gatti said before fighting Mayweather in 2005. "But I've never been in a fight where my opponent was talking like he is. He has no class, to speak about another fighter like he does."

The June 28, 2011, kick-off press conference for Mayweather-Ortiz began with a promotional film that praised Floyd as "pound-for pound, the best fighter in the universe; [a man who] always fights the best and stands alone as the shining star in boxing."

Promoter Richard Schaefer advised the assembled media that Floyd is a "gentleman" and promised that Mayweather-Ortiz would be "the greatest pay-per-view card in the history of boxing."

Not to be outdone, World Boxing Council representative Jill Diamond said that Floyd "bleeds green" but has "a heart of gold."

The "bleeding green" was understandable, given the sanctioning fees that the WBC expected to reap from Mayweather-Ortiz. There are some battered women who might disagree with the "heart of gold" part.

Ortiz seemed a bit overwhelmed by it all.

The "high point" of the pre-fight marketing campaign was a profanity-laced confrontation between Floyd and his father on the first episode of HBO's *Mayweather-Ortiz: 24/7*. Floyd's conduct in that exchange was reminiscent of Mike Tyson's tirade at the Hudson Theater after he assaulted Lennox Lewis onstage during the build-up to Lewis-Tyson.

The low point of the promotion was Mayweather's attack on Oscar De La Hoya after Ortiz said in the second episode of *24/7* that Oscar is his idol. That engendered a Mayweather tweet: "De La Hoya is a drug user, dresses in drag, committed adultery, and drinks alcohol; and Ortiz looks up to this guy."

At that point, Richard Schaefer balanced the competing interests of De La Hoya (his dear friend and partner) and Mayweather (a source of income) and resolutely declared, "I'm not going to get into the middle of that. I have a very nice relationship with Floyd. We work very well together. When Oscar came out with his statement [admitting to having been photographed by a stripper while wearing women's lingerie at a time when he was under the influence of cocaine], there were a lot of people who were very supportive of Oscar and wished him all the best with rehab. There are always those who will have a different opinion."

Meanwhile, it should be noted that, whenever De La Hoya and Mayweather appear jointly at a media event, Oscar has the look of a man who is trying to smile while chewing on glass.

Mayweather was established as a 7-to-1 betting favorite over Ortiz. Thereafter, Victor's chances (such as they were) took another hit when the Nevada State Athletic Commission designated Joe Cortez as the referee for the fight.

Cortez (who has legally trademarked the phrase "I'm fair but I'm firm") was once regarded as one of boxing's better referees. But in recent years, there have been times when "unfair" and "infirm" have attached to his name. More specifically, he has engaged in questionable conduct that altered the flow of several big fights; most notably, Mayweather vs. Ricky Hatton and Amir Khan vs. Marcos Maidana.

The assumption was that Cortez's style of refereeing was likely to favor Mayweather over Ortiz. Carlos Acevedo put the matter in harsh perspective, writing, "Cortez, whose incompetence has been steadily growing, is now one of the perpetual black clouds of boxing. Among his peculiar habits is an inability to break fighters at the appropriate moment. Why let Cortez, whose reverse Midas touch has marred more than one big fight recently, in the building at all on Saturday night?"

Fight-night attendance at the MGM Grand Garden Arena was 14,687; well short of a sellout.

Mayweather dominated the first three rounds, which was bad news for Ortiz, who has a history of slowing down as a fight progresses and seemed to be breaking down both physically and mentally.

In round four, the following sequence of events occurred:

(1) Ortiz cornered Mayweather and, frustrated by his inability to land a clean shot, deliberately head-butted Floyd.

(2) Cortez called "time."

(3) Ortiz acknowledged his wrongdoing, hugged Mayweather, and kissed him on the cheek.

(4) Cortez walked Ortiz away from the corner, holding him by the arm, and appropriately deducted a point (for the head-butt; not the kiss).

(5) While Cortez was circling the ring, signaling the deduction to each judge and still holding Ortiz by the arm, Victor reached out with his free hand and touched Mayweather's left glove in another gesture of apology.

(6) Mayweather went to a neutral corner, and Cortez led Ortiz to the opposite side of the ring.

(7) Cortez motioned the fighters to ring center and then, inexplicably, turned away from the action, losing control of the moment.

(8) Ortiz moved to touch gloves again. Mayweather moved as though he was going to respond in kind and whacked Ortiz with a left hook (that neither Ortiz or Cortez saw coming) followed by a straight right hand that ended the fight.

Legal or illegal, it was a sucker punch.

After the fight, Mayweather was defiant. "Shit happens in boxing," he declared. "Protect yourself at all times."

He also got into an ugly shouting match with Larry Merchant, when the HBO analyst questioned him about the propriety of the knockout blow:

Mayweather: You'll never give me a fair shake. You know that. So I'm gonna let you talk to Victor Ortiz. All right? I'm through. Put somebody else up here to give me an interview.

Merchant: What are you talking about?

Mayweather: You never give me a fair shake. HBO needs to fire you. You don't know shit about boxing. You ain't shit.

Merchant: I wish I was fifty years younger. I'd kick your ass.

Given the Mayweather family history, one might say that Merchant has become a "father figure" to Floyd.

Meanwhile . . . How should the boxing community assess Mayweather's sucker punch?

First, it should be noted that, as a general rule, Floyd conducts himself well in the ring. That was exemplified when chaos broke out during his 2006 fight against Zab Judah. While both trainers and Zab were throwing extracurricular punches, Floyd stood calmly in a neutral corner.

Also, one can argue that, when Ortiz took the fight into the gutter with a flagrant foul, he was inviting an equally unsportsmanlike response.

And let's be honest. If the reverse had happened; if Mayweather had deliberately head-butted Ortiz and Victor responded with a sucker-punch knockout, many people would be saying today that Floyd got what he deserved.

That said; Mayweather-Ortiz was another proverbial black eye for boxing. Bill Dwyre (the veteran boxing writer for the *Los Angeles Times* and a man not given to hyperbole) wrote afterward, "The boos rang into the night and may not stop for months to come. Mayweather won his mega-fight against Ortiz, and each ought to be ashamed of himself. Any resemblance between sportsmanship and boxing vanished on a night of mugging and dirty play. This was more freak show than sporting event."

And Jim Lampley opined, "If you're the best fighter in the world and you like to claim that you're the best fighter in history, you shouldn't have to do that."

In a post-fight interview, Bernard Osuna of ESPN asked Mayweather, "What does this fight do for you?"

"It adds to my legacy," Mayweather responded.

It certainly does.

Outside the ring, Segio Martinez radiates elegance and grace. Inside the ring, look out.

Martinez–Barker: A Night at the Office Gets Complicated

In many sports today, the great athletes are getting younger. In boxing, the other end of the age spectrum is being extended. Sergio Martinez is thirty-six years old. In a sport with multiple phony beltholders, he's the real middleweight champion of the world.

On October 1, 2011, Martinez defended his championship against Darren Barker in Atlantic City. Sergio was a 20-to-1 betting favorite. The prevailing view was that it would be just another night's work. Then things got complicated.

Martinez won "Fighter of the Year" honors in 2010 by virtue of victories over Kelly Pavlik and Paul Williams. He began 2011 by knocking out Sergiy Dzinziruk in impressive fashion.

But too often in boxing, the right connections matter more than ring performance. The supersized purses continued to elude Martinez. He was placed on a back-burner by HBO. In May of this year, he was approached by third parties who told him that he would be better off without his adviser Sampson Lewkowicz and promoter Lou DiBella. The lobbying peaked in early June, when Sergio was in Los Angeles for the June 4th match-up between Julio Cesar Chavez Jr and Sebastian Zbik. It was suggested to Martinez that he could get a $2,000,000 signing bonus if he signed with another promoter. Other inducements were offered.

The maneuvering troubled Martinez, who has a strong sense of loyalty to Lewkowicz and felt that DiBella had done a credible job on his behalf. It also raised issues of tortious interference with contract, since Sergio's promotional agreement with DiBella extended until February 12, 2012.

On June 14th, Martinez put the matter to rest, signing a six-fight contract extension with Lewkowicz and DiBella. Then, with no big-money opponent in sight, he signed to fight Darren Barker.

Barker, age twenty-nine, is a likable man with little pretense about him. He hails from London and was advertised as the "undefeated British Commonwealth and European middleweight champion." His nickname is "Dazzling Darren" and he came into the bout with a 23–0 record against opposition of questionable provenance. To the American public, he was a fungible challenger.

Barker said all the right things during the build-up to October 1st: "If the fight was a formality and the favorite always won, boxing wouldn't be much of a sport, would it? . . . As much as I respect Sergio, I believe I have what it takes to pull a massive upset . . . He's underestimating me. If he wants to do that, fine. I'll make him pay for taking me lightly and looking past what's right in front of him . . . There's not many things in life that I'm good at, but boxing is one of them."

In recent years, the United Kingdom has produced champions like Lennox Lewis, Joe Calzaghe, and Ricky Hatton. It has also produced challengers like Michael Jennings and Gary Lockett. The prevailing view was that Barker fit into the latter category and didn't pose much of a threat to Martinez.

Sergio gave his opponent the respect that he was entitled to as an undefeated professional fighter. "When I came to the United States," the champion offered, "nobody knew me and people thought I was nothing as a fighter. I had to prove myself the same way that Barker wants to prove himself now."

Still, the feeling at the final pre-fight press conference three days before the fight was that Barker couldn't win without help from Martinez. In that vein, it was noted that the champion had a deep bruise beneath his left eye, courtesy of a punch thrown by sparring partner Israel Duffus.

And there was another potential problem. More on that later.

On fight night, Martinez entered his dressing room at Boardwalk Hall shortly after 8:00 PM. The first televised fight of the evening (Andy Lee vs. Brian Vera) was scheduled to start at 10:10. The earliest that Sergio would be called to the ring was 10:20. An eleven o'clock starting time was more likely.

Martinez sat on a folding metal chair with his feet propped up on another chair in front of him. Sanctioning body officials and HBO personnel moved in and out of the room. He had a smile and gracious word for each of them.

At 8:30, the room emptied out as most of Team Martinez left to watch a preliminary bout between heavyweights Magomed Abdusalamov and Kevin Burnett. Abdusalamov, a Martinez stablemate, was 9-and-0 with nine knockouts. Burnett, once considered a prospect, had lost three fights in a row and been reduced to opponent status.

Sergio and three others were now the only people in the room. There was relaxed conversation. Word filtered back that Abdusalamov had won on a first-round knockout. Team Martinez returned from ringside: Sampson Lewkowicz, trainer Pablo Sarmiento, cutman Dr. Roger Anderson, and cornermen Cecilio Flores and Russ Anber.

The mood in the dressing room was light. Heavy metal music played at low volume in the background. By nine o'clock, Sergio had been sitting for an hour, no more active than if he'd been at home watching a ballgame on television.

Anber began wrapping Martinez's hands, left hand first. Sergio sipped from a cup of Starbucks coffee that he held in his right hand. Sometimes in the dressing room before a fight, he eats nuts and dried fruit. A can of mixed nuts was within reach, but he ignored it.

Anber finished wrapping the left hand, and Martinez nodded in satisfaction.

"Excellent or fucking excellent?" the cornerman queried.

Sergio smiled. "Fucking bueno."

At 9:30, the right hand was done. Martinez took off his sneakers and put on his boxing shoes. Sarmiento moved a chair beside him and they engaged in quiet conversation.

The preparation continued. Sergio shadow-boxed in the center of the room for several minutes. Then he lay down on a rubdown table in the adjacent shower area. Flores stretched his legs and massaged his upper body for five minutes.

More shadow-boxing.

The HBO telecast began.

Martinez put on his protective cup and trunks. Anber gloved him up. From now until the fight was over, Sergio would unable to tighten his shoe laces, go to the bathroom, or even help himself to a drink of water. The only thing he'd be able to do with his hands was fight.

More stretching exercises.

At 10:20, with Lee vs. Vera in round three, Martinez began hitting the pads with Sarmiento; his first strenuous exercise of the evening.

During the last week of training camp, Sergio had strained a muscle in his left leg. Now, he appeared to be favoring the leg. It wasn't a debilitating condition. But it was the sort of thing that could shade matters a bit. The straight left hand and overhand left are Martinez's power punches. If he had trouble planting and pushing off his left foot, those punches would have less power than is normally the case. If the condition worsened during the fight, his timing might be affected.

The padwork ended. Martinez sat down. Flores draped a white towel over the fighter's head and another across his chest. Roger Anderson put Vaseline on his face.

More padwork.

Flores helped Sergio into his robe. There was nothing to do now but pace back and forth and wait. A heavily favored champion going to the ring is like a police officer responding to a 911 call that a man with a gun is running down the street. No matter how careful and well-prepared the cop is, something bad might happen.

There were some vocal Barker fans in the arena, but the crowd of 4,376 was largely pro-Martinez.

The first round was quiet and belonged to Sergio on the basis of a ten-to-five edge in punches landed. But it was a good round for the challenger in that it raised his confidence level a bit. Round two was more of a same. Then the momentum shifted.

If a fighter isn't right in the ring, he's the first person to know. Then his opponent figures it out.

Martinez's modus operandi is to stand just outside of punching range with his hands down. As the opponent readies to punch, Sergio moves in and gets off first. More than most boxers, he fights with his legs. And he lures opponents into his power. Fighting aggressively against him opens a boxer up to counterpunches.

With that in mind, Barker moved cautiously forward for most of the fight, hands held high in a defensive posture. But in round three, he started jabbing more effectively and became more aggressive, landing several lead right hands. Martinez's nose seemed to bother him. It bled from round four on and looked to be broken.

Sergio regained the initiative in round five. He also won six and seven, fighting the way he often fights; hands down, drawing Barker into punching range before getting off first. But his timing was off. He appeared to be lunging with his punches rather than moving with the fluidity and grace that characterize his art. And the blood in his nose was affecting his breathing.

Twenty-two seconds into round eight, Martinez's right heel got entangled with the instep of Barker's left foot and Sergio fell hard to the canvas. Referee Eddie Cotton correctly ruled it a slip. Sergio rose slowly and his corner held its collective breath as he tested his left leg.

Then Barker came on again, doing damage in rounds eight and nine. The challenger was fighting as well as he could. With more power, he might have been able to turn the fight. But he was a heavy underdog for a reason.

Round ten was the biggest round of the fight for Martinez. Halfway through it, he landed a sharp straight left that shook Barker and had him holding on. Forty seconds later, a solid jab landed just right and staggered the challenger. Darren covered up, and, over the next twenty seconds, Sergio fired a barrage of thirty-three unanswered punches before Barker fired back.

The champion came out confidently in round eleven. Barker was weary; his left eye was closing. Now Sergio was measuring his opponent. Seventy-seven seconds into the stanza, a right hook landed partially on Barker's upraised left glove and partially just above his ear. The challenger went down, struggled to rise, and was counted out.

"I can't remember the punch," Barker acknowledged afterward. "I remember, my legs just fell from under me. I was trying to get up, but couldn't."

The judges had Martinez ahead 99–91, 97–94, and 96–94 at the time of the stoppage. This writer scored it 96–94, giving Barker the third, fourth, eighth, and ninth rounds.

In truth, Martinez looked flat. After a number of scintillating outings, his performance was less-than-spectacular, more workmanlike than inspired. But he did what a champion is supposed to do, digging deep and gutting it out to win on a night when he was less than his best.

"I must be realistic," Sergio said at the post-fight press conference. "It was a tough fight and a close fight." He paused, then added, "It is never an easy fight. There is never a small enemy in the ring."

As for what comes next; Martinez symbolizes the conundrum that boxing finds itself in today. Boxing fans know how good he is. The rest of the world has no idea who he is; let alone, how good.

Sergio can compete in two weight divisions without sacrificing speed or power. He's a "small" middleweight, who could go down to 154 pounds with relative ease. As DiBella points out, "He weighed in for Barker at 158 after eating all week like Gary Shaw." But the fighters with names that generate big money don't want to get in the ring with him.

Martinez is beatable. Before fighting Barker, he'd faced moments of doubt in each of his five previous fights. At times, Kelly Pavlik, Sergiy Dzinziruk, Kermit Cintron, and Paul Williams (twice) fought with him on even terms. But he's a gifted athlete with a fighting heart. And he can punch. In his last three outings, he has knocked out three opponents with a composite record of 99-and-1.

In sum, Martinez is a symbol of excellence in boxing. "I don't know how many more fights I'll have," he told Gabriel Montoya recently. "But I know I can fight for more. I'm going to continue to work until my body says no more."

Sergio will be thirty-seven years old in February. He doesn't have that much time left. Boxing fans should get to know him better before he's gone.

When Bernard Hopkins faced off against Chad Dawson, a referee was again at the center of controversy. This time, I thought that the third man in the ring got it right.

The Controversy Surrounding Hopkins–Dawson

There are times when it seems as though Bernard Hopkins views the past twenty years in boxing as *The Bernard Hopkins Story*, with all of the promoters, television executives, and other fighters playing bit roles in the drama of his life.

Patrick Kehoe has referenced Bernard's "idealistic glorification of himself as the American Dream" and noted "time itself seems to collapse into the black hole of his insatiable yearning for self-definition."

Hopkins told Tom Gerbasi, "I wanted to be the Bill Russell of my time. I wanted to be the Muhammad Ali, the Jim Brown, the Satchel Paige. I wanted to be a guy known in history."

"Hopkins," Gerbasi wrote afterward, "is an idiot, but he's a smart idiot."

He's also a superbly talented fighter, who has built a hall-of-fame career on a will of iron, extraordinary conditioning, and remarkable technical skills. Bernard doesn't get hit solidly often. When he does, he's protected by one of the great chins in boxing.

But the Hopkins resume has been thin over the past three years. He has beaten Jean Pascal, Enrique Ornelas, and Roy Jones Jr.

Thus, it has been suggested that two things distinguish Bernard from other fighters: (1) his remarkable performance at an advanced age; and (2) he's one of the few quality fighters in boxing who can't knock Jones out.

The October 15, 2011, match-up between Hopkins and Chad Dawson was marketed as the next building block in the Hopkins legend. Bernard thrives against fighters who are mentally weak. At the August 9th kick-off press conference in New York, he declared, "In boxing, either you fight or you quit. What happens in the ring when things don't go [Dawson's] way? Any adversity, he bails out. I just have to give him some problems. We know what will happen. I already diagnosed him."

At the close of the press conference, when the fighters faced off for the ritual staredown, Bernard stood with his hands at his side. Chad's hands were clasped behind his backside.

Ticket sales for the fight were poor. Steve Kim reported that the Staples Center was cold-calling and sending emails to past customers, offering significant discounts. Two days before the fight, Gary Shaw (Dawson's promoter) tweeted, "1st 50 people to email me: gary@ garyshawproductions.com, wish Dawson good luck, I'll leave 2 tix @ will call to fight. Must submit full name."

Then the hour of reckoning arrived.

To say that round one of Hopkins-Dawson was "slow" overstates the drama. In round two, Chad picked up the pace, with Bernard trying to blunt the action. One minute forty-five seconds into the stanza, HBO analyst Max Kellerman opined, "So far, the fight is a stinker."

Then, with twenty-two seconds left in round two, Hopkins missed with a right hand, leveraged himself onto Dawson's upper back, and appeared to deliberately push his right forearm down on the back of Chad's neck. At the same time, he wrapped his left arm around Dawson's torso to steady himself and apply additional pressure to Chad's neck.

"Bernard was on his back and was more physical than he should have been," HBO commentator Emanuel Steward noted later.

Consider for a moment what it feels like to have Bernard Hopkins climb onto your back and jam his forearm into your neck. The intelligent response is to throw him off as fast as possible, which is what Dawson did. Chad rose up and, using his shoulder, shoved Bernard up and off. At one point, Dawson's left arm was around Hopkins's right thigh. But Chad let it go before shoving Bernard off.

Hopkins fell backward to the canvas, landed hard on his left elbow and shoulder, and lay there in pain. In response to questioning from a ring physician and referee Pat Russell, he said that he couldn't continue unless it was "with one hand."

Russell then ruled that Bernard's trip to the canvas was not caused by a foul and declared Dawson the winner by knockout at 2 minutes and 48 seconds of the second round.

"I do not have a foul," Russell said. "I'm not calling that a foul. He was pushing down on top of [Dawson], and [Dawson] lifted him off. It was not a foul. It's a TKO."

"He ran from me for three years," Dawson declared in a post-fight interview. "I knew he didn't want the fight. He keeps talking about Philly and about being a gangster. He's no gangster. Gangsters don't quit. He's weak physically and mentally. He has no power. I was going to get on him, and he knew it."

If the decision stands, it will be the first "KO by" on Bernard's record.

As for what comes next; there are two threshold issues. The first is whether Hopkins was really injured. The general consensus is that he has employed his thespian talents in the past to feign injury and buy time when he found himself in trouble (for example, against Joe Calzaghe). Dawson, for his part, said flatly after the fight, "He was faking."

According to a spokesperson for the Hopkins camp, Bernard was taken to California Hospital Medical Center after the fight and diagnosed as having a dislocation of the joint that connects the collarbone to the shoulder blade. Presumably, if he waives the confidentiality that attaches to his medical records and allows the examining physician to speak freely with the California State Athletic Commission and the media, that would lay one issue to rest.

The thornier question is whether referee Pat Russell acted correctly.

Section 33 of the *Referee Rules and Guidelines* adopted by the Association of Boxing Commissions states, "The referee must consult with the ringside physician in all accidental injury cases. The referee, in conjunction with the ringside physician, will determine the length of time needed to evaluate the affected boxer and his or her suitability to continue. If the injured boxer is not adversely affected and their chance of winning has not been seriously jeopardized because of the injury, the bout may be allowed to continue."

Here, Hopkins told Russell and the ring physician that he couldn't continue unless it was "with one hand." Thus, the fight was properly stopped.

After the stoppage, Max Kellerman muddied the waters when he told the HBO-PPV audience, "It should be something like a no decision or no contest because clearly it was an injury [caused] by a non-boxing move. He was thrown to the ground even if he was on top of Chad Dawson."

But Dawson only did what he had to do to keep Hopkins (who was fouling) from damaging the back of his neck.

Before the fight, Hopkins proclaimed, "Chad Dawson said I'm dirty. All fights are dirty to me. Some are dirtier than others. The referee is in the ring that will oversee anything that he does or I do. When you're in the fight, things happen he might say is an accident. Things happen I might say is an accident. It's up to the referee. I don't have to be dirty to win a fight, but I'm in a fight."

Whatsoever a man soweth, that shall he also reap.

It has been argued that a title shouldn't change hands on a ruling of this nature. But it would be wrong to have rules relating to the conduct of a fight that favor a champion over the challenger. Yes, it's hard on Hopkins for him to lose his title in this manner. But it would be just as unfair to allow him to keep his title and consign Dawson to the wilderness of boxing because of an unfortunate situation that Bernard himself created.

Hopkins will file an appeal of Russell's decision with the California State Athletic Commission, where his promoter (Golden Boy) has considerable influence. If the outcome is changed to "no contest," he will retain his WBC and *Ring* magazine titles. Either way, the WBC can be expected to order a rematch "for the good of boxing" and the lucrative sanctioning fee involved. It will be interesting to see how *The Ring* (which is owned by Golden Boy) handles the matter.

In sum; there can be no completely satisfactory resolution of the situation that arose in Hopkins-Dawson. But Pat Russell made a reasonable decision. And the view from here is that it was the right one.

Bernard Hopkins was primarily responsible for the injury that he suffered. Is a rematch appropriate? Yes; but with Chad Dawson as the defending champion.

Building a star in boxing is easier said than done.

Nonito Donaire Hits a Speed Bump

Drivers see them all the time. They're bumps in a roadway (typically painted yellow, three-to-four inches high, six-inches-or-so deep) designed to reduce the speed at which cars are driven. Think of Nonito Donaire as a finely tuned Porsche with Bob Arum revving up the engine for a test drive toward super-stardom.

Donaire is charismatic in and out of the ring. The WBC-WBO 118-pound champion is on virtually every pound-for-pound list. His record is 27-and-1 with 18 knockouts (the loss came ten years ago in his second pro fight). In the age of Manny Pacquiao, it doesn't hurt that Nonito's nickname is The Filipino Flash.

On October 22nd against Omar Narvaez at Madison Square Garden, Donaire hit a speed bump. He didn't career off the road, but it slowed him down a bit.

Donaire was born in the Philippines on November 16, 1982; the third of four children. "We were poor," he says. "We weren't starving, but lots of times we were hungry. If there was a chicken to split up, it was an occasion."

Nonito's parents immigrated to the United States when he was eight years old, bringing his younger brother with them. Nonito and two older siblings stayed behind with their grandparents.

"My grandfather called me 'midget' because I was tiny," Donaire remembers. "As a kid, you take that very seriously. I thought I was nothing. I was an extra mouth to feed; that's all. I grew up in the streets and got picked on a lot because I was so small. I'd fade away into corners and try not to be noticed. I tried to befriend everyone so I wouldn't have to fight. No one saw the fighter in me, including me."

When Nonito was ten, his parents brought him to America.

"I remember very vividly looking out the window of the plane right before it landed in San Francisco," he recalls. "It was night. I saw all the city lights and wondered, 'What is that? Fireflies?'"

The transition to life in America was hard. Nonito spoke Visayan; not a word of English. When he was eleven, his father put him in an after-school boxing program to keep him off the streets.

"I worked hard at it because I wanted my father to be proud of me," Nonito says. "I remember walking to the ring for my first fight. I was so scared, I pissed in my pants. I literally pissed in my pants. But the moment I got hit, I wasn't afraid anymore. That's what courage is; facing your fears and giving your all, no matter what. When I got hit, it was like another person took over my body. I had to defend myself and the courage came out. I scored three eight-counts and won the decision. After I won, my father smiled and gave me a hug. That was the first time in my life that I felt special."

Donaire has an exuberant personality and an enthusiasm for life. He loves to talk. His mind darts back and forth. He's easy to like.

He's also a gifted impersonator with innumerable accents and dozens of characters in his repertoire: Robert DeNiro in *Taxi Driver* ("You talkin' to me?") . . . Mel Gibson in *Braveheart* ("They may take our lives, but they'll never take our freedom!") . . . Bruce Lee in *Enter the Dragon* ("Boards don't hit back!") . . . He could do stand-up comedy and be a success.

But Donaire's most obvious gifts are as a fighter. He's blessed with great athleticism and explosive punching power. Make a single mistake against him, and your night can be over. He also has a good boxing mind that is currently being honed by trainer Robert Garcia.

"I pay attention to detail in everything I do," Nonito says. "A friend of mine drinks beer and always moves his glass in a circle. I've noticed that. When we sit down together, I know what he'll do. If I know what my opponent's habits are, everything in the ring becomes like a slow motion chess match to me."

Donaire has two signature victories to his credit. The first was a one-punch knockout over then-undefeated Vic Darchinyan in 2007.

"Against Darchinyan, I fought with anger because I felt that he had disrespected me," Nonito says. "When I knocked him down, I was hoping he'd get up so I could hit him again. After the fight, he said it was a lucky punch that knocked him out; but I don't believe in lucky punches. When I get hit, it's because my opponent did something right and I made a mistake. When I hit my opponent, it's because I did something right and he made a mistake."

Donaire's other signature win came against Fernando Montiel in February of this year. Again, one punch made the outcome a foregone conclusion. Montiel rose from a brutal knockdown but was unable to continue.

"The punch I knocked Montiel down with was the best punch I've ever thrown," Nonito says. "The respect I have for him, that he got up and wanted to keep fighting; it's hard to express the respect I felt."

Donaire is good, and the consensus is that he'll get better. "I'm always learning," he says. "And a lot of what I learned came from studying Bruce Lee. Watching him taught me that, every day, I can become better and go beyond what I already am; that there's always another lesson to learn; that I have to be dedicated and do things right to succeed in life."

"I love boxing," Nonito continues. "I love the beauty of boxing, the purity of boxing. I give my whole being to the sport. Being a great fighter isn't about belts. To me, greatness is the smile you leave on people's faces and in their hearts, the way you inspire them. I want to win belts; I want to make a lot of money. But I hope that, a long time from now, people smile when they think about me as a fighter and that I inspire them to want to be the best at whatever they choose to do in their life."

After Donaire knocked out Montiel, he was on the verge of stardom. Then Golden Boy tried to lure him away from Top Rank. Nonito was told that Top Rank (which had been building his career and still had him under contract) was keeping him under wraps to advance its own economic agenda with Manny Pacquiao. At one point, Donaire signed a contract with Golden Boy. That led to legal action and an ugly war of words.

"Facts are facts," Top Rank CEO Bob Arum declared. "He's not a pay-per-view fighter. Filipinos don't support him. When we put him on pay-per-view, we did no buys. When he fought Montiel, it was all Mexicans. He has not connected with the Filipinos. I don't think the Filipino people like him and that is largely because of his wife [who reportedly was advocating for Golden Boy]. She criticizes the way Jinkee [Pacquiao] dresses and she's all tarted up. Jinkee dresses like a lady."

That led to a self-righteous rebuttal from Golden Boy CEO Richard Schaefer, who raged, "Nonito Donaire and Rachel Donaire are first-class people. They really don't deserve this sort of vicious and uncalled for attacks from Bob Arum. Bob Arum may be angry that they left him, but such is life. There is no reason for these idiotic comments. Bob Arum's true colors came out, and they always will. That's just the kind of person that he is. If Bob Arum thought that he still had [a binding contract] with Nonito and he was making these comments, then wouldn't that make him an even bigger idiot? You just don't say these kinds of negative things. That's just a low-life who does that; and that's what Bob Arum really is."

A contract extension heals all wounds. The war was resolved when Donaire signed a contract that binds him to Top Rank for a minimum of four more years. Top Rank can further extend the contract if certain contingencies occur.

"It went out of control," Arum said after peace with the Donaire camp had been restored. "I should know with all my experience that it's self-defeating to carry on battles like this through the media. I apologized to Rachel, which is more than most politicians do when they say something wrong. I apologized sincerely and she accepted my apology. We're all on the same page now."

With the hostilities at an end, Arum began planning for the future. "You can't be a superstar if you have only a regional following," he noted. "You can have a regional base or an ethnic base. But to be a real superstar, which means that you generate a large number of pay-per-view buys whenever you fight, you have to have a much broader following."

Toward that end, Top Rank brought Donaire to New York for the East Coast media exposure that would accompany his fighting in the Big Apple.

"Our goal is to make him a superstar," Arum said during a pre-fight conference call. "We think that Nonito is such a great exciting fighter and such a pleasing personality that, as he rises in weight, he will become a major superstar in the sport."

"Donaire is telling us that he wants to go up in weight and fight the toughest guys out there," Top Rank director of public relations Lee Samuels added. "He wants to fight Mikey Garcia. He wants to fight Juanma and Yuriorkis Gamboa. I said to him, 'These guys are good and they fight back.' Nonito told me, 'No problem.'"

But first there was the matter of Donaire defending his belts against Omar Narvaez in The Theater at Madison Square Garden. The good news for boxing fans was that Narvaez was undefeated (35–0–2) and a "champion." The bad news was that the Argentinean was thirty-six years old, lacked power (19 knockouts in 37 fights), was moving up in weight, and had won his WBO 114-pound bauble in one of those contests for a vacant title.

Donaire said all the right things in the days leading up to the fight. "Narvaez is a tremendous fighter. He has a great heart. He knows how to win."

At the final pre-fight press conference, people were throwing around the names of Argentinean fighters like Carlos Monzon and Sergio Martinez. Perhaps the most relevant name from a promotional point of view was that of Carlos Baldomir, who came into Madison Square Garden as a prohibitive underdog against Zab Judah in 2006 and emerged with the WBC welterweight crown.

But the truth of the matter was that Donaire-Narvaez had been put together as a showcase for Nonito with Narvaez as a sacrificial lamb.

The Theater was close to sold out with 4,425 fans in attendance. The fight began with Narvaez fighting cautiously and Donaire biding his time, waiting for his opponent to make a mistake. The fight continued with Narvaez fighting cautiously and Donaire biding his time, waiting for his opponent to make a mistake. And the fight ended with Narvaez fighting cautiously and Donaire biding his time, waiting for his opponent to make a mistake.

In sum, it was like a twelve-round sparring session with few solid punches landed. Narvaez, a clever boxer, was there to survive and spent the entire night in a defensive shell. Each of the judges scored the bout 120–108 in Donaire's favor. This observer's scorecard read 118–110.

The encounter didn't do much to advance Nonito's ring career, but it didn't damage it much either. He was in the ring with a fighter who knew how to protect himself. And Donaire already has good highlight-reel footage from his earlier knockouts of Darchinyan and Montiel.

As for the future; Arum proclaims, "We fully intend to make Nonito a pay-per-view attraction. It's silly to guess how long that will take. It will come when it comes. And it's silly to compare Nonito with Manny Pacquiao. They're both Filipino, but Nonito has lived in the United States since he was ten years old. Every fighter is different. Top Rank will promote Nonito as his own person in his own way."

In other words; the issue isn't whether Donaire will be "the next

Manny Pacquiao." Pacquiao (like Muhammad Ali, Sugar Ray Leonard, George Foreman, Mike Tyson, and Oscar De La Hoya) is a one-of-a-kind phenomenon. The issue is, "How big can Nonito become in his own right?"

We still don't know how fast and how far the car can go.

Pacquiao-Marquez III was the most anticipated fight of 2011.

Pacquiao-Marquez III: The Rivals

Great rivalries elevate their participants and link them forever in the pages of history. Manny Pacquiao and Juan Manuel Marquez are great rivals.

Neither man was pre-packaged and handed a road map to stardom. Pacquiao turned pro at age sixteen and fought his first twenty-three fights in the Philippines. Marquez debuted in Mexico City at age nineteen and was disqualified in round one of his first pro fight.

Since then, Pacquiao has risen to global superstar status. Marquez will be a first-ballot Hall of Fame inductee when his time comes. They've met in the ring twice in classic fights that were everything boxing should be. On November 12th, they'll meet again at the MGM Grand Garden Arena in Las Vegas.

There's no way that Pacquiao-Marquez III can be as good as its predecessors.

Or is there?

Pacquiao-Marquez I (contested on May 8, 2004) was a non-stop action fight with a dramatic ebb and flow. Midway through round one, Pacquiao put Marquez on the canvas with a straight left hand. Two more knockdowns followed, each one leaving Marquez more dazed than the one before. But Marquez did more than survive. Fighting for eleven-and-a-half rounds with blood streaming from his nose, he worked his way back into the fight and left the ring with a much-deserved draw.

Pacquiao-Marquez II (on March 15, 2008) featured more non-stop action from beginning to end. In round three, a straight left hand put Marquez down. He rose and fired back. By the middle rounds, each man was badly cut on the right eyelid with blood dripping into his eye. Round eight was Marquez's best of the night. He hurt Pacquiao with body shots and scored repeatedly to the head. Manny had the look of a beaten fighter. "I'm really hurt in that round," he acknowledged afterward. But

Pacquiao fought his way back into the fight and won a split-decision by a single point.

Marquez thinks that he should have been awarded the decision in both fights. There are knowledgeable observers who agree with him. Everyone agrees that the two men battled on even terms.

Six judges scored twenty-four rounds of boxing between Pacquiao and Marquez. Their composite score gives Pacquiao a 679-to-678 edge in points and Marquez a 41-to-31 lead in rounds.

Rounds twenty-five through thirty-six of Pacquiao-Marquez are now at hand.

The conventional wisdom is that Pacquiao has gotten bigger, stronger, and more skilled over the past three years, while Marquez has gotten older and slower. Juan Manuel is now thirty-eight years old. That's old for a fighter; particularly one who fights the way he fights. Pacquiao will be thirty-three in December.

Their first two fights were contested at contract weights of 126 and 130 pounds. This one is at 144. Pacquiao is used to the 144-pound weight. It's natural for him at this stage of his career. Marquez is a natural light-weight. His one foray into the higher weight classes was against Floyd Mayweather Jr, when he weighed in at 142 pounds and was never in the fight.

Also, Pacquiao is a much smarter fighter now than he was before. He has been taught by Freddie Roach . . . and by Marquez.

Let's assume for the moment that Marquez "figured out" Pacquiao after round one of their first encounter. The question now is whether, even with that knowledge, he can deal with Manny's increased firepower and improved weapons delivery system.

Three-and-a-half years is a long time in boxing. Seven-and-a-half years is longer. Pacquiao-Marquez I and II are ancient history.

Alex Ariza (Pacquiao's strength and conditioning coach) elaborates on that theme, saying, "Manny is going to knock Marquez out. He's a whole different fighter now from what he was then. Freddie gave him the right game plan for those first two fights, but Manny wasn't physically prepared to execute it. I started working with him after that. Manny will be prepared physically this time and his technical skills are better. He and Marquez are in different leagues now."

"I know there have been doubts over the last two fights," Pacquiao said at the September 3rd kick-off press conference in Manila. "There have been debates on who won them. This fight should end all doubts. This fight should end all debates."

In sum, Pacquiao wants to close the books on his rivalry with Marquez and put to rest any doubt regarding his ring supremacy. His fans are expecting a coronation. But Juan Manuel has a different ending in mind.

For every great fighter, there's always that one opponent who poses particularly formidable obstacles no matter what logic says. The question that gives Pacquiao-Marquez III its buzz is, "Does Marquez have Pacquiao's number?"

A fighter studies his opponent on tape and, sometimes, live from a ringside seat. But when they get in the ring to face each other, the opponent's speed and power can be very different from what the fighter thinks they'll be. Marquez knows that firsthand from having fought Pacquiao twice. Round one of Pacquiao-Marquez I was a shock to him. Subsequent to that, he made adjustments.

Counterpunching is Marquez's greatest technical strength, and it served him well in his previous fights against Pacquiao. He made Manny pay for his mistakes and, at times, took him to school.

"When you let your hands go, you leave yourself open," Freddie Roach acknowledges. "When you exchange and throw punches like Manny does, you put yourself in harm's way."

Emanuel Steward puts the matter in perspective, saying, "Pacquiao is bigger and stronger now than he was before, so there will be a big difference in natural strength. Also, Marquez has slowed down a bit and his reflexes aren't what they used to be."

"But as good as Pacquiao is," Steward continues, "he makes mistakes. And he gambles in the ring. That means he's more likely to do damage, but he's also more likely to get hit. And Marquez has the skills to take advantage of Pacquiao's mistakes better than anyone that Pacquiao has ever fought. Marquez has great balance and great positioning. He can take that half step to the side and make an opponent miss. He can change his style on the spur of the moment and alter the flow of a fight as seamlessly as any fighter I know. And Marquez will be sky high for this fight. He'll come into the ring emotionally charged because believes that he beat

Pacquiao twice. I think Pacquiao wins, but it won't be easy. I would not take Marquez lightly."

So let's end with a cautionary tale about the third fight in another famous boxing trilogy; a fight that took place in the Philippines three years before Manny Pacquiao was born.

Muhammad Ali and Joe Frazier split their first two encounters. Then they met in Manila for Ali–Frazier III. Ferdie Pacheco (who was Ali's cutman and physician) later recalled, "You have to understand the premise behind that fight. The first fight was life and death, and Frazier won. Second fight; Ali figures him out. Then Ali beats Foreman, and Frazier's sun sets. And I don't care what anyone says now; all of us thought that Joe Frazier was shot. We all thought that this was going to be an easy fight. Ali comes out, dances around, and knocks him out in eight or nine rounds. That's what we figured. And you know what happened in that fight. Ali took a beating like you'd never believe anyone could take. When he said afterward that it was the closest thing he'd ever known to death—let me tell you something; if dying is that hard, I'd hate to see it coming."

The outcome of Pacquiao-Marquez III is by no means certain.

Pacquiao-Marquez III reminded boxing fans that, no matter how hard a fighter punches, he can't knock his opponent out if he can't hit him with solid blows.

Pacquiao-Marquez III: Postscript

Christopher Columbus discovered America and changed the face of the world forever. Five hundred years later, Bob Arum discovered the Philippines in the persona of Manny Pacquiao. Since then, boxing hasn't been the same.

Pacquiao's life has been a perfect storm since he beat Oscar De La Hoya in 2008. His last seven fights have engendered more than 7,500,000 pay-per-view buys. Tickets for his November 12, 2011, match-up against Juan Manuel Marquez sold out in a matter of days. By contrast, when Floyd Mayweather Jr (Pacquiao's chief rival for boxing dollars) fought in the same arena against Victor Ortiz on September 17th, 1,268 complimentary tickets were given away and an additional 3,052 tickets went unsold.

In other words, Manny created a scalper's market; Floyd fought in front of three thousand empty seats.

Pacquiao has become part of the culture of boxing. But his impact extends far beyond the ring. His business portfolio now includes ventures ranging from cell-phone plans to Manny Pacquiao Broccoli. His endorsement deals run the gamut from Nike to Hennessy cognac ("I have tasted it, but I drink responsibly," Manny says).

More significantly, in 2010, Pacquiao was elected to Congress by the voters in Sarangani province. Since then, he has been a vocal proponent of measures to combat poverty and has spoken out on various social issues. In May of this year, as reported by *Time Magazine,* he joined with officials from the Catholic Bishops' Conference of the Philippines to oppose legislation that would liberalize national birth control laws. Speaking on the floor of the House of Representatives, Pacquiao noted that, if his parents had practiced "artificial" birth control, he wouldn't have been born.

That earned a word of caution from David Greisman, who wrote, "Oh, Manny, Manny, Manny. You're a boxer. Whatever happened to protect yourself at all times?" But Pacquiao remained firm in his conviction and urged his supporters to "follow God's command, not man's."

One week before Pacquiao-Marquez III, Pacquiao was featured on the cover of *Newsweek*'s Philippine and Latin American editions. "To call Manny Pacquiao a 'boxer,'" the article began, "is one of those descriptions that don't quite fly; like calling Mahatma Gandhi a 'Hindu lawyer.'" *Newsweek* went on to reference Pacquiao as "a kind of sacral celebrity" with "a religious aura."

"As a Congressman," Pacquiao said recently, "I represent the interests of the people who elected me. When I fight, I represent a nation and a people."

How pervasive has his influence been?

Nonito Donaire (who came to the United States at age ten) says, "Manny has been a big part of my success. As a Filipino, he inspired me. And he opened the door of opportunity for me. When I turned pro [in 2001], all I heard was, 'I'm sorry, kid; I can't use you; you're not Mexican. I'm sorry, kid; you don't speak Spanish.' No one was interested in Filipino fighters. Now my being born in the Philippines is a marketing advantage for me."

As Pacquiao's fame has grown, he has become more polished outside the ring as well as in it. His hair is longer and more styled than in the past. He converses easily in English. Few people remember that post-fight interviews after his first few fights on HBO were conducted in Visayan through an interpreter.

Time management has become a major issue. It seems as though everybody wants a piece of Manny. There are moments when he seems a bit weary of it all; as though a period of anonymity might not be such a bad thing. But overall, he's enjoying the ride.

Meanwhile, Pacquiao's growing fame has been accompanied by the burgeoning myth that, inside the ring, he's Superman. Thus, the Pacquiao-Marquez trilogy was expected to end the way it began; with Juan Manuel on the canvas (as he was three times in round one of their first fight).

The fighters were respectful toward one another during the build-up to Pacquiao-Marquez III. Each man has pride and carries himself like a champion. Pacquiao talked about his desire to "answer all the doubts about who is better that come from our first two fights." Marquez spoke of the judges' decisions in the same fights as "a thorn in my side that I want to pull out."

But the tea leaves favored Pacquiao. Since he and Marquez had last met in the ring (on March 15, 2008), Manny had devastated David Diaz, Oscar De La Hoya, Ricky Hatton, Miguel Cotto, Joshua Clottey, Antonio Margarito, and Shane Mosley. Marquez had struggled in victories against Joel Casamayor, Juan Diaz (twice), and Michael Katsidis, was whitewashed by Floyd Mayweather Jr, walked through Likar Ramos (in a fight that left some observers questioning the extent of Ramos's effort), and been seen on television drinking his own urine.

Physically, Pacquiao and Marquez had been roughly equal to each other the first two times they fought. Now Pacquiao was seen as the naturally bigger man in addition to being faster, stronger, and a harder puncher.

There was even a school of thought that Marquez was simply showing up on November 12th for a paycheck. This would be his largest purse ever. He's a prizefighter; he fights for money. Against Mayweather (the only other time he'd ventured into welterweight terrain), he'd lost all but one round and showed little regret afterward.

There was a flurry of interest when a *Pacquiao-Marquez: 24/7* telecast showing Marquez working with a strength-and-condition coach identified as "Angel Hernandez" was followed by a "tweet" from Victor Conte.

Conte (who spent four months in prison as a consequence of his role in the BALCO scandal) informed the world, "J.M. Marquez is working with admitted steroid dealer Angel 'Memo' Heredia ('Hernandez' on 24/7). Heredia testified he supplied PEDs to Marion Jones. Angel Heredia was the star witness for the government against many athletes. He got no time in return."

When asked about the matter, Marquez responded that Heredia's checkered past "was news to me" and "we work very well together."

Bob Arum further downplayed the issue, telling the media, "For a period of time, people like Victor Conte and this guy Hernandez dealt in steroids with major athletes, but that's old news. You can achieve all of the benefits that you used to achieve with steroids without any risk of illegality or without any dangers that steroids caused. Wake up and see what the conditioners are saying. They are using natural and totally legal supplements and using state of the art conditioning methods. There have been advancements in the legal methods. The steroid problem is fading into the past."

That earned a rejoinder from Bart Barry, who wrote, "This year's leading slugger belted forty-three home runs. In 2001, Barry Bonds hit seventy-three. That's the difference between the natural substances and sophisticated training methods now used and steroids. And before anyone offers up a loony rebuttal that boxing trainers have discovered some secret the rest of the sports world knows nothing about, he should visit a boxing gym. Eating ice chips, rubbing one's body with Albolene, and training in a garbage bag is the way most boxers still make weight. From such a laboratory, next year's Nobel Laureate in chemistry is not likely to emerge."

Be that as it may; the suggestion that Marquez might be using PEDs was regarded in some circles as a plus in that, were it true, it would increase the likelihood of a competitive fight. The conventional wisdom was that Juan Manuel might know how to beat Pacquiao but that, at age thirty-eight, he couldn't do it.

"I've never been more confident before one of Manny's fights than I am now," Freddie Roach (Pacquiao's trainer) said. "Manny is going in one direction, and Marquez is going in another. Manny's footwork is much better now than it was before. He's a better-conditioned athlete. His right hand is more effective. He's stronger. He's a different fighter from the guy that fought Marquez before. We had a great training camp. I've never seen him this intense. I think Manny will knock him out. I'll be surprised if it goes more than six rounds."

"I don't think the last two fights will help Marquez for this fight," Pacquiao added. "I've changed a lot. The problem before was, I never studied the style of a counterpuncher. Since then, I have studied how to fight a counterpuncher; I learned more technique; and I improved my power."

The feeling was that, if Pacquiao won, each man's legacy would stay the same. But if Marquez won, his legacy would rise and Manny's would be deflated.

The pre-fight odds at the MGM Grand Sports Book were 8-to-1 in Pacquiao's favor. A Marquez victory by decision was considered no more likely than a first-round Pacquiao knockout. Bettors were offered 10-to-1 odds on either proposition.

But as Angelo Dundee noted after Pacquiao upset Oscar De La Hoya, "In boxing, sometimes the best laid plans of mice and men go bye-bye."

Fight week kicked off after Pacquiao appeared on *Jimmy Kimmel Live* for the fifth time. Manny had wanted to sing "Let It Be" on the telecast. "I learned about the Beatles in the 1990s," he says. "I like the spirit of their music." But rights to the song couldn't be cleared, so he sang "How Deep Is Your Love" instead.

Then he and his entourage (which seems to grow with every fight) traveled from Los Angeles to Las Vegas in a caravan that included twenty-six cars plus the official Manny Pacquiao bus.

The first two times that Pacquiao and Marquez did battle in Sin City, Manny was thought of almost exclusively as a fighter. Times change. Now he's an icon. Pacquiao-Marquez II engendered 407,000 pay-per-view buys (a record for fights under 147 pounds at the time). The goal for Pacquiao-Marquez III was 1,400,000.

The feeling in fight circles was that boxing needed an entertaining evening to wash the sour taste left by the pay-per-view cards featuring Floyd Mayweather vs. Victor Ortiz (September 17th) and Bernard Hopkins vs. Chad Dawson (October 15th) out of everyone's mouth.

Bob Arum presided over the week's proceedings. His voice has a lot of Brooklyn in it. He still identifies fighters as "champeen."

"Before Manny Pacquiao," Arum told the media, "we heard about Imelda Marcos and her shoes. We knew that Muhammad Ali and Joe Frazier fought a great fight in the Philippines thirty-five years ago, but that was just one fight. Manny Pacquiao has brought the Philippines front and center in the eyes of the world."

Pacquiao showed incredible patience, answering the same questions again and again. During a series of satellite interviews conducted two days before the fight, he was remarkably upbeat.

"Hi, CNN. How are you? . . . Hi, ESPN . . . Hi. Fox Sports . . . This fight is important to me . . . Marquez is a very good fighter. I want to show that I am better . . ."

"Nick News on Nickelodeon is next," publicist Ed Keenan told Pacquiao. "It's a news segment on a kid's channel. You'll be talking with Linda Ellerbee. That's Leonard sister."

For the uninitiated, Leonard Ellerbe is Mayweather's business manager. Pacquiao's eyes widened.

"Just kidding," Keenan added.

Ellerbee asked Pacquiao about overcoming failure.

"The first failure in my life was not to finish my education," Manny told her. "But sometimes failure teaches you the road to success. When I fail to win a fight, I feel very sad, but I accept it and pray and work harder."

The interviews continued.

"The first fight with Marquez was a good fight; very tough. The second fight; same thing . . . I think I will win this fight. Marquez says he will win. Somebody is wrong; somebody is right."

"Okay, Manny. This next one is a Spanish-language station. Could you count to ten for a microphone check."

An impish look crossed Pacquiao's face.

"Uno, dos, tres, cuatro, cinco . . ."

When the interviews ended, Manny seemed troubled.

"What's the matter?" he was asked.

"I feel bad that the [NBA] owners and players are fighting. There might not be basketball this year."

★   ★   ★

As he often does on the night of a big fight, Freddie Roach arrived at the dressing room in the arena four hours before the main event.

There are times when it seems as though Roach can't go anywhere without a boom microphone hovering above him. He's an integral part of several Pacquiao documentary projects and also the subject of a six-part TV-reality series that will debut on HBO in January 2012.

"I'm pretty boring," Roach says. "Outside of boxing, I don't do a lot."

Regardless; an overhead microphone was there.

Roach was confident. One day earlier, Marquez had weighed in at 142 pounds while Pacquiao tipped the scales at 143.

"I think the weight that Marquez put on will hurt him," Freddie said. "Manny filled out over time. Marquez did it all at once. He doesn't know how to use his new body. It will affect his timing, his balance, his speed. His arms will get tired from the extra weight. He might look good, but that's about all. And he'll look even better when he's lying down on the canvas."

"Muscle is not for speed," Roach continued. "It's not for counter-punching; it's not for timing. It's to exchange. I think Marquez will come out to trade punches, and Manny will oblige him. Manny is ready and he really wants this one. When I was fighting, I never let an opponent last longer than I had to. You don't want take the risk of a fight going on and getting hit with something that hurts you or opens a cut. Manny is more compassionate during a fight than I was, but I don't think we'll see that tonight. I wouldn't be surprised if he knocks Marquez out in the first round."

Bottom line: it's easy for a trainer to say "do this" and "do that." When a fighter is in the ring, it's different. No one knows if a fight plan will work until it's tested in battle. Anyone can be wrong in boxing.

By the time the fighters entered the ring, the sell-out crowd was at a fever pitch. Rock music and sixty-four rotating spotlights had been fused into a spectacular sound-and-light show. Two fervent constituencies were on hand. Marquez had his partisans, but it was a pro-Pacquiao crowd.

After twenty-four rounds of non-stop punching, round one of the third encounter between Pacquiao and Marquez was the first between them without much action. Juan Manuel proceeded cautiously, and Manny showed his opponent more respect than it had been thought he would.

Rounds two and three were also tactically fought, with Marquez dictating the distance between the fighters and Pacquiao appearing a bit frustrated. The sense was that, if Manny could just land solidly, he'd be able to take Juan Manuel out, whereas Marquez couldn't change the flow of the fight with one or two punches. But as the rounds passed, Marquez continued to land sharp clean counters and Pacquiao was unable to successfully blitz his foe.

The action picked up in the middle rounds, with both men fighting more aggressively and Marquez giving as good as he got. Pacquiao is most effective when he gambles in the ring. Juan Manuel had exploited those gambles in their earlier fights. This time, Manny seemed less willing to take risks.

By round ten, Pacquiao was fighting with a touch of desperation but still couldn't solve the puzzle in front of him. Midway through the stanza, an accidental headbutt sliced open the skin beneath his right eyebrow. Twenty-eight stitches were required to close the cut after the fight, but it didn't affect the flow of the action.

During the last twenty seconds of the bout, Marquez's partisans rose as one and roared their appreciation. At the bell, Juan Manuel raised his arms in triumph and was hoisted into the air by his handlers. Pacquiao walked dejectedly to his corner.

Then came the decision of the judges.

Robert Hoyle, 114–114, even.

Dave Moretti 115–113 and Glenn Trowbridge 116–112; both for Manny Pacquiao.

Earlier in the week, Pacquiao had said, "I like to hear the fans screaming." Now he heard a different sound. Boos resounded throughout the arena. The crowd chanted Marquez's name. The image of Pacquiao being interviewed appeared on the giant overhead screen. The boos grew louder.

Most members of the media scored the fight for Marquez. Some had it even. In fairness to Pacquiao, he outlanded Marquez by a 176-to-138 margin. Also, there were a lot of close rounds, and one can argue that a close round should go to the aggressor (Manny threw 142 more punches). But Marquez landed the cleaner harder sharper blows. This observer favored Juan Manuel by a 116–113 margin. He gave Pacquiao a boxing lesson.

"Everybody comes in with a plan," Emanuel Steward said afterward. "But Marquez's plan worked. Pacquiao might have landed more punches, but this is professional boxing. You don't score it like an amateur fight."

The surprise of the night was that Marquez, at age thirty-eight and after lackluster showings in several recent outings, performed as well as he did. A fighter is measured by his skills and also by how he deploys them. Juan Manuel was superb.

"I'm happy about my performance tonight," Marquez said at the post-fight press conference. "I won this fight more clearly [than the first two]. I don't know what I need to do to change the mind of the judges."

"We won, but this guy still has our number," Roach said.

So what happens next?

Pacquiao will keep fighting for the foreseeable future. Being in the ring furthers his political ambitions. And it's nice to make tens of millions of dollars a year; particularly when one spends as generously as Manny does.

To that, Roach adds, "Everything in Manny Pacquiao's life is because of boxing. He hasn't forgotten that. And it's still what he does best."

There are two particularly attractive alternatives for Pacquiao's next fight. The first, obviously, is a fourth bout against Marquez.

Forty-four months ago, in the ring after he defeated Marquez, Pacquiao was asked, "Do you think you'll fight him again?'

"I don't think so," Manny answered. "I think now the business is over."

But it wasn't. And Pacquiao-Marquez III failed to bring the expected closure. "It's a fight I don't want to do again," Roach said at the post-fight press conference. "But I think we have to."

Marquez maintains that he's unwilling to fight Pacquiao again in Las Vegas and suggests Mexico as the site for a proposed fourth encounter. That's as likely as Pacquiao-Mayweather taking place in the Philippines. Cowboys Stadium in Texas would be a nice compromise.

The other attractive possibility, of course, is that Pacquiao-Mayweather will finally happen. The consensus view is that Floyd has avoided the fight; possibly waiting for Manny to wear down, at which time Pacquiao will have lost his hard edge and Mayweather's own sounder fundamentals will carry him to victory.

Pacquiao-Marquez III might have whetted Mayweather's appetite, given the fact that he disposed of Marquez so easily two years ago. But keep in mind; styles determine the outcome of fights. It's like rock-paper-scissors. Ali beats Foreman; Foreman obliterates Frazier; Frazier gives Ali trouble every time. Mayweather beats De La Hoya on a split decision. Pacquiao destroys De La Hoya. Mayweather dominates Marquez. Pacquiao squeaks by him.

Meanwhile, the Pacquiao-Marquez rivalry should be celebrated for what it is; two dignified highly skilled boxers engaging in the noble art of prizefighting at the highest level.

As for the thought that Pacquiao has now lost some of his luster: every fighter, no matter how good, has an off night. If Manny beats Marquez or Mayweather in his next outing, he'll shine just as brightly as before.

The rematch between Miguel Cotto and Antonio Margarito had a story-line that went beyond the norm.

Cotto–Margarito II:
This Fight Is About Honor

On July 26, 2008, at the MGM Grand Garden Arena in Las Vegas, Miguel Cotto and Antonio Margarito entered the ring for one of the most-anticipated fights in years.

Cotto was grouped with Manny Pacquiao, Floyd Mayweather Jr, and Joe Calzaghe at the top of most pound-for-pound lists. He was undefeated in 32 fights with 26 knockouts. Margarito was worthy challenger. There was a school of thought that Mayweather had ducked both men to preserve his unblemished record.

Cotto was a 2-to-1 favorite. He had a well-earned reputation in boxing circles for being a destroyer. Margarito beat Miguel down brutally and took all the fight out of him. He beat Cotto into submission. Miguel took a knee to end the fight.

Cotto–Margarito II will be contested at Madison Square Garden on December 3, 2011. Both men will be fighting for money. More than in most fights, they'll also be fighting for honor.

Make no mistake about it. No matter what anyone says, Cotto–Margarito II is in large part about Antonio's handwraps.

Six months after annihilating Cotto, Margarito fought Shane Mosley in Los Angeles. Prior to the fight, illegal inserts were found in Antonio's knuckle-pads. They were removed and Mosley knocked out Margarito in the ninth round. Antonio was subsequently precluded from fighting in the United States for one year. His trainer, Javier Capetillo, has been banned for life.

Bob Arum (who promotes both Cotto and Margarito) has staunchly defended Antonio, saying that he doesn't believe Margarito knew that Capetillo put the inserts in his knucklepads. That's possible. It's also possible that (1) Margarito knew; (2) it happened (and went undetected) in previous fights; and (3) Antonio's gloves were loaded for the first Cotto-

Margarito fight. In that bout, counter to custom, Evangelista Cotto (who was Miguel's chief second) didn't send anyone to Margarito's dressing room to watch Antonio's hands being wrapped.

Early in the promotion of Cotto-Margarito II, Miguel said of the issue, "I have been, the whole way, a man. I accepted my defeat and tried to get better. You have never heard something about the handwraps coming out of my mouth. The only people who can tell you is him and anyone on his team."

But more recently, Miguel has voiced a different view, declaring, "He used the plaster [knucklepad inserts] the night of the fight with me. He looks and he acts like a criminal."

The prevailing view in boxing circles is that Margarito's gloves were loaded and Antonio knew it. Margarito will be the villain on December 3rd. Promoter Don Elbaum speaks for many in the sweet science when he says, "Margarito should have been banned for life. I think it's a disgrace that he's getting a big payday like this. And I can't wait to see this fight."

Margarito carries himself like a man who has convinced himself that he won the first fight fair and square regardless of what was (or wasn't) in his gloves. "I'll give you the same result," he told Cotto at the September 20th kick-off press conference in New York. "But it will be sooner this time."

Neither fighter is what he once was. Significantly, their downward curves are intersecting at a point that is expected to make for a particularly dramatic encounter.

Emanuel Steward trained Cotto for his two most recent fights (against Yuri Foreman and Ricardo Mayorga). On October 4th, Steward was replaced by Pedro Luis Diaz, who has worked extensively with the Cuban national amateur team. Four days prior to his dismissal, Steward told this writer, "There are three keys to this fight: Miguel's conditioning, Miguel setting down on his punches, and Miguel's confidence."

"If you look at Miguel's past fights," Steward explained, "he wore down late against Margarito. He wore down late against Pacquiao and Mosley and Clottey. Miguel's weak point is stamina, which is one of Margarito's greatest strengths. Margarito beat Miguel the first time with pressure. He made Miguel fight at a faster pace than Miguel was used to. So Miguel has to be in better condition this time. He has to be able to fight the whole twelve rounds at a fast pace."

"Second, Miguel has to punch through his target more than he did the last time, so he hurts Margarito when he hits him. He can't be punching and moving away at the same time. It's important that he get Margarito's respect, and it's important that he get that respect early."

"But the biggest key," Steward continued, "will be Miguel's confidence. Margarito has a huge psychological edge going into the fight. Let's be honest about it. When a fighter goes to his knees and submits, which is what happened the first time against Margarito, that's worse for his confidence than if he gets knocked out by one punch. So a lot of this fight has to do with Miguel's mental state. He believes that Margarito's gloves were loaded the first time, and that will help Miguel's confidence. But until Miguel gets hit hard a few times, you don't know what will happen on December 3rd."

Cotto looked troubled at the kick-off press conference in New York. "I'm going to give my body and soul to make a great fight," he said. But he seemed less confident than Margarito. It's possible this is a fight that Miguel didn't want but felt that he had to take.

"I think Cotto wins," say Don Turner, who trained Evander Holyfield for his two victories over Mike Tyson. "But Margarito takes a better beating, and it might come down to that. Margarito won't quit, and Cotto might."

That's where the crowd comes in. After much *sturm und drang* over whether or not Margarito would be licensed to fight in New York because of the condition of his right eye, the bout will proceed at Madison Square Garden.

There won't be a buzz at The Garden on December 3rd. There will be a roar. This is the ultimate Puerto Rican Passion play for Miguel's adoring followers. It will be like those nights when Felix Trinidad lit up the Garden. If Cotto wins, there will be unbridled joy. If he loses, it will feel like Trinidad vs. Bernard Hopkins all over again.

"The crowd can't fight," says Emanuel Steward. "But I truly believe that this will be one of those rare occasions when the crowd inspires a fighter and makes him better. The crowd at Madison Square Garden is always for Miguel, but this will be something more. The atmosphere at The Garden will be crazy on fight night. You'll have twenty thousand fans, virtually every one of them for Miguel, screaming for blood."

Cotto has some great victories to his credit, including back-to-back triumphs over Zab Judah and Shane Mosley. But the most-talked-about fights in his career have been his two losses (to Pacquiao and Margarito). Cotto-Margarito II is the most important fight of Miguel's life. It will be his greatest victory or his most bitter defeat.

Eric Raskin wrote recently, "This fight stirs emotion. It's a fight that lends itself perfectly to hype and is also about ninety-nine percent certain to live up to that hype. One guy hates the other and believes his opponent spent eleven rounds beating him about the head with loaded gloves. The other guy feels that burning hatred and either lives with soul-melting guilt everyday or is fighting the uphill battle of the wrongfully accused. You've never seen a man fighting for redemption to the extreme that Margarito will be. You've never seen a man fighting for revenge to the extreme that Cotto will be."

Each fighter has to win. Most people in boxing will feel better if the winner is Cotto.

Some mountains are harder to climb than others.

Cotto–Margarito II: The Hardest Thing to Do in Boxing

Sugar Ray Robinson once said that the hardest thing for a fighter to do is win a rematch against a man who beat him badly in their first fight.

A bad beating lingers in a fighter's mind longer than most losses. It isn't something that he puts behind after a good night's sleep. His body aches for days, if not weeks. Sometimes there's permanent physical damage. He remembers it for the rest of his life.

"It goes down on tape," former heavyweight champion Jersey Joe Walcott said. "And you play it back at funny times, when you're dreaming or just walking down the street."

Miguel Cotto took a beating at the hands of Antonio Margarito in their first fight. He wasn't outpointed. It wasn't a quick knockout or a question of one punch turning the tide. It was a brutal beatdown. Miguel fought with everything that was in him and was beaten into submission.

It's hard to come back from a beating like that; and harder still, to do it against the man who administered the beating. On December 3rd, Cotto will try to do just that.

One reason trilogies are rare in boxing is that the fighter who wins the first fight between two men usually wins the second.

There are notable exceptions. In 1936, Joe Louis was brutally beaten by Max Schmeling. In round four, The Brown Bomber found himself on the canvas for the first time in his professional career. "I really don't know what happened the rest of the fight," he said later. "I didn't know where I was. I didn't know nothing. I took such a terrible beating that [when I was knocked down in the twelfth round] I just couldn't get up. The only thing I remember is, when I went out of the ring, my trainer said, 'Cover up his face.' That's because my face, my jaw was out like this where I had stopped so many right hands."

Two years later, Louis and Schmeling fought again. Louis was in bet-

ter shape. He held his left hand higher. And he was Joe Louis. He annihilated Schmeling in the first round.

Floyd Patterson was knocked down seven times in a three-round loss
to Ingemar Johansson in 1959. One year later, Patterson evened the score
on fifth-round knockout that left Johansson unconscious on the ring canvas. But Floyd was helped by the fact that Ingemar had lived a hedonistic
lifestyle after winning the title. And he was a better fighter than Johansson.
Patterson had markedly less success in a rematch against Sonny Liston
(who knocked him out twice in the first round).

Emanuel Steward (who trained Cotto for his most recent two fights
but won't be in his corner for this one) says, "If a guy beats you up, chances
are it happened because he's better than you are. Lennox [Lewis] came
back and beat Oliver McCall and Hasim Rahman after they knocked
him out. But those were one-punch knockouts, not beatings. Wladimir
[Klitschko] came back and beat Lamon Brewster. But I believe, and
Wladimir believes, that he was drugged the first time they fought. And
whatever Wladimir's condition was the first time, Lamon was a shell of
himself by their second fight. If you look at things historically, most fighters
who take a beating the first time do worse in the rematch. The other guy
is just too good for them."

In applying the above lessons to Cotto-Margarito II, we'll come to
the issue of Antonio's handwraps shortly. Let's start with the fact that
Miguel won five of the first six rounds in their initial encounter by
circling, getting off first, and landing sharp crisp counterpunches. But
Margarito continued to apply non-stop pressure and took everything that
Cotto hit him with. Regardless of what was (or wasn't) in Antonio's
handwraps, he didn't have knuckle-pads in his chin.

Margarito and Cotto have each now absorbed two bad beatings.
Margarito, at the hands of Shane Mosley and Manny Pacquiao; Cotto, at
the hands of Pacquiao and Margarito. At this point, Antonio might be
more physically damaged than Miguel. And he's coming off major eye
surgery, which could be an issue in the ring on December 3rd.

But the beatings that Margarito took weren't from Cotto. And the
beatings that Miguel absorbed seemed to break his spirit. Indeed, after losing to Pacquiao on a twelfth-round stoppage in 2009, Cotto acknowledged that he'd asked his corner to stop the bout after the seventh round.

"I didn't know from where the punches come," he admitted. "I couldn't protect myself. After round seven, I tell Joe [Santiago] to stop the fight, but I think better and I prefer to fight."

Miguel is frequently referred to as "stoic; that is, a person who endures hardship and pain without complaint or visible emotion. But that's a misleading description.

"People can say what they want to say," observes Emanuel Steward. "When a fighter takes the kind of beating that Miguel took against Margarito, it has a huge psychological affect on him. Miguel has to put that fight behind him, but that's easier said than done."

"I would have liked it for Cotto's sake if Emanuel was in his corner for this fight," says matchmaker Ron Katz. "Having a new trainer who doesn't know what buttons to push, no matter how good that trainer might be, makes things harder. And Emanuel is good with guys' heads."

As of the kick-off press conference for Cotto-Margarito II (three years after their first encounter), Miguel had still not watched a tape of the fight. That says something about his state of mind, although no one is quite sure what.

Still, Cotto will have a lot of things going for him on December 3rd. He's a better boxer than Margarito. If the fight is decided on skill alone, Miguel is likely to prevail. Also, three years have passed since their first encounter. The passage of time should help Cotto.

Paulie Malignaggi views Cotto-Margarito II from a unique perspective. Five years ago, Paulie fought Miguel when Cotto was at his peak. He suffered a brutal beating but stayed the course and won four of twelve rounds (five on one judge's scorecard).

"When I lost to Cotto, I was dying to fight him again," Malignaggi says. "It was an obsession with me. It took a long time for me to let go. Other fighters might feel differently about something like that, but that's the way I am."

"Miguel has all the motivation in the world going into this fight," Paulie posits. "Margarito took a lot from him. Status, money. And he took things out of him physically that Miguel can never get back. But the key to this fight will be Miguel's confidence. As a fighter, I'm always battling with myself mentally. It's not just when I lose. Most fighters are like that. So Miguel has to overcome the mental obstacles before he can overcome the physical challenge that Margarito presents in the ring."

That's where the handwraps come in.

"Miguel has to build in his mind on the good things he did in the first fight," Malignaggi continues. "He knows he won the first six rounds by outboxing Margarito. He was boxing great until Antonio's punches wore him down. And he knows in his heart that Margarito's gloves were loaded."

"As long as Miguel's belief stays strong," Malignaggi concludes, "he'll win this fight. But if it comes to round seven, round eight, round nine, and Miguel is taking some hard shots, he'll start having doubts. Margarito can punch. He had Pacquiao doubled over from a body shot in round six of their fight, and his gloves weren't loaded then. And let's face it; Miguel is known for a lot of good things, but having a great chin isn't one of them. So when Miguel is getting hit, he'll have to say to himself, 'It's different this time. Margarito's gloves aren't loaded tonight. Even if I can't do anything differently, Margarito can't do as much as he did last time.'"

Naazim Richardson is the man who discovered the illegal inserts in Margarito's knuckle-pads before Antonio fought Shane Mosley. The inserts were removed, and Mosley knocked Margarito out in the ninth round.

"It's hard for a fighter to come back from a beating," Richardson says. "It's hard physically and it's harder mentally. But because of the handwraps, you can't see this fight the way you usually would. The handwraps allow Cotto to explain the beating to himself and also give him confidence that it won't happen again."

"I watched a tape of Margarito against Cotto before Shane fought Margarito," Richardson continues. "It was intimidating. Then, in the dressing room, I found the knuckle-pads and it was like, 'Okay; now I understand everything.' Cotto moves like a boxer, but he stops to punch. Guys like Ali and Roy Jones could punch from their toes. Cotto can't do that effectively. And what happened against Margarito was, there came a time when Cotto couldn't stop to punch because the punishment he was taking was too heavy. So right now, Cotto has to say to himself, 'Yes, he beat me up; but he did it illegally.' Cotto saw what Shane and Pacquiao did to Margarito. And he knows that, for six rounds, he was landing on Margarito with everything he threw. I think it goes the distance this time, and I think Cotto will outbox him to win."

"You can't oversell the idea to Miguel that Margarito's gloves were loaded," says Pat Burns, who trained Jermain Taylor to a pair of upset victories over Bernard Hopkins. "You're preparing now for this fight, not the last one. You talk about it because the issue is there, but you don't dwell on it. You use it to build Cotto's confidence; so he feels that, yes, he was cheated in the first fight but this time the playing field will be level. And you build on his anger. He wants to beat the crap out of Margarito. You don't want him to fight recklessly, but you encourage him to channel his anger and use it as a positive force."

Cotto-Margarito II is personal for Miguel in a way that no fight has been before. People close to him say that, when he and Antonio share a dais, they can feel the anger seething within.

When bad blood exists between two fighters, beating the crap out of the other guy is the best revenge. Still, no one but Cotto knows what he's thinking now. And not even Miguel can be sure what he'll be thinking on fight night.

Does Cotto believe in his heart that he's the better fighter? When the bell rings, what thoughts will flow through his mind? When he gets hit, will he say to himself, "These punches don't feel like they did last time." Or will the punches hurt just as much? What will happen when Margarito whispers in his ear, "It's the same gloves as last time."

Fighters can be respectful toward one another during the build-up to a fight or they can be ugly. Either way, it's a fistfight.

Cotto-Margarito II:
The Moment of Truth

David Greisman recently wrote, "A storyline can take a boxing match, transcend it beyond a cookie-cutter popcorn flick, and turn it into a can't-miss prizefight. Character development can establish a reason to root for heroes and against villains. Plot twists can bring a bout from competitive to compelling."

The December 3rd rematch between Miguel Cotto and Antonio Margarito at Madison Square Garden fit that description perfectly. On paper, Cotto and Margarito were fighting for Miguel's WBA junior-middleweight title. But they were really fighting for the championship of each other.

Cotto was wounded physically and emotionally by their first fight. He lost his WBA welterweight crown and undefeated record. He was beaten up and forced into submission before the eyes of the world. Thereafter, questions arose as to whether Margarito entered the ring for that encounter with illegal knucklepads in his handwraps. "I'm a clean fighter," Antonio declared. "There was nothing illegal. And that's it."

Cotto and most of the boxing community thought otherwise.

A $5,000,000 guarantee enticed Miguel into a rematch. Margarito was guaranteed $2,500,000. But the primary currencies were vindication and revenge.

Bart Barry framed the matter nicely, writing, "Once you admit this fight appeals to a sense of vengeance, you can suspend other moral considerations and all the Cotto-Margarito II pieces fall happily into place. It is about satisfying the bloodlust Puerto Ricans feel because of the ruin Margarito brought to their guy's career in 2008. Cotto has not been the same since his match with Margarito. He says he was criminally assaulted in their first fight. Whatever else Cotto might be, he is not a salesman. He would rather see Margarito in jail than across a boxing ring from him."

Despite its commercial potential, the rematch almost didn't happen. The New York State Athletic Commission was initially unwilling to license Margarito because of myriad concerns (including an artificial lens implant) regarding his right eye. There was still the option of moving the card to another jurisdiction. But economically, that would have been a disaster. Then, twelve days before the bout, Cotto took even that option off the table, telling reporters that he wouldn't fight Margarito outside of New York. Finally, the NYSAC declared Margarito medically fit to fight, and fight week proceeded as planned.

Margarito appeared to relish the role of villain. He wore sunglasses for most of the proceedings in The Big Apple and still managed to look shifty-eyed. His first words from the dais at the final pre-fight press conference were, "Here comes the criminal."

As Margarito spoke, Cotto's face hardened. When it was Miguel's turn to speak, he began with, "I'm going to talk in Spanish so Antonio can understand me." He then told Margarito precisely what he thought of him, closing with the sentiment, "You are an embarrassment to boxing."

There was no ritual staredown for photographers at the end of the press conference. Instead, the fighters posed with promoter Bob Arum standing between them.

The bad blood was real and wouldn't wash away when the fight was over.

"Margarito is just another human being," Cotto said. "I don't have to like him. I just have to fight him."

Cotto was a 2-to-1 betting favorite, but he'd also been favored 2-to-1 in their first encounter.

Miguel's backers felt that their man was the better fighter; that "loaded" gloves had been a key factor in the previous fight; that Antonio's right eye would make a nice target for Cotto's power punch (his left hook); and that Miguel's hatred would strengthen his resolve.

As for Margarito's trash-talking, Cotto declared, "I don't pay attention to what my opponents say; only to what they do in the fight."

Margarito's partisans believed that Antonio had won the first fight fairly and that, once again, his brutal swarming assault would beat Miguel down. Cotto would be coming to box. Margarito would be coming to fight. No matter how good Miguel's defense was, he would be hit and hit hard.

Margarito is a tough SOB. Last year, AFTER his orbital bone was broken and his right eye was swollen shut, he doubled Manny Pacquiao over with a body shot that almost took Pacquiao out of the fight. What would happen if he hit Cotto like that?

The moment of truth would come in the ring when Miguel was on the receiving end of punches from the man who'd beaten him into submission before.

"We're different," Margarito said. "Cotto will take a knee, and I won't."

December 3rd was boxing at Madison Square Garden the way it used to be. The arena was sold out, with an announced attendance of 21,239 (which included media, suite patrons, et al.).

Cotto arrived at 8:30 PM and walked largely unnoticed into the arena, where he accompanied his wife to her seat. Then he retired to his dressing room to prepare for the night ahead.

At various times during the evening, images of Miguel and Antonio were shown on large video screens above the ring. Cotto's image was greeted with cheers; Margarito's, with boos. The crowd also booed when the Mexican national anthem was sung and when Antonio's wife was seen overhead.

The undercard was good and added to the excitement. The atmosphere had the frenzy and nationalistic pride of a World Cup soccer match.

Margarito entered the ring at the stroke of midnight; the witching hour, when all manner of things happen. Boos and jeers resounded throughout the arena. Cotto followed to a thunderous roar. One could imagine the fighters as gladiators in The Coliseum in ancient Rome.

Now only the fight mattered.

Margarito fights as though finesse in the ring is a sin of the highest order. He comes forward, takes punches, throws punches; and more often than not—by virtue of his stamina, power and iron chin—grinds opponents down like a crushing millstone at work.

Cotto-Margarito II began like its predecessor. Miguel, circling and jabbing. Antonio, coming forward, willing to take punishment, throwing punches in return.

Chants of "Cotto! Cotto!" resounded from the first minute on. As was the case in their initial encounter, Margarito appeared to be the larger man. When Miguel stopped to trade punches, Antonio relished the exchanges and went to the body well.

But there were two differences between this fight and their epic first battle. Margarito's punches didn't have the same devastating effect on Cotto the second time around; not even when the fighters were trading bombs. And the area around Antonio's surgically repaired right eye began to swell in the third round. By the end of round six, Dr. Anthony Curreri (the ring doctor assigned to Margarito's corner) was monitoring the damage under the supervision of chief ringside physician Dr. Barry Jordan. Just before the start of round ten (with Cotto leading 89–82 on each scorecard), they instructed referee Steve Smoger to stop the fight.

Cotto walked across the ring toward Margarito, cast a scornful look in his defeated adversary's direction, and walked away.

"I just wanted to savor my victory," Miguel said afterward. "And I wanted him to see me savoring my victory with the one eye that he had."

Later, Dr. Curreri explained the stoppage, saying, "His eye was gradually closing throughout the fight to the point where there was no vision. Between the vision and the lid closing, I felt it was best to stop the fight. He had no vision in the right eye, meaning he had no peripheral vision."

But others took a contrary view. Dr. Margaret Goodman (former chief ringside physician and medical director for the Nevada State Athletic Commission) has been a leading proponent of fighter safety for years. Commenting on the stoppage, Dr. Goodman says, "A fighter can fight with a shut eye if he can see out of the other eye and is protecting himself."

And Steve Smoger (who did an excellent job of refereeing the fight) put the matter in perspective, recounting the night's events as follows.

"When I went to Margarito's dressing room to give him his pre-fight instructions, I told him, 'Antonio; in my mind, you're a complete fighter. I know there was an issue regarding your eye. But you've been found medically fit to fight, and I'll treat you the same way I treat every other fighter.' I could see the relief on his face when I said that. Then you had the fight. From the middle rounds on, I could see that Dr Curreri was looking at the eye. But it never crossed my mind to stop the fight. Margarito never took a backward step. He was competitive. He was defending himself. He wasn't taking unnecessary punishment. In fact, near the end of round nine, I sensed a change of momentum and thought that Margarito might be coming on. And remember; I refereed Pawel Wolak's first fight against Delvin Rodriquez, which was also in New York. Pawel's eye was worse than Margarito's. But he was allowed to finish the fight, and now it's a candidate for 'Fight of the Year.' So I was in a situation after round nine where Antonio and his corner were pleading for one more round. If it was my call, I wouldn't have stopped it. But I'm not an eye doctor. And in the great State of New York, the ring doctor has the authority to stop a fight. People have said there was confusion at the end, but that wasn't the case. The delay in stopping the fight before the start of the tenth round was my doing. I wanted to make totally sure that Dr. Curreri and Dr. Jordan wanted me to stop it; because once I wave my hands that it's over, that action can't be undone."

As for the future; it's unlikely that Cotto will recover the stature he enjoyed in the pound-for-pound rankings before his 2008 loss to Margarito. But his victory over Antonio will go a long way toward ensuring his place in the hearts of his countrymen.

And he has closure.

"I am very happy to finally get it over with," Miguel said at the post-fight press conference.

"How do you feel about Antonio Margarito now?" he was asked.

"He means nothing to me," Cotto answered. "He has his own life. I have my own. He can keep with his life. I'm going to keep with mine."

The better man won. So did the better fighter.

Curiosities

A tradition continues . . .

My 85-Year-Old Mother
Meets Don Elbaum

Four years ago, I brought my mother to a press conference and introduced her to Don King. Several days later, "My 81-Year-Old Mother Meets Don King" was posted on the Internet.

Thus, a tradition was born. Once a year, I bring my mother to Portobello's (at 83 Murray Street in Manhattan), where Anthony Catanzaro hosts a pizza party for my mother and assorted boxing dignitaries.

Last year, the guest list included Paulie Malignaggi. Later, in an article I wrote about the gathering, I quoted my mother as saying, "Paulie is adorable; a little cocky, but as cute as can be."

The next time I saw Paulie, he told me, "Tell your mother I think she's cute but a little cocky."

This year, the tradition continued on July 11th with Don Elbaum as the primary celebrity guest. Readers with a good memory might recall that Elbaum was to have been a guest last year but stood my mother up.

"Is this like a blind date?" he asked when I called to re-extend the invitation.

"Don; I love my mother. I'd never do anything like that to her."

"So explain to me again what this lunch is about?"

"My mother likes meeting boxing people. She started with Muhammad Ali. Then she met Don King. Now it's you, and we're planning a special honor for you."

"What's the honor?"

"The honor is, if you stand my mother up again, I'll send Paulie over to beat the crap out of you."

"That doesn't scare me. Paulie can't punch."

"I'll give him a gun."

"I'll be there; I promise."

The guest list included Elbaum, Frank Macchiarola (who oversees the

Arthur Curry Scholarship Program at St. Francis College in Brooklyn), Steve Albert, Seth Abraham, and Lou DiBella.

As homework, my mother read "Bordello Boxing" (an article detailing Elbaum's efforts to promote a fight card at a Nevada brothel called Sherry's Ranch).

When my mother and I arrived at Portobello's, Seth Abraham was already there. As is his custom, he was wearing a boutonniere on his jacket lapel.

"I was fifteen years old when I went to college," Seth explained to my mother. "Most of the girls were two years older than I was and I couldn't get dates. I confessed my frustrations to a fraternity brother named Paul Hill; and Paul told me that another part of my problem was that I was a slob. He took me to a clothing store and helped me pick out some nice shirts and a few pairs of slacks. Eventually, I started getting dates and I've paid attention to my appearance ever since."

Steve Albert was the next to arrive. "I wouldn't pass up this opportunity," he proclaimed.

"To meet my mother?"

"No. Free pizza."

Then, to the accompaniment of trumpets with seraphim flying through the air (I'm making that part up), Don Elbaum entered and handed my mother a blue gift bag.

"I have a lot of respect for mothers," Don told her. "The way I was brought up, you open doors for women and treat them right. Even if the woman I'm with is a hooker, I'll open the door for her."

Over the next half hour, Frank Macchiarola and Lou DiBella rounded out the group. In keeping with the spirit of the day, Lou brought his mother.

For the record, Anna DiBella is an elegant woman with three published volumes of poetry to her credit.

Anthony Catanzaro is fond of saying, "I'm just a guy who makes pizza." He's a lot more than that. But what pizza!!!

As lunch progressed, Seth told old war stories about Don King and Mike Tyson. My mother is fascinated by both of them. "I know that Don King has done bad things," she said. "But I liked him when I met him. I can't explain why."

"When Don is being nice," Elbaum offered, "he's absolutely incredible. You have to love him. The problems come when he's being Don."

As for Tyson, Steve Albert was behind the microphone when Iron Mike bit off part of Evander Holyfield's ear.

"That must have been exciting," my mother said.

"Actually, it was disgusting," Steve recalled.

Lou DiBella spent most of the time talking on his cell phone and eating pizza off his mother's plate. Anna DiBella offered the information that Lou could speak in full sentences when he was eleven-and-a-half months old.

"And I dropped by first F-bomb when I was two," Lou added.

Later in the conversation, Lou told my mother, "Everyone in boxing who has a heart has a love-hate relationship with the business. I love what I do and I hate what I do. There's more evil in boxing than in any other sport. If you stay in the business long enough, you get fucked as many times as a porn star."

"Lou is passionate and there's a human quality about him," my mother told me afterward.

Elbaum is co-promoting a July 30th fight card at John F. Kennedy High School in Paterson, New Jersey. "I've got three guys from Peru fighting that night," he advised my mother. "You can't believe how good these guys are. Jonathan Maicello has the appeal of a rock star and his record is 15-and-0. He's the next Manny Pacquiao. Juan Zegarra is undefeated. And Carlos Zambrano is 13-and-0, but I've got an even better story for you about Zambrano. His wife's mother is fifty-seven years old. She has twenty-four children and all of them are girls. What are the odds of something like that?"

"Does this women really have twenty-four children who are all girls?" my mother asked me later.

"I doubt it. But with Don, anything is possible."

"You ought to come as my guest to see the fights," Elbaum offered. "These three guys will make Peru the boxing capitol of the world."

"It's not for me," my mother answered, declining the invitation. "I don't understand, and never will, why all of you love this sport so much."

"I saw Willie Pep fight when I was young," Don explained. "It was like a beautiful ballet. I was totally mesmerized by the way he moved and slipped punches. Since then, all I've wanted out of life is to be in boxing. There have been good times and bad times, but I've loved every minute of it."

Later, while I was talking with Steve Albert, I heard bits and pieces of further conversation between my mother and Elbaum. Don was speaking with great animation: "You can't believe how educated some of the women at Sherry's Ranch are . . . The people that run the place fly helicopters back and forth from Los Angeles . . ."

"It was a lot more interesting than talking with my friends about their manicures," my mother told me afterward.

Being a gentleman, Don drove my mother home when lunch was over. During the ride, he reminisced about meeting Frank Sinatra ("I forget the year, but it was before he died") and the time in 1979 when he was staying in the Mayflower Hotel on Central Park West in Manhattan. Two cops appeared at his door, investigating the theft of a horse.

"I've done some things in my life that might not have been one-hundred-percent kosher," Elbaum told the cops. "But I swear to you; I never stole a horse."

By the way; the gift that Don gave my mother was a magic ball called "rattleshake." If she wants to make a wish, she shakes it and it sounds like a baby's rattle. On the outside, it says, "You thrill me."

And a final thought . . .

"Your mother is fantastic, a real doll," Don said when he called to thank me that night. "And tell Lou that I liked his mother too."

In the past, I've recounted the memories of fighters and others in the sweet science who spoke fondly of their greatest moment in a sport other than boxing. The recollections of ten more "boxing people" follow.

"My Greatest Moment in Another Sport"

SUGAR RAY LEONARD

About ten years ago, I was playing golf at TPC Summerlin [in Las Vegas]. I hit a five iron off the tee that I thought was going way out of bounds. I turned my back. That's how bad I thought the shot was. Then someone said, "Ray; you hit an F'in hole in one." I didn't believe him. But somehow, the ball came back. It was crazy; I felt like a little kid. By the time I got to the club house, they had a plaque made up for me with "hole in one" and my name on it. That was my moment of golf glory. If I play course management, I can shoot in the eighties, but I never play course management. My short game is the best part of my game. My putting comes and goes. But put in your article that my putting is better than Oscar's. Oscar's putting sucks.

FREDDIE ROACH

When I was twelve years old, I was on the [Dedham, Massachusetts] All-Star team in the Pop Warner League. I wasn't very good. My brother Pepper was a year older than me. He was the starting halfback and safety. We were playing a team from Aliquippa, Pennsylvania. It was freezing cold and we were losing something like 35 to 0. I'd been sitting on the bench the whole game. My feet were numb. I couldn't feel my feet. That's how cold it was. Aliquippa fumbled on their own one yard line. We recovered, and the coach put me in the game for Pepper. The quarterback called play 44; the four back, which was me, running through the four hole [between tackle and guard]. That was my moment of glory. For the first time in my life, I was going to score a touchdown. The quarterback gave me the ball.

I fumbled. The other team recovered. And when I got back to the bench, Pepper told me, "I could have done that."

HASIM RAHMAN

I didn't do much athletically outside of boxing, so there's not a lot to choose from. But there's one thing I remember that was special. I was twelve years old, playing for a team called the Cubs in the James Mosher Little League. It was near the end of the season. We were undefeated, but we were losing the game by one run. I was at bat with a man on base. The pitcher threw a fastball, and I hit it over the fence in leftfield for my first home run ever.

I didn't know it was gone when I hit it because I'd never hit a home run before. There were times before when I'd hit the ball hard and thought it was gone, but it never went out. So I didn't know it was a home run until the ball hit the dirt on the other side of the fence. I was ecstatic. I was so happy. I ran extremely slowly around the bases so I could stretch out the moment. We scored one more run in the game and won by two, so that home run was the difference. That was my only home run ever.

And there's another moment, now that you got me thinking. When I was fifteen, I was playing basketball outdoors in a pick-up game at the Deer Park school [in Baltimore]. It was a full-court game, five on five. I was being lazy and didn't go down to the other end of the court to play defense. We got a steal. One of my teammates threw me the ball. I was all alone. I'd never dunked a basketball before. But I said to myself, "I might as well try it." So I went up and WHAM! I mean, I dunked it with power. The other guys were looking at me, and they were like WOW! I felt just like Charles Barkley.

EMANUEL STEWARD

In 1981, we were in New York on the publicity tour for Hearns-Leonard, and someone set up a softball game in Central Park between the New York sportswriters and Kronk.

We had some good players on the Kronk team. Prentiss Byrd had played professional ball in the minor leagues. He was our shortstop. Milton McCrory's best sport in high school was baseball. He was in center field. Tommy could play. He was at first base. And Dan Duva was on our team because Main Events was promoting the fight. Dan was a player. That surprised me.

Anyway; Kronk was short one guy, so I took off my sport jacket and agreed to play. I hadn't had a bat in my hands in about fifteen years. But I hit a triple, a double, and a home run. Each one was on the first pitch. The home run was in my last at bat and it won the game. I think the score was 13-to-11.

Afterward, Tommy came over to me and said, "Whoah! You were something." He couldn't believe it. I got a real kick out of that game.

BOB ARUM

It was in college, at NYU in a fraternity basketball game. I was nowhere near good enough to play varsity ball, but I wasn't bad as a fraternity player. Zeta Beta Tau, which was my fraternity, was playing Sigma-some-thing-or-other. Their guys were bigger than we were. But that game, I could do no wrong. They had guys hitting me, fouling me, doing anything they could to keep me from scoring. And whatever they did, I'd throw the ball up and it went in. You can believe me or not; but I'm telling you, I hit sixteen shots in a row and we won the game. It was a magical night. Nothing like that had happened to me before and nothing like that happened to me again. That was more than fifty years ago, but I remember it like it was yesterday. So when Kobe or LeBron has a memorable game, I say to myself, "I know how that feels."

DON TURNER

I'd say it was winning the fifty-yard freestyle championship in junior high school intramurals when I was in seventh grade. This was in Cincinnati. I'd learned to swim in a place behind our house called Chemical Creek. When I got good, I started going to the Lincoln Center, where they had three pools. In practice there, we had to flutter kick a mile every day. Anyway; they had the intramurals and I won by a body. I felt pretty good that day. I didn't feel like I did when Evander Holyfield knocked out Mike Tyson or when Larry Holmes beat Ray Mercer. Those were probably my two greatest moments in sports. But as far as moments outside of boxing are concerned, it was that time in seventh grade.

HAROLD LEDERMAN

I played football when I was at Stuyvesant High School [a public school for academically gifted students in New York]. The team was called the Peg Legs. Our uniforms were blue and gray. Sometimes I started as an offensive guard, but mostly I played linebacker. I intercepted a couple of passes and recovered a few fumbles. But I never scored a touchdown and there were no moments of glory to speak of.

The team wasn't bad; we won more than we lost. What I remember most is that it was a lot of fun. We'd practice after school along the East River Drive. Afterward, there was always a long walk to the subway and a longer ride home. But we were teammates and we got as close as kids can get. The camaraderie was the best part. I graduated in 1956 when I was sixteen years old. God, that was a long time ago.

CEDRIC KUSHNER

When I was growing up in South Africa, rugby was a big part of my life, both as a player and a fan. In 1967, when I was seventeen years old, I put together a team called the Muizenberg Spurs.

Muizenberg was a suburb of Capetown. We played in a league that consisted of similar pick-up teams from different parts of Capetown and a few university teams, which was the closest I ever got to university. There were several hundred spectators at each game; mostly family and friends.

The season ran for about fourteen weeks. I was captain of the team. We played every Sunday afternoon and won more than we lost. I was strong and powerfully built; 5 feet 7 inches tall, about two hundred pounds and in good condition back then.

I always enjoyed bringing people together and I was passionate about rugby; so the joy of putting the team together and the excitement of playing was very special to me. There's no one game that stands out in my mind. But I still remember the thrill of it all.

BUDDY McGIRT

I was on a team of eleven-year-olds called The Cheyennes in the Brentwood Youth Association. We were playing against a team from Bayshore-Islip and had the ball on their five-yard line. Normally, I played cornerback. But it was late in the fourth quarter and we were winning by a lot, so the coach let me carry the ball. The play was called "21 quick pitch." I'd run the play once before in an earlier game and been stopped. This time, I took a pitch from the quarterback and I didn't care if they had the whole damn defense there. I was going to score. But there wasn't much there. No one touched me. I could have walked in. That was my only touchdown. I didn't carry the ball again that season; and the following year, I started boxing.

MARGARET GOODMAN

I have a fulltime practice as a neurologist. But when I resigned from the Nevada State Athletic Commission [in January 2007], I needed something to fill the void that leaving boxing created in my life. My mother had taken me riding a few times when I was very young. I'd only done it once or twice after that. But I love animals; and in October 2007, Flip [longtime friend Dr. Flip Homansky] bought me a horse.

Mo was four years old when we got him. I'm very competitive, so it wasn't enough for me just to pleasure ride. I wanted a competitive discipline. And I wanted to do English riding, which is based on using your body and legs rather than the reins to control the horse.

The choices I had for a discipline were dressage, which is very technical fancy riding; eventing, which I'm not insane enough to do because it's like steeplechase times ten; and hunter competition, which is slow jumping where the emphasis is on form and the beauty of the jump.

I chose hunter competition. Mo and I entered our first competition in Los Angeles in May 2008 and won two first places. That was a great moment for me; although if you want me to spill my guts, most of the competitors were between the ages of seven and twelve. One of the kids was a snotty little brat, who was riding what looked like a hundred-thousand-dollar horse. After I won, she started whining, "It's not fair." And I told her, "Grow up, kid; this is life."

Note for fashion-conscious readers: Dr. Goodman reports that, in her victorious riding competition, she wore beige riding breeches, a gray plaid hunter coat cut like an Armani jacket, a black helmet, black leather boots, and black leather gloves accessorized by a black riding crop.

2011, like its predecessors, brought its share of miscellaneous insights and humor.

Fistic Nuggets

Now that promoter Gary Shaw and Alfredo Angulo have parted ways, it's worth revisiting comments that Shaw made following his fighter's first-round knockout of Joachim Alcine on July 17, 2010.

Shaw: I'll fight anybody with Angulo from 154 pounds to heavyweight.

Q: What about Sergio Martinez?

Shaw: I have a 154-pounder. So if Sergio Martinez wants to fight at 154 . . .

Q: It would be at 155 pounds for the middleweight title.

Shaw: I represent a junior-middleweight. When we're ready to move up, I'll make that decision. Nobody makes me move up. Will Angulo fight him? Yes, at 154 pounds.

Q: I thought you just said you'd fight him from 154 to heavyweight.

Shaw: I don't believe in catchweights. I believe in real weights. Catchweight is bullshit. It's just made-up stuff.

Less than a month later, Chad Dawson (another Shaw fighter) was readying to defend his WBC light-heavyweight belt against Jean Pascal. At the final pre-fight press conference on August 11th, Shaw declared, "After Chad Dawson beats Pascal, I'd like to see him fight Lucian Bute. They could do it at a catchweight of 172 pounds."

★   ★   ★

Words of Wisdom from the 1960s New York Boxing Scene

Cus D'Amato: "Lots of managers grab the nickels and dimes. They put their fighter in a tough fight because a dime is more than a nickel and they want the dime. My job is to maneuver the fighter to a dollar. Once he's ready to win a title, all the money the manager wants will be there."

Harry Markson: "When a fighter starts out as an amateur, he wants to win medals and cups and plaques. When he turns pro, he wants to win in Madison Square Garden. When he wins in the Garden, he wants to win a championship. When he wins a championship, he wants to make a lot of money. And when he makes a lot of money, he wants to win medals and cups and plaques."

Teddy Brenner: "Ask any great fighter who his toughest opponent was and, nine times out of ten, he'll name someone he beat."

Floyd Patterson: "The best thing about being a fighter is that, outside the ring, you don't have to fight."

★   ★   ★

Three Things You'll Never Read on a Boxing Website

(1) Dan Goossen is on *Dancing with the Stars* tonight.

(2) "The WBC has decided that it will no longer collect sanctioning fees," Jose Sulaiman told the convention delegates. "For the good of boxing, we will let the fighters keep that money."

(3) It was another well-scored fight in New Jersey.

★   ★   ★

Freddie Roach has a tattoo of a Celtic cross with the legend "Five Angels" on his left biceps. How did that come about?

"I got it on my thirty-fifth birthday, which means I was old enough to know better," Roach says. "I wasn't drunk. I don't know why the fuck I did it, except I was dating a girl who had a lot of tattoos and it seemed like a good idea at the time. That's life. It's better than being in a bad car accident."

Don King has said of himself, "I am like a cork in the ocean that goes down and keeps bouncing up."

Don King at Philippe Chow

It's a half-mile from the Rainbow Room high above Rockefeller Center to Philippe Chow (a Chinese restaurant in midtown Manhattan). For Don King, those destinations are decades apart.

When King was in his glory years, the Rainbow Room hosted some of the most remarkable press conferences in boxing history. Major media feasted on all manner of cuisine as the promoter held court with Muhammad Ali and others.

On October 25, 2011, King was back in New York on the second floor of Philippe Chow. He was there to plug a night of boxing that will be televised by a small cable network called WealthTV.

Let's get the administrative details out of the way. On November 5th at the Seminole Hard Rock Hotel and Casino in Hollywood, Florida, GUILLERMO JONES (King shouts the name when he says it) will defend a cruiserweight belt that he won by defeating someone named Firat Arsian against the challenge of Mike Marrone. Three other bouts will also be televised. WealthTV is distributed by a limited number of cable systems, so the fights will be available on various other electronic platforms as well.

King loves a challenge. That night, he will be going up against Alfredo Angulo vs. James Kirkland on HBO; Lucian Bute vs. Glen Johnson on Showtime; and LSU vs. Alabama (college football's match-up of the year) on CBS.

Anthony Evans once wrote, "I seldom get a buzz from meeting famous people. The hot girls are never as hot in person, and the funny guys are never as funny when they aren't paid to be. The action heroes are so small that it ruins the illusion. But whenever I meet Don King, he's Don King."

King is eighty years old now, but he still has a magnetic personality. Wearing his trademark "Only in America" jacket accessorized with mountains of bling, he entered the room waving sixteen flags representing the nations of fighters who be on the eleven-bout card.

"We'll have great fights," King told his audience. "We'll have dancing girls. We'll have Harold Melvin and the Blue Notes [a Philadelphia rhythm-and-blues group that was popular in the 1970s]. We'll have GUILLERMO JONES. And I guarantee you that, unlike another television network, we will show our National Anthem being sung as a matter of respect for our brave troops overseas. We must respect those who defend the glory of America, the greatness of America, the grandeur of America. Our troops overseas are fighting for our safety and freedom. Because of them, we know that we can be here and eat lunch at Philippe Chow without something bad happening to us."

Follow Don King around as he works a room, and you will be rewarded. Among the words of wisdom that he offered were:

* "I've never done anything dishonest in boxing, but I have outmaneuvered many."
* "Everybody loves you when you're on top and can help them make money, but I'm a true friend to those in dire need and distress."
* "Robin Hood stole from the rich and gave to the poor. I don't steal from anybody, but I certainly give to the poor."
* "If you want to see dancing, show me Ginger Rogers and Fred Astaire, not Bernard Hopkins and Chad Dawson."
* "I don't talk trash. I speak in an uplifting manner with respect toward all people."
* "The one thing a man can give and still keep is his word."
* "The best thing about Tom Hauser is his momma." [I had to get that one in.]

Don King is no longer ringmaster of the boxing circus. The man who promoted Ali-Foreman in Zaire and Tyson-Holyfield in Las Vegas is now regarded by many as a benign sideshow. But he's still Don King. And like Elvis Presley in his later years, he is still capable of great performance art.

Issues and Answers

Manny Pacquiao's move to Showtime raised the possibility that 2011 would be a transformative year behind the scenes in boxing.

How HBO Lost Manny Pacquiao

Manny Pacquiao is going to Showtime. On January 20, 2011, Top Rank (Pacquiao's promoter), Showtime, and CBS signed a contractually binding three-way deal memorandum that calls for the May 7th fight between boxing's reigning pound-for-pound king and Shane Mosley to be televised on Showtime Pay-Per-View.

Showtime and CBS are owned by the media conglomerate, CBS Corporation. CBS is a terrestrial network.

Pacquiao's last eight fights have been televised by HBO-PPV.

Top Rank CEO Bob Arum has long been intrigued by the idea of synergy between a pay-per-view provider and a terrestrial network. He'd explored the idea in the past with Showtime and CBS, but nothing came to fruition.

The idea was revisited in December 2009, when Arum, Les Moonves (CEO and president of CBS Corporation), and attorney Allen Grubman were vacationing with their wives in Mexico. It percolated while Pacquiao fought Joshua Clottey (March 13, 2010) and Antonio Margarito (November 13, 2010) on HBO-PPV. Then Moonves made an oral presentation to Arum outlining what CBS and Showtime were prepared to offer.

Among the things that Moonves ultimately promised were (1) advertising spots and live cutaways during the NCAA men's basketball championship tournament and other CBS Sports programming in April and the first week of May; (2) a four-part *Fight Camp 360* countdown series, with one or more of the episodes airing on CBS; and (3) appearances for pay-per-view undercard fighters on CBS talk shows.

Also, when HBO produces a *24/7* series to engender pay-per-view buys, the promoter bears the cost of production. That will be true here too for *Fight Camp 360*. But Top Rank will be given commercial time on CBS during the shows that it can sell to partially underwrite its costs.

In sum, the move to Showtime isn't simply about choosing one pay-per-view platform over another. It's about getting the broadest possible exposure for Pacquiao, Pacquiao-Mosley, and boxing. Manny is Top Rank's vehicle for breaking down some of the barriers that have separated boxing from large segments of the American public for the past thirty years.

Showtime and CBS offered Top Rank more than HBO. Not more up-front dollars. The currency here is awareness and exposure; 115,000,000 homes in the United States to promote the fight. That contrasts favorably with the 30,000,000 households that subscribe to HBO.

However, sources say that Arum's disenchantment with the leadership at HBO Sports also played into the decision-making process. Arum was angered by what he felt was a tilt by HBO in favor of Golden Boy and Al Haymon. In recent years, HBO has turned down opponents for Kelly Pavlik and Miguel Cotto (two elite Top Rank fighters) who were just as good as the opponents that the network accepted for boxers who were promoted by Golden Boy and managed by Haymon. The maneuvering by HBO that hastened the transit of Floyd Mayweather Jr from Top Rank to Golden Boy infuriated him. And he was saddened by the fact that no one from HBO attended the memorial service in Seattle in honor of his son, John (who was killed in a mountaineering accident last August).

"No one—and I mean, no one—has had a longer relationship with HBO than Bob," notes one observer, who has been a friend to both Arum and HBO Sports president Ross Greenburg over the years. "That Ross and Kery [HBO Sports vice president for programming, Kery Davis] didn't get on a plane was callous and disrespectful."

Planning for 2011 brought more of the same. Arum suggested putting Yuriorkis Gamboa on a February 26th HBO telecast. Davis told him that HBO was holding that date for a possible fight between Shane Mosley and Andre Berto and asked if Top Rank would schedule Gamboa for March 5th. Arum said yes. Then he read on the Internet that HBO had given the March 5th date to Golden Boy for Saul "Canelo" Alvarez.

Arum told Greenburg that he planned to promote an interim fight for Miguel Cotto (possibly against Vanes Martirosyan) on March 12th and match Cotto against Antonio Margarito in June. Ross said that he wasn't interested in the first Cotto fight and Arum should do it on his own as an independent pay-per-view show. Then HBO announced that it was holding March 12th for a Sergio Martinez fight (which would cut into Arum's pay-per-view buys). Davis told Arum, "We didn't know that you were going on March 12th."

When crunch time came, there was no reservoir of good will for HBO to draw upon.

Meanwhile, it was known to many in the boxing industry that Arum and Moonves were talking. And Top Rank president Todd DuBoef had made no secret of his interest in exploring options other than HBO for Pacquiao. Indeed, last June, DuBoef stated, "I should have explored making a deal with ESPN for Pacquiao-Clottey. HBO brought nothing to the promotion. They wouldn't even do a *24/7* series. They did *The Road to Dallas* as a promo piece. One show. ESPN would have given us four "Roads to Dallas" in 90,000,000 homes. If I had it to do over again; absolutely, I'd discuss Pacquiao-Clottey with ESPN, with CBS, with Showtime. I'm not looking to rock the boat. But I am looking to grow the audience."

A visionary television executive would have taken DuBoef's remarks as a signal to seriously explore the possibility of synergy between HBO and either TNT or TBS (which are in 90,000,000 homes and, like HBO, are part of the Time Warner empire). Greenburg didn't do that.

Moreover, as negotiations between Top Rank and CBS Corporation were reaching a critical juncture, HBO Sports essentially shut down for an extended Christmas holiday.

"They knew they didn't have Pacquiao-Mosley locked in," Arum says. "I kept waiting for a serious proposal from them that would address my concerns, and it never came. Ross was off skiing, I guess."

Finally, word filtered back to HBO that the network might really lose Pacquiao-Mosley.

On Wednesday, January 5th, Greenburg telephoned Arum and told him that he wanted to fly to Las Vegas as soon as possible to meet with him. They agreed to have dinner on Monday, January 10th; just the two of them.

DuBoef was scheduled to meet with Showtime boxing tsar Ken Hershman in New York earlier in the day on January 10th to finalize a term sheet. HBO had become Arum's safety net in the event that negotiations with CBS and Showtime failed.

On January 7th, Arum called Greenburg and cancelled their Las Vegas dinner engagement. His reason, unstated, was that he felt it would be wrong to have Ross make the trip given the fact that he hoped to close a deal with Showtime and CBS. The promoter suggested that, snow permitting (six-to-twelve inches were predicted for the following Tuesday) they meet for dinner in New York on Wednesday, January 12th.

The snow didn't permit. Arum's dinner with Greenburg was rescheduled again; this time for Tuesday, January 18th.

By Friday, January 14th, Top Rank's deal with Showtime had been finalized. A few issues with CBS needed to be nailed down. "I have to know that CBS will deliver what it's promising," Arum told one confidante. "I don't want 'best efforts.' I want a full contractual commitment."

Arum arrived in New York on Monday, January 17th. The following night, he and Greenburg had dinner at San Pietro (an upscale Italian restaurant).

"Ross thinks he has to act fast because the ship is getting ready to sail," one observer of the unfolding drama said before the two men met. "Trust me; the ship has sailed."

According to one report, the Arum-Greenburg dinner was civil. Bob told Ross that there were a number of reasons for a move to Showtime and CBS, but the primary reason was his desire to give boxing a presence on terrestrial television. He also cited his obligation to Pacquiao and Mosley to maximize their income from the fight. "If it was a question of choosing HBO or Showtime," Arum said, "I'd choose HBO. But CBS brings an entirely new element into the equation."

"Then at the end," the source recounts, "things fell apart. As they were getting ready to leave the restaurant, Bob told Ross what some of his grievances were, including the fact that HBO had played the situation with Floyd Mayweather Jr in a way that was calculated to take Floyd away from Top Rank. Ross said, 'That wasn't me; that was Seth [former HBO Sports president Seth Abraham].' Arum told him, 'No; that was you. Seth was gone by then.'"

"Ross is trying to play chess with Arum," the source concluded. "But he's moving his pieces like they were checkers."

On Wednesday, January 19th, Arum hosted a press conference at B.B. King's in New York to formally announce a March 12th fight between Miguel Cotto and Ricardo Mayorga.

Mayorga is promoted by Don King, and there was a lot of talk about the reunion of the two promoters being the equivalent of a Hollywood buddy movie. Think Bob Hope and Bing Crosby, Oscar Madison and Felix Unger, or Thelma and Louise.

More significantly, Cotto-Mayorga will be on Showtime-PPV. Among other things, it's a trial run to get the glitches out of the system for Pacquiao-Mosley.

Ken Hershman was in Los Angeles with Todd DuBoef, putting the finishing touches on what Arum hoped would be the CBS portion of the Pacquiao-Mosley television contract. In his Hershman's absence, Showtime upped the ante. Arum proudly told the assembled media, "To demonstrate Showtime's commitment to boxing, we don't have the head of the sports department here today. We don't have the head of pay-per-view. We have the actual head of Showtime [CEO Matt Blank]."

After the press conference, Arum walked several blocks from B.B. King's to HBO, where he met for two hours with Greenburg and HBO senior vice president Mark Taffet (who oversees the network's pay-per-view programming). Following that meeting, Ross asked Bob to accompany him to Richard Plepler's office.

Plepler is the president of HBO. He's liked and respected throughout the company.

Arum was impressed with Plepler. But at that point, there was nothing HBO could do to halt the tide of events.

"A 'Hail Mary' pass might work when you're down by six points at the end of the game," one source who was following the negotiations noted. "But it won't work if there are ten seconds left on the clock and you're behind by three touchdowns. What's HBO going to do? Offer Bob a *36/7?*"

On Thursday, January 20th, Arum was in Puerto Rico for another Cotto-Mayorga press conference. Meanwhile, contracts with CBS Corporation were finalized in Los Angeles.

On Friday, Arum returned to New York. Early in the afternoon, he telephoned Greenburg and told him that the deal was done and he was taking Pacquiao-Mosley to Showtime and CBS. Greenburg offered a curt response and hung up.

Ross told several staff members about the development. Then he called Al Haymon, Golden Boy CEO Richard Schaefer, and a few others, saying that he looked forward to continuing to do business with them in the future.

"Ross was very dejected," one person said of their conversation. "I felt sorry for him."

As for what comes next; the first thing to note is that, on its face, the Top Rank-Showtime-CBS alliance is largely about one fighter (although Miguel Cotto is also in the mix).

Fighters move from Showtime to HBO all the time. Naseem Hamed, Ricky Hatton, and Joe Calzaghe all developed on Showtime as attractions in the United States. Then they jumped ship. So did Chad Dawson.

But the move of Pacquiao to Showtime-PPV for at least one fight symbolizes the drift at HBO Sports. The HBO Boxing brand has been in decline for almost a decade and there are more storm clouds on the horizon.

Over the years, this writer has referenced the issues facing HBO Sports on numerous occasions. Non-competitive fights, low ratings, inconsistent announcing, and stale production values have been ongoing problems.

The network that brought boxing fans the scintillating Gatti-Ward and Barrera-Morales trilogies now can't even make the first in what would be a trilogy-worthy series of fights.

2011 looks to be a repeat of the erratic programming that has typified HBO boxing in recent years. A lot has been made of the upcoming bout between Timothy Bradley and Devon Alexander. In a vacuum, it's an intriguing fight. Bradley and Alexander are good young fighters. But HBO is spending close to $4,000,000 on the license fee, marketing, and production costs for a fight that most likely will draw a poor rating because only hardcore boxing fans are interested in it. Also, styles make fights and this could turn out to be a boring styles match-up.

Worse, HBO has mortgaged its future to make Bradley-Alexander. Each fighter (in tandem with his respective promoter) has been guaranteed a second fight for a license fee of at least $3,000,000. This means that, unless their first encounter warrants a rematch, three fights involving these two boxers will command almost 25 percent of HBO's license fees in 2011.

Some of HBO's problems also flow from what is perceived by many to be a culture of disdain within the sports department. There are many good caring people at HBO Sports. But there's a widespread feeling within the boxing community that too many of those at the top of the pyramid are aloof and look down their nose at "boxing people."

"The guys running the show now," says former 140-pound champion Paulie Malignaggi, "don't care that every decision they make has the power to turn someone else's life right side up or upside down. The way they make fights; sometimes it feels like they're playing chess and all we are is pawns. They don't think twice that someone else's livelihood is on the line. The only fighter they've shown any real respect for since I've been in boxing is Oscar."

No one from HBO attended Arturo Gatti's funeral in Montreal.

Former middleweight champion Kelly Pavlik fought seven times on HBO. In April 2010, he lost his title to Sergio Martinez. Late last year, he spent several months in rehab for drinking-related problems. No one from HBO wrote to Kelly to wish him well while he was undergoing treatment.

"They don't care about anybody but themselves," a member of Team Pavlik grumbled. "They don't even pretend to care."

Often, when HBO executives are onsite for a fight, they're booked into a hotel other than the fight center. For example, at Pacquiao-Margarito, HBO personnel stayed at The Four Seasons rather than the Gaylord Texan. One week later, fight headquarters for Sergio Martinez vs. Paul Williams in Atlantic City was at Caesars-Bally's. HBO put its people in The Chelsea. That might mean more elegant surroundings, but it's isolating and symptomatic of a failing that has led to the decision-makers at HBO Sports not being fully grounded in the sport and business of boxing.

"There were a lot of warning signs on Pacquiao," says one person who followed the negotiations. "But HBO missed them because the guys there don't have their ear to the ground. By the time they woke up to the problem, it was too late. And there's an arrogance. It's like, 'We're HBO. We can buy what we want. We're too big to fail.' But when they can't get what they want by throwing money at people, they have no idea how to deal with the situation. Look how helpless they were when they tried to make Mayweather-Pacquiao."

"Ross and Kery brought this on themselves," says Arum. "They're not bad people, but they're in the wrong jobs. Ross is a producer, not a television executive. Kery has no feel for boxing and cares less. And they don't treat people with respect. Look; I know what HBO has done for Top Rank over the years. If Ross had treated me differently, it would have been very hard for me as a matter of personal loyalty to bring Manny to Showtime and CBS. I carry a lot of Jewish guilt."

Pat English has represented Main Events for almost thirty years. He's one of the most respected attorneys in the boxing industry.

"There's an incredibly high degree of frustration toward the actions of certain representatives of HBO," English says. "Right now, some promoters have become so angry that they'd just as soon see HBO sink into the sea. There is an element of wanting to see HBO fail. I share some of that resentment, but I think that's the wrong reaction. I want HBO to be successful in boxing. I want Showtime to be successful in boxing. It pains me more than it angers me to see some of the decisions they've made at HBO in recent years. I was there [as the attorney for Main Events] during the heyday of boxing at HBO. Unfortunately, those days are past."

"Can they be rekindled?"

"I think so," English answers.

"How?"

"One; they have to regain credibility as decision-makers with the people that they deal with in the industry. The industry as a whole has to perceive that there's a rational basis for decisions that are made at HBO. And the general perception in the industry now is that there is not."

"Two," English continues, "people in the industry have to believe that the individuals with whom they are dealing at HBO are dealing with them honestly. They have to believe what is said to them, and that doesn't exist right now. There is a serious credibility issue at HBO."

"Three; HBO has to get back an understanding of what its subscribers and potential subscribers want to see. There is a fundamental lack of understanding at HBO that people have to care about the fighters who are on HBO if HBO is going to get good ratings. There should be a premium on fights and fighters that are fan-friendly. There should not be an award for being associated with certain people who are in favor at HBO."

Then English is asked, "Do you think that Ross Greenburg is capable of doing that?"

"I don't know."

"What about Kery Davis?"

"No."

"Ross's arrogance led to this," says a promoter who has done extensive business with HBO. "He fiddled while HBO Sports burned. HBO has the largest checkbook in the business, so he's used to buying whatever he wants. If Ross had put together a package that gave Manny a platform on TBS or TNT, the fight could have stayed with HBO. But Ross didn't see the need for that and he isn't that creative. He's creative in a production sense, but not as a businessman. Ross doesn't understand boxing as a business or a sport, so he can't help find ways to make it better. He understands what makes a compelling documentary, but not a compelling fight. He has lots of Emmys, but Emmys are about art, not business.

The loss of Pacquiao to Showtime coupled with the decline in ratings for HBO's boxing programming has sent ripples throughout HBO. There's a growing feeling internally that the sports department as presently constituted will be unable to fully solve its problems.

The point person in any overall evaluation of the situation is likely to be Richard Plepler. In all probability, he would work with Michael Lombardo (president of HBO programming and West Coast operations). Ultimately, HBO CEO Bill Nelson could become directly involved.

In recent years, Plepler has been aware of issues within the sports department, but he has had more pressing concerns to address.

In November 2010, after a three-part series about HBO was posted on this website, Plepler had separate meetings with New York City Police Department commissioner Ray Kelly (a former chairman of the New York State Athletic Commission) and Edwin Torres (a retired New York State Supreme Court judge currently serving as a member of the athletic commission) to solicit their thoughts on how to revive HBO's boxing program.

People who care about boxing hope that Plepler will now become more deeply involved in the situation and cast a wider net. He and Lombardo rebuilt HBO's programming staff on the west coast after Chris Albrecht's departure in 2007. They might decide do the same thing with HBO Sports.

Meanwhile, HBO has to fashion a coherent plan for the future. In some areas, immediate action is required.

The network needs a constructive strategy, not a punitive one. It should not counter-program Pacquiao-Mosley with a "free" fight on May 7th. Nor should it retaliate against Top Rank.

In that regard, Arum says, "I would hope Ross understands that we've approached decisions about Pacquiao-Mosley the same way that HBO makes the decision to not buy some of our fights. I didn't refuse to do business with HBO because they wouldn't televise Julio Cesar Chavez Jr or any number of other Top Rank fights. If we offer a fight to HBO in the future and it meets their criteria, I assume that HBO will buy it. If not, they'll be short-changing their subscribers."

Next, HBO has to understand that there are issues here that go far beyond one fighter. HBO survived the loss of Mike Tyson to Showtime in 1995, and it will survive the loss of Manny Pacquiao even if he never comes back. The big prize in many people's eyes is Pacquiao-Mayweather (if it happens). But keep in mind; Mayweather vs. Oscar De La Hoya engendered a record 2,400,000 pay-per-view buys four years ago, and HBO boxing is worse off now than it was then. It would be a mistake for HBO to focus on Mayweather and Pacquiao-Mayweather to the detriment of other fighters and fights. The most constructive thing that HBO Sports can do to get healthy again is to televise more entertaining fights.

HBO has to explore an alliance with Turner Sports now.

There should be some soul-searching and fence-mending.

But regardless of how HBO reacts, Pacquiao to Showtime is one of the biggest out-of-the-ring boxing stories in a long time and the most significant development in the sport since HBO's boxing program went into decline. What happens next depends in large measure on whether the tandem of CBS and Showtime is successful in engendering pay-per-view buys.

The target that Arum is pursuing here is the general sports fan and the public at large. But successfully marketing a pay-per-view fight is more complicated than simply getting on-air promotion. There's a great deal of behind-the-scenes nuts-and-bolts work that has to be done with cable system operators and other entities. HBO does that better than anyone else in boxing. Most of the people at Showtime who did it successfully for Mike Tyson's fights more than a decade ago are gone. Top Rank has done it with some success (and some failure) for its small independent pay-per-view shows. Pacquiao-Mosley is a far more ambitious undertaking.

If Miguel Cotto beats Ricardo Mayorga on March 12th, Cotto vs. Antonio Margarito on Showtime-PPV might follow. Strong numbers for Pacquiao-Mosley could lead to ABC-ESPN, NBC-Versus, and Fox-FX pairings for similar ventures. That would break HBO's control over major pay-per-view shows.

In other words; if the Top Rank-Showtime-CBS alliance is successful, it will mark a seismic shift in the boxing landscape. The be-all-and-end-all for fighters will no longer be a fight on HBO-PPV.

When ABC passed on Larry Holmes vs. Mike Weaver in 1979 and HBO purchased the fight, it marked the beginning of the end of ABC's supremacy in boxing. Pacquiao-Mosley could mark another changing of the guard.

"For far too long," says Arum, "boxing promoters have been puppets doing whatever HBO tells them to do. At times, I've been guilty of that too. But that's over now. We're taking back the business from HBO."

A television network can get into boxing for a minimal investment. This isn't the National Football League. Two other premium cable networks are currently in discussions with promoters about adding boxing to their programming. Hopefully, Pacquiao-Mosley will lead to the return of boxing to terrestrial television as well.

"I don't know yet what the ramifications of this will be," says Pat English. "No one does. If this opens up a new market and helps popularize the sport, it's a good thing. We have to see how successful it is and how wide-ranging the involvement of CBS in the sport will be after this."

Whatever happens though, it's going to be an interesting few months. People who thought that boxing was dead thirty days ago are once again paying attention to the sport.

Dallas Cowboys owner Jerry Jones has one of the keenest business minds in sports. "Don King and I are lucky this guy didn't get in boxing when we did," Arum said last year. "He would have run us both out of the business."

Earlier this month, Jones spoke publicly about the ongoing National Football League labor negotiations.

"Every place in the world is revisiting how they do business," Jones said. "Everybody is doing it. It is almost irresponsible not to do it. The time to address the adjustment in your business model is now; not when you are driving off the cliff."

In recent years, boxing and HBO have been driving toward a cliff. Bob Arum just got out of the car.

After the loss of Manny Pacquiao to Showtime, it was clear that HBO
Sports had to change course if it was going to once again be "the heart
and soul of boxing."

What HBO Should Do Now

Part One

Eight years ago, I wrote an article entitled "What's Going on at
HBO?" In part, that article read, "Boxing at HBO is at a crossroads. There's
an axiom in the sweet science that, if a fighter isn't getting better, he's getting worse. And the same might be said of those who televise fights. To a
degree, HBO is living off the good will that attaches to the HBO brand.
And because HBO sets the standard, if it gets sloppy it will allow everyone
else's standards to drop."

Four years after that, in 2007, I wrote, "This is a watershed moment
for HBO Sports. And it comes at a time when HBO can no longer take
its favored position with boxing fans for granted. Until recently, there was
a presumption that, if a fight was on HBO, it was worth watching. That's
no longer always the case. The powers that be at HBO have to sit down
with a blank piece of paper and ask themselves, 'What do we want HBO
Sports to look like five years from now?' And when they do, they should
examine the underlying philosophy that drives their boxing program."

Since then, I've remained an admirer and also a critic of HBO Sports.
Among the points I've made are:

(1) HBO Sports should televise better fights.

(2) Rather than pre-select "stars," HBO Sports should let stars emerge
from exciting competitive match-ups.

(3) HBO Sports has been bidding against itself and overpaying for
fights.

(4) HBO Sports should stop tilting the playing field in favor of certain promoters and managers. In recent years, that tilt has been toward
Golden Boy and Al Haymon.

(5) HBO Sports should reserve the HBO-PPV label for special events and give pay-per-view buyers better undercard fights.

(6) The HBO Sports announcing teams (which are crucial to branding its boxing program) should be revamped.

(7) HBO Sports needs to eliminate the arrogant condescending attitude that several of its key executives manifest toward the boxing community.

(8) The decision-makers at HBO Sports have to immerse themselves in the boxing community and become better informed with regard to boxing matters.

These things didn't happen. As a result, HBO Sports let its subscribers, Time Warner's shareholders, and boxing down.

Recent events have been extremely discouraging to the many people who have worked so hard over the years to build HBO Sports. The announcement that Manny Pacquiao is leaving the network to fight Shane Mosley on Showtime Pay-Per-View has led to serious soul-searching at the highest levels of HBO. But Pacquiao-Mosley is only the tip of the iceberg. There's a growing understanding, as evidenced by years of declining ratings, that the problems at HBO Sports go far beyond one fight.

The key players at HBO Sports are Ross Greenburg (president), Kery Davis (senior vice president for sports programming), Mark Taffet (senior vice president for sports operations and pay-per-view), and Rick Bernstein (senior vice president / executive producer).

Their future and the future of HBO Sports will be determined by three men.

Bill Nelson is HBO's chairman and CEO. Richard Plepler is HBO's co-president. Michael Lombardo is president of HBO programming.

Greenburg reports to Lombardo. Above that, the chain of command runs through Plepler to Nelson. Sources say that Greenburg did not inform Nelson, Plepler, or Lombardo that HBO was in danger of losing Manny Pacquiao until it was too late for HBO to marshal its resources and make a proposal that would be competitive with Showtime and CBS.

Other sources say that Nelson, Plepler, and Lombardo have decided that HBO will remain involved with boxing on a long-term basis and that they are committed to restoring excellence to HBO's boxing brand.

In furtherance of that goal, Plepler and Lombardo have embarked upon a fact-finding mission. When it's complete, Plepler (with significant input from Lombardo and subject to Nelson's approval) will decide who is best qualified to run HBO Sports in the future. All other HBO Sports personnel decisions will flow from that choice.

No final decision has been made yet with regard to Greenburg's future. But a number of leaders in the boxing community have said privately that, if Plepler and Lombardo ask for their opinion, they will tell them that both Greenburg and Davis are better suited for positions other than the ones they currently hold.

"The handwriting is on the wall," says one person with knowledge of the situation. "It's more than handwriting; it's graffiti. Ross and Kery are on a very small island and the water is rising. I'd be very surprised if either one of them is with HBO Sports six months from now."

Commenting on another person's job performance is a serious matter. But it's a responsibility that resides with the media at appropriate times. *Time Magazine* and CNN (which, like HBO, are components of the Time Warner empire) critique the performance of government officials and corporate executives on a regular basis. HBO Sports grades the performance of fighters and others in the boxing industry all the time; often harshly.

Certainly, a journalist has the right to critique the leaders of HBO Sports.

For far too long, the people running HBO Sports have been like trust fund babies with a constant flow of budget money from above who aren't in touch with the financial realities of the boxing industry. There has been a collective failure to identify, acknowledge, and take responsibility for problems. As one industry veteran notes, "They're like guys at a very exclusive country club. They sit around enjoying the good life, telling each other what a wonderful job they're doing, and nothing that goes wrong is their fault."

When Roger Goodell was interviewing for the job of commissioner of the National Football League, he gave the owners this piece of advice: "Change before you're forced to change."

The leaders of HBO Sports have been slow to change. Indeed, because HBO Sports was so successful during the last two decades of the twentieth century, they've resisted change in the new millennium. And they've seemed oblivious to the decline of HBO's boxing franchise. The problem isn't that HBO lost Pacquiao-Mosley. The problem is everything that led to the loss of Pacquiao-Mosley.

Ross Greenburg took over the helm of HBO Sports ten years ago. During his tenure, HBO has turned a deaf ear to large segments of the boxing community. In July 2008, when Bob Arum was raising some of the same issues he has raised during the past year, HBO issued a statement that read, "We've grown weary of Bob Arum's tirades against HBO Sports. They are foolish, unproductive and marginal in accuracy."

In recent weeks, Arum has been cast as Moses leading boxing out of bondage into the promised land with Greenburg playing the role of Pharaoh. It's not that simple. Arum is far from perfect and Greenburg has redeeming qualities. But Arum is able to see beyond his own personal preferences, and Greenburg seems to have difficulty doing that.

"Ross personalizes everything," says a former HBO employee. "He doesn't understand that what appeals to him doesn't necessarily appeal to HBO's subscriber base. Ross likes baseball, so he thinks that everybody likes baseball and he won't run boxing against the baseball playoffs. There are run-of-the-mill college football games that do better ratings than the baseball playoffs."

Also, there are times when Greenburg allows his personal feelings to override sound business judgment.

"Ross has stopped speaking to me altogether," Arum said in 2008. "He won't take telephone calls from me anymore because he's mad that I've criticized him. I've called him five or six times in the past few weeks, and he won't return my calls. That's not how a responsible television executive behaves. It's worse than unprofessional. It's fucking moronic. I'm supplying Manny Pacquiao, Kelly Pavlik, Miguel Cotto, Antonio Margarito. None of them are tied to HBO, which means they can bolt at any time. Ross might despise me. But doesn't he have an obligation as the head of HBO Sports to talk with me? Don King and I were mortal enemies at times, but we always talked. [Former HBO Sports president] Seth Abraham was pissed off at me more times than I can count, but we always talked. Even when Seth and I were fighting, he'd pick up the phone and call to say 'congratulations' after a great fight."

"Ross made it personal with Bob," says someone who knows both men well. "His approach was, 'Hey; let's dump all over the promoter who has the best, most marketable fighter in boxing because he has nowhere else to go.' That's not a very good strategy."

"You can like Bob Arum or not like Bob Arum," says another industry insider. "But Bob has one of the longest-running relationships that exists between a supplier and HBO. Not just HBO Sports; all of HBO. Bob has supplied HBO with more fights than any other promoter. If you add up the revenue from pay-per-fights-over the years, HBO has made more money with Bob than with any other promoter. And look what Ross has done to that relationship."

Greenburg's first response to the loss of Manny Pacquiao should have been to sit back and reflect on the question, "What did we do wrong?" But people who've worked closely with him say that he has difficulty admitting to having made a mistake. Being stubborn in the face of a contrary reality is rarely a virtue. The Bourbon Kings (who were known for their stubbornness) ruled France from the late-sixteenth century until the French Revolution. Talleyrand said of them, "They have learned nothing, and they have forgotten nothing."

For the past decade, like its Emmy–award-winning *Sports of the 20th Century* series, HBO Sports has often seemed to be rooted in the past.

More significantly, Greenburg and the business of boxing are a poor fit.

Lou DiBella (who was the point person for HBO's boxing program during the glory years) observes, "Other networks have been heavily into boxing in the past, and other networks will be heavily into boxing in the future. But their sports departments haven't been built on boxing. Boxing is the core of HBO Sports. Not documentaries; not *Real Sports*. Boxing."

Eight years ago, I wrote, "Seth Abraham was a forceful advocate for boxing within Time Warner. Greenburg is a great producer. But Greenburg doesn't know the sport of boxing, the business of boxing, or the players in boxing the way Abraham did. Nor is he expected to be as strong an internal advocate for the sweet science. Boxing might well be just another sport to him; something to be thrown into the mix."

"You need a boxing guy to run boxing at HBO," Bob Arum said in 2008. "Not a bunch of TV guys who think they know boxing. The biggest problem with Ross, far worse than his personal animosity toward me and one or two other promoters, is his lack of knowledge and lack of interest in boxing. Ross was a good producer, but that doesn't qualify him to be the head of a major department at a major premium network. I'm sorry to say it, but Ross is ill-equipped for the job and he's certainly ill-equipped to run HBO's boxing program. If someone has no understanding of boxing and no love for the sport, he gets hooked on names he's heard of, even if those names belong to fighters who are way past their prime or could never fight to begin with. That's why you see so many horrible fights and so many of the same tired old faces on HBO. Make up a quiz about boxing and give it to all the executives who've been involved in buying fights for the television networks over the past ten years. I guarantee you; Ross would come in last."

Years ago, Seth Abraham reflected on the first professional fight he ever saw. At the time, he was a young man working as a special assistant to Bowie Kuhn (then the commissioner of Major League Baseball).

"There was nothing remarkable about the fight, but I found it thrilling," Abraham recalled. "I'd seen countless fights before on television. But sitting at this one, I was struck by the realization that every other sport has some type of time frame; either a clock or a given number of innings or whatever. And a fight can end at any moment. I suppose that's obvious, but it was an epiphany for me and the excitement of that night stayed with me. A year later, I went to HBO, believing that boxing had all the elements of great drama and great television."

But that drama often seems lost on Greenburg, who has made delay telecasts an integral part of his programming philosophy. Here, Arum observes, "The whole idea that it doesn't matter if people watch a fight live because we're showing it on tape and we count the cumulative total from all of the telecasts and re-telecasts is nuts. The whole point of watching a fight is that you can't take a break like you do if you're watching the first quarter of a football game. Because if you do, when you come back, the fight might be over. To watch a fight when you already know the result takes most of the excitement and drama out of it. Can you imagine someone saying, 'I'm not watching the Super Bowl live. I'll watch it on tape a week later.' You can't have a major sport like that."

Greenburg's critics also point to numerous missteps which were avoidable.

For example, in 2008, I wrote, "HBO is on the verge of signing a long-term output deal with Golden Boy. The proposed deal is, by definition, for fights and fighters unknown. It would undercut HBO's leverage in future negotiations with Golden Boy because the promoter would already have certain dates, which in and of itself is a major negotiating point."

In the same article, Seth Abraham was quoted as follows: "It's hard to believe that HBO would commit to buying a specified number of fights from Golden Boy for a specified number of dollars over a [long-term] period. Teddy Brenner once said, 'Fights make fights.' How could you know what fights and fighters you're buying?"

Greenburg finalized the output deal with Golden Boy. It's now widely acknowledged (even within HBO) that it was a huge mistake.

Prior to that, in 2006, Greenburg vetoed a deal that would have had HBO, in effect, partnering with Versus and using the cable network (which is part of the Comcast empire) as a development ground for HBO fighters. An opportunity for synergy with a network that's seen in tens of millions of homes was lost.

In 2009, Ross nixed a proposal that HBO bring boxing's leading promoters together for a "summit" to discuss the sport's problems.

And over the years, Greenburg has evinced a sense of entitlement that has soured a number of people in the boxing and entertainment industries.

A case in point— Last year, Jim Lampley proposed that HBO work with his production company on an unscripted documentary-reality series about trainer Freddie Roach. Greenburg turned the project down. The following recitation of what happened thereafter has been pieced together from multiple sources.

Ted Chervin is the head of worldwide television at ICM (one of the largest and most influential talent agencies in the world). He's also Lampley's agent. Chervin was instrumental in eliciting an offer for the Freddie Roach project from AMC. In May 2010, Greenburg was given one last chance to pick up the project and declined.

Ultimately, Greenburg was overruled by Michael Lombardo, who purchased the series for HBO with funds from the network's entertainment division (rather than the sports department). But in the interim, filming began.

In October 2010, Manny Pacquiao arrived at the Wild Card Gym in Los Angeles to begin training with Roach for his November 13th fight against Antonio Margarito. HBO's *24/7* production team was there. At that point, HBO executive producer Rick Bernstein called Nick Khan (who works for Chervin and is Roach's agent) and told him, "Our camera crew says there's an AMC crew there. They have to leave."

Khan said that the AMC crew had every right to be there.

Five minutes later, Greenburg called Khan, demanding, "How dare you do a show like this? You're shutting that AMC project down now [expletives deleted]."

Khan told Chervin about the conversation, including the fact that Greenburg had referred to the two of them as "morons."

Ted Chervin is a former assistant United States attorney, who made his name in legal circles by prosecuting organized crime figures (including members of Colombia's Cali drug cartel). He didn't like being called a moron.

Chervin instructed Khan to have the *24/7* crew thrown out of the gym.

Soon after, Arum and Top Rank president Todd DuBoef called Khan and told him, "This puts us in a difficult spot. We have a contract with *24/7*. We'd take it as a personal favor if you let them back in the gym."

Khan called Bernstein and said that, as a courtesy to Top Rank, the *24/7* crew would be allowed in the gym when Pacquiao was there. He also telephoned Greenburg and told him that, if Ross didn't apologize to Chervin, Ted would complain about the incident to Richard Plepler.

Greenburg called Chervin, apologized, and asked, "Is it all square between us now?"

Maybe it is; maybe it isn't.

Ross's right-hand man on boxing matters is Kery Davis. Like Greenburg, he declined to be interviewed for this article.

Davis had a hard act to follow. As I wrote in 2003, "Lou DiBella essentially ran HBO Boxing for Seth Abraham on a day-to-day basis. He was proactive when it came to the sport. He loved the fight world. He understood, cared about, and subordinated his life to boxing. He also operated in a very personal way with everyone from the media to the fighters themselves. DiBella constantly bounced ideas off people and solicited their advice. He fought to change HBO from a network that showcased its stars in mismatches in order to groom them for pay-per-view events to a network that put fighters in tough and stood by them when they lost as long as they lost with honor. He championed the lighter-weight fighters; a commitment that's paying dividends now in the form of Naseem Hamed, Erik Morales, and Marco Antonio Barrera. And he was up-front with his feelings about corruption in the sport. To a degree, his passion for cleaning up the sweet science inoculated HBO against some of boxing's broader scandals."

DiBella had his flaws (as all of us do). "He ruffled feathers in-house," I wrote. "There were times when he upstaged some of his compatriots and neutered others. Because boxing at HBO was enormously successful under his watch, the powers-that-be gave him wide latitude. But now that DiBella is gone, there appears to be a new attitude at HBO. Kery Davis is the new 'boxing guy' at HBO. Davis comes out of the music business and appears to lack DiBella's passion for and knowledge of the sport. Whenever there was a [pay-per-view] fight in Las Vegas on a Saturday, DiBella was likely to be in attendance at the ESPN2 card the night before. Kery is more likely to be enjoying a leisurely dinner. Davis may well grow into his role. But right now, he doesn't have the personal rapport with fighters, managers, and the media that DiBella enjoyed."

"Part of Seth's genius," says a longtime HBO employee, "was that he let Lou be Lou. Part of Ross's problem is that he lets Kery be Kery."

Davis has voiced anger that I've questioned the practice of HBO Sports executives not staying at the host hotel for certain fights and, instead, staying at more luxurious accommodations away from the action. My own view is that corporate employees are entitled to travel in comfort. But when HBO Sports pays for one of its executives to be on-site for a fight, the purpose of the trip is not eat expensive dinners, play golf, and hang out at the best hotel in town with friends.

I might add that *Time Magazine,* CNN, and other Time Warner subsidiaries appropriately criticize the extravagant perks given to management at Wall Street brokerage houses and other corporate executives.

Also, Davis is enormously engaging and charming when he chooses to be. But a lot of people in the boxing industry feel that he acts disrespectfully toward them. A small example: there was a time when Kery was said to have a policy of not returning telephone calls from Internet writers because of their lowly position. If Dana White had adhered to that policy, UFC might not exist today.

More important, a promoter who does business regularly with HBO says, "A lot of us don't feel that we can rely on what Kery tells us. Sometimes that's because he's telling the truth as he sees it and then Ross undermines him. And sometimes it's because—let's put it this way—Kery equivocates."

But the heart of the matter is that, in recent years, HBO has televised too many mediocre fights. "Kery is in a job where he has to know boxing," the same promoter notes. "And he doesn't. He doesn't know what will make for a good fight and he certainly doesn't know which fighters have the potential to become stars. Kery knows music; he has passion for music; he respects music people. But he doesn't get it when it comes to boxing. Kery should be in the music business, not in boxing."

Bob Arum sounded a similar theme last year, when he opined, "Kery isn't a boxing guy. To do that job, you have to love boxing and be part of boxing and get boxing. Kery has no feel for the sport. He would dispute that, but I've been in boxing for a long time and I know what I'm talking about."

It's time for a change in leadership at HBO Sports. That isn't something I write lightly. As noted earlier, commenting on someone else's job performance is serious commentary. I'm mindful that people's livelihoods are at stake; just as they're at stake every time that HBO Sports makes a decision regarding which fights to buy and how much to pay for them.

Ross Greenberg and Kery Davis make decisions every day that affect the trajectory of people's careers.

Last year, HBO Sports dismissed Lennox Lewis as a commentator on *Boxing After Dark*. The decision wasn't motivated by personal ill will. Rightly or wrongly, there was a judgment that Lennox wasn't performing up to par. Very few jobs come with lifetime tenure.

"The solution is simple," says one observer of the unfolding drama. "It's fixable, but not by the incumbents. HBO Sports reminds me of an overfunded incompetently run sports franchise. Omar Minaya with the Mets and Isiah Thomas with the Knicks are examples of executives who were continually outmaneuvered by guys who had much smaller budgets but knew what they were doing. Just as in other sports, you hire a new general manager and a new coach and get to work."

"If you've gone from being the unquestioned leader in boxing to a floundering giant, you've fucked up," says a promoter who has done business regularly with HBO. "They've taken the premier franchise in boxing and turned it into an ordinary product. It's like when the New York

Yankees went from the greatest dynasty in baseball history to just another team. The Yankees came back, but it took new leadership."

There are people who think that Ross Greenburg and Kery Davis have done a good job. Their opinions should be given the same careful consideration as those voiced above.

As for the other leaders of HBO Sports; Mark Taffet is respected in the boxing industry. He's comfortable communing with the powers that be. And when HBO has a big pay-per-view fight, he spends as much time in the media center as many of the writers. He's studying, exchanging ideas, and learning because he views it as part of his job.

"Taffet is a politician," Bob Arum said two years ago. "But at least he's a bright politician."

Rick Bernstein's tenure as executive producer has been more problematic.

The HBO Sports production team has many advantages, including the platform and money to do virtually anything it wants as it relates to boxing. It has better access to the athletes it covers than the producers of almost any other network sports department. It also has the services of some enormously talented people like director Marc Payton and creative young producers (who haven't been given the opportunity to fully show what they can do). There is a technical support staff comprised of people who are as good, if not better than, any of their industry counterparts.

But in recent years, HBO Sports programming has lost its edge. It has become formulaic. It's far less innovative and daring now than the documentaries produced by Sheila Nevins (president of HBO Documentary Films), not to mention such offerings as *Boardwalk Empire*. It has become tired and less appealing to young viewers, who will make up the next generation of premium-cable subscribers.

That's also true of HBO's boxing telecasts, which have gotten stale. Last year's fights at Cowboys Stadium and Yankee Stadium saw some interesting innovations; particularly with regard to lighting. But those were largely the work of the promoter.

Rick Bernstein's defenders say that he hasn't been allowed to deviate from certain templates that Ross Greenburg has set in stone. One assumes that Richard Plepler and Michael Lombardo will explore the matter.

All of this prompts the question of, "Who will lead HBO Sports and its boxing program into the future if Ross Greenburg and Kery Davis are replaced?"

The role of HBO Sports president will be more complex in the future than in the past because HBO's boxing program will face competition from multiple networks and alternative media platforms; not just Showtime.

The next president of HBO Sports has to appreciate the fact that boxing has been the anchor of HBO Sports for decades. If he intends to continue on that course, he must clearly communicate this fact, both internally and externally.

Because of boxing's primacy, he should be grounded in boxing, not just sports, and understand the strength of the brand of boxing.

He must be a visionary leader with the ability to plan for the future.

Once the blueprint for the future is fashioned, he must have the ability and credibility to sell the new HBO Sports to the boxing community, hotel-casinos, other potential sites, sponsors, and the media.

He must understand that ratings (which are a measure of subscriber satisfaction) are more important than Emmys.

He must be a good administrator who knows how (and to whom) to delegate authority.

He must put his own personal comfort aside and get on a plane to close a deal when necessary.

He has to listen to people carefully enough to understand their point of view and accept the fact that his own personal preferences for programming might be different from those of HBO's subscribers.

His conduct must be such that he restores morale and a sense of pride where it has been lost.

He must realize that he is not the star. He is occupying a position of power in a fiduciary role to benefit others; not just himself.

The new president of HBO Sports will be chosen before the point person on boxing is selected. A National Football League team doesn't hire a new head coach and tell him who his offensive coordinator will be.

The number-two slot (HBO's "boxing guy") isn't just a matchmaking job. The person who fills it needs a passion for boxing and an understanding of what makes an entertaining fight. It's imperative that he (or she) have respect for fighters and all of the other "boxing people" he comes in contact with in the performance of his duties. He also has to be able to transition back and forth between the boxing world and the corporate environment of HBO and understand the profit-and-loss end of the business. He needs negotiating skills and an understanding of the legal environment that he's operating within. People can like him or not like him, but they have to be able to trust his word. He can't play favorites.

No one can learn the boxing business in six months or a year. It takes at least five years of close study. Even then, a person needs an aptitude for it. Given the current crisis at HBO, both positions have to be filled by people who can hit the ground running.

Ideally, HBO will have a new team in place and be ready to act decisively in the market place by May 8th (the day after Mosley-Pacquiao). Given the realities of today's world and the detailed nature of the study that Richard Plepler and Michael Lombardo are undertaking, that might not be possible.

Part Two

2011 began poorly for HBO. On January 29th, the network televised Timothy Bradley vs. Devon Alexander.

The bout was billed as "The Super Fight." At the December 8, 2010, kick-off press conference in New York, co-promoter Gary Shaw told the media, "Other than Pacquiao-Mayweather, there's no bigger event in boxing than Bradley-Alexander." Ross Greenburg declared, "This is a star-power fight."

Greenburg also championed the fight internally. At one of his weekly HBO Sports staff meetings, he expressed the view that Bradley-Alexander would be "one of the best HBO fights in years."

HBO did its best to prop up the promotion with an expensive marketing campaign. Then reality intervened.

Greenburg had agreed to pay a $2,750,000 license fee for Bradley-Alexander. As part of the deal, win or lose, each fighter was guaranteed a seven-figure payday for his next bout. As I wrote on January 23rd, "In a vacuum, it's an intriguing fight. Bradley and Alexander are good young fighters. But HBO is spending close to $4,000,000 on the license fee, marketing, and production costs for a fight that most likely will draw a poor rating because only hard-core boxing fans are interested in it. Also, styles make fights and this could turn out to be a boring styles match-up. Worse, HBO has mortgaged its future to make Bradley-Alexander. HBO hopes that its 140-pound festival will evoke memories of the glory years when Sugar Ray Leonard, Thomas Hearns, Roberto Duran, and Marvelous Marvin Hagler fought each other. Unfortunately, Bradley, Alexander, [Amir] Khan, and [Victor] Ortiz aren't Leonard, Hearns, Duran, and Hagler."

In the end, HBO couldn't make the public care about the fight or the fighters.

The Silverdome in Pontiac, Michigan (where the bout was held) seats 80,000 people. The announced attendance was 6,247. That number was an exaggeration and the promoters acknowledged that many of those in attendance were admitted for free.

As the bout progressed, it was clear that no amount of hype could cover up the fact that it was an ordinary fight. One of the elements of a compelling match-up in boxing is the feeling that a viewer can't turn away because, at any moment, something exciting might happen. With Bradley-Alexander, viewers had the sense that they could turn away at any time and not miss a thing.

Bradley made the fight such as it was. Alexander fought in safety-first fashion, secure in the knowledge that, regardless of the outcome, he had another seven-figure payday ahead. Had that guarantee not been in place, perhaps he would have fought harder.

The bout ended in the tenth round after an accidental head-butt. Bradley was declared the winner on points. Regarding the possibility of a rematch, Larry Merchant told HBO's viewers, "There's no reason that we have to see this fight again." Bradley said of his opponent, "If that's the best in the world, that's weak."

The media were not kind in their appraisal of the fight.

Dan Rafael: "Talk about a disappointment. Bradley-Alexander was supposed to launch the winner, and maybe even the loser, to stardom. Instead, it was a giant dud. All the hype and all the hope went up in smoke."

Michael Woods: "It was billed as The Super Fight, and let us not mince words. It was not."

Michael Rosenthal: "I won't dismiss it as a disaster because I enjoy a good tactical fight. But it served up precious few moments that got the heart racing. It certainly wasn't the kind of scrap that brings fans to boxing."

David Greisman: "Most of the fight was clinching or wrestling or missed punches. HBO paid money for a fight that might have had casual viewers changing the channel halfway through. It invested millions of dollars in boxers who are now less marketable than they were before they fought each other."

Sports Illustrated fired a double salvo. First, Bryan Graham called Bradley-Alexander "a crummy fight and a crummier ending." Then Chris Mannix weighed in. "They wanted to believe they could create a superstar," Mannix wrote. "They wanted to believe that, with a lot of hype, a fight between Timothy Bradley and Devon Alexander would produce boxing's next big thing. What they forgot is that true greatness is measured by more than spotless records. It's measured by an ability to deliver a resonating performance. And in their shining moment, Bradley and Alexander could not. For a fight billed as all action, this one had precious little."

Insiders say that Greenburg was hoping for a 4.0 rating for Bradley-Alexander. The final number was 2.3 (with a 2.6 peak). That's one of the lowest rating-points-per-dollar numbers in the history of HBO Sports.

Worse, there was a sentiment among some viewers that, if HBO really thinks that Bradley-Alexander is "boxing at its best," then there's no reason for boxing fans to subscribe to HBO.

In the aftermath of Bradley-Alexander, HBO Sports found itself in an uncomfortable position. It was public knowledge that Pacquiao-Mosley was going to Showtime. And HBO's plans for the first half of 2011 were unsettled.

Richard Plepler is said to have instructed Greenburg that there was to be no retaliation against Bob Arum for taking Pacquiao to another network. "Be remedial, not punitive," was the gist of the HBO president's message. Thus, Top Rank shows scheduled for *Boxing After Dark* on February 19th and March 26th were kept in place. A March 5th *Boxing After Dark* date for Golden Boy was also on the schedule. The rest of HBO's dance card for the first half of 2011 had to be filled.

The first piece in the puzzle to be put in place was a March 12th date for middleweight champion Sergio Martinez, who earned "fighter of the year" honors in 2010 with a decision-victory over Kelly Pavlik and a thrilling one-punch knockout of Paul Williams. Greenburg and Kery Davis told the Martinez camp that the only available opponent they would accept for Sergio was Sergiy Dzinziruk. There's a school of thought that Ross promised Gary Shaw two fights for Dzinziruk as part of HBO's package deal for Bradley-Alexander.

Martinez-Dzinziruk figures to be a competitive fight. Whether it's entertaining is another matter. Kevin Iole called it "exactly the kind of match that fans will ignore" and added, "Dzinziruk is completely unknown in the U.S., even to the boxing media, and has a defensive jab-oriented style. There is almost no way to imagine it turns into a compelling fight."

Bob Arum was more direct, saying, "HBO has an emerging superstar [in Martinez] and they've compromised his future by putting him in a fight that it's virtually impossible for him to look good in and no one will care about. And for what? To make a deal with Gary Shaw for a fight between Bradley and Alexander in an empty barn."

April 16th has been set aside for a delay-telecast of Amir Khan vs. Paul McCloskey and a proposed bout between Andre Berto and Victor Ortiz. Khan-McCloskey is widely perceived as a mismatch. Berto-Ortiz is an intriguing fight.

Greenburg hopes to showcase Paul Williams in a comeback bout on April 30th. It would be nice if he insisted upon a competitive opponent.

As for Bradley and Alexander; Ross is counting on matching Timothy against Amir Khan this summer. Bradley and promoter Gary Shaw are said to be locked into the fight for $1,500,000 to be divided between them. But Khan is said to be questioning the $1,500,000 (to be shared with Golden Boy) that has been allocated by HBO for his side of the ledger.

As for Devon Alexander; the previous assumption was that he would fight Marcos Maidana with the two sides sharing a (vastly inflated) $3,000,000 license fee. Now Maidana is slated to face Erik Morales on HBO-PPV, and HBO might look for a less expensive dance partner for Alexander.

Greenburg is also said to covet a heavyweight fight between Tomasz Adamek and Vitali or Wladimir Klitschko. Adamek against David Haye, Alexander Povetkin, or one of many other heavyweights would be a compelling match-up. Adamek against either Klitschko is a mismatch.

The most disturbing news to come out of HBO in the past month is the report that the network is contemplating multi-fight contracts with the trio of Bernard Hopkins, Chad Dawson, and Jean Pascal. Contract signings have not been announced as of this writing. But multiple sources say that Greenberg has offered $3,700,000 for a May 21st doubleheader featuring a rematch between Hopkins and Pascal (who fought each other on Showtime last December) coupled with Chad Dawson vs. either Librado Andrade or Adrian Diaconu. If Dawson wins, he would fight the winner of Pascal-Hopkins. Depending on the outcome of various fights, the deal could lock in as many as three fights on HBO for Hopkins and two for Pascal and Dawson.

Hopkins is forty-six years old. Dawson has drawn consistently poor ratings. Indeed, Greenburg's decision to spend $3,200,000 plus production and marketing costs for the 2009 rematch between Dawson and Antonio Tarver (their first fight drew 911 paying customers) has become one of the symbols of his reign. As for Pascal; hall-of-fame matchmaker and promoter Russell Peltz opines, "Jean Pascal is an ordinary fighter who's lucky he lives in Canada."

There's value to HBO in going to Canada, where the proposed May 21st doubleheader would be held. The enthusiastic hometown crowd would provide a good backdrop for television. But if HBO wants to go Canadian, unbeaten middleweight David Lemieux (25–0, 24 KOs) has a far greater upside than Jean Pascal in terms of entertainment value. And he's available now at a fraction of the cost.

Lemieux is fighting Marco Antonio Rubio on ESPN2 on April 8th for a license fee said to be between $50,000 and $60,000. If you're running boxing at a television network, do you want Lemieux-Rubio for $60,000 or Pascal-Hopkins for roughly fifty times that amount?

"What are they building?" asks Kathy Duva (one of boxing's savvier promoters). "What are they doing? I don't understand the thought processes there. How do you attract young people to the sport with Bernard Hopkins?"

"It's one catastrophe after another," says another promoter. "If this is some sort of twelve-step program to rehabilitate boxing at HBO, I'd skip what they're doing now and go to the next step."

The contracts that Greenburg negotiated with regard to Bradley and Alexander coupled with the proposed deals involving Hopkins, Dawson, and Pascal have the potential to eat up 40 percent of HBO's license-fee budget for an entire year.

So why is Greenburg doing it?

"Ross thinks he's punishing Showtime by buying the Pascal-Hopkins rematch," says an industry veteran who negotiates regularly with HBO. "He's furious at Showtime because of Pacquiao-Mosley. So he's taking the rematch of one of their fights and using it to counter-program Showtime's super-middleweight tournament [the semifinals are scheduled to conclude on May 21st with Carl Froch vs. Glen Johnson]. But what he's really doing is cutting off his nose to spite his face. In attacking Showtime, he's directing his energies toward someone else's business rather than his own."

Counter-programming Showtime's boxing offerings seems to have become a key component of HBO's programming strategy. Greenburg won't televise boxing opposite the Major League Baseball playoffs. But he has counter-programmed four of Showtime's last five super-middleweight championship tournament telecasts.

CBS and Fox are rivals. But they don't counter-program each other with the Jets and Giants. When those two teams play on the same day (as they often do), it's in different time slots. That's because, when it comes to the National Football League, intelligent grown-ups are running the show.

Counter-programming Showtime hurts HBO's ratings too. Here, the thoughts of Pat English (the attorney for Main Events) are instructive.

"If you want the highest possible ratings," English observes, "you don't counter-program. Sometimes counter-programming is unavoidable. But where it's avoidable, then the intent is anti-competitive. That doesn't seem like a wise use of money since you decrease your own viewership."

There's increasing concern among people loyal to HBO that Greenburg is now making deals that will encumber his successor (if he's replaced) and make it more difficult to raise ratings in the year ahead.

"All Ross is doing now," says one observer, "is spinning his wheels and digging HBO further into a snowdrift."

Recent events have made people wonder if some form of oversight or interim leadership might be in the best interests of HBO Sports.

Meanwhile, morale is low at HBO Sports and a gallows humor pervades the scene: "They gave Ross and Kery lemonade, and they made lemons out of it . . . Is Ross a lame duck? I'm not the guy who makes that decision. But when I saw him this morning, he was limping and going 'quack quack' . . . Who leaves first: Ross or Hosni Mubarak?"

You can't put out a fire with a hammer.

So let's get constructive. What should be done to restore HBO Sports to greatness?

There's no quick fix. HBO has to work to regain the trust of the boxing industry and its subscribers.

The first step is to televise better fights.

Ross Greenburg has said again and again that the biggest problem he faces is that promoters aren't building stars like they used to.

No! The biggest problem is that HBO is trying to tell the public who the stars will be.

"A television network cannot anoint stars," Lennox Lewis said years ago. "You have to earn it in the ring."

Four years ago, I wrote, "Boxing fans might want to see 'stars,' but they want to see them in competitive fights. HBO is in the entertainment business. In boxing, great fights are entertainment. One-man-show fights get boring fast. HBO has to get away from the star-at-any-cost mentality and televise better fights; not just fights as a vehicle for one fighter. Every fight on HBO should be good enough to stand on its own. *Boxing After Dark* should not be a developmental league for *HBO World Championship Boxing*. *HBO World Championship Boxing* shouldn't be a developmental league for HBO Pay-Per-View. Better fights will attract younger viewers in addition to more old ones. There aren't many great fighters today, but that doesn't mean there can't be great fights. Matchmaking is an art, not a science. Fights don't always turn out the way they look on paper, but HBO is more likely to have great fights if it starts out with match-ups that are great to begin with."

As Cassius (Shakespeare's, not Louisville's) said to his companion in Act 1, Scene 2, of *Julius Caesar*, "The fault, dear Brutus, is not in our stars, but in ourselves."

The focus at HBO Sports should shift from who's an HBO-level fighter to what is an HBO-level fight. Don't buy bad fights to get to good ones. Buy good fights to get to great ones. And understand that there's a difference between an A-list fighter and an A-list attraction.

Over the years, promoter Dan Goossen has been a stalwart defender of HBO. "The key now," Goossen says, "is not what happened in the past. It doesn't serve any constructive purpose to grade HBO on what it did and didn't do until now. It's where HBO goes from here that counts.

A change in philosophy and direction is more important than assigning blame for the past."

Then Goossen puts his finger on the heart of the matter and says, "HBO has gotten away from the things we applauded over the years; good exciting competitive fights. It's right in front of our face with *The Fighter* [the recently-released feature film about Micky Ward]. Ward and Gatti weren't great fighters, but fans knew they were going to get what they wanted when they watched them fight. Lots of action from two guys with do-or-die attitudes; no one looking for an easy way out. HBO has to go back to basics. Put two evenly matched guys who want to fight in the ring against each other and you have excitement. Those are the fights we should be seeing on HBO. That's what we had for years and, somehow, HBO got away from it. The guys there got complacent and what happened happened."

Lou DiBella is in accord, saying, "If you're boring and you fight going backwards, I don't care what your pound-for-pound ranking is; you shouldn't be on HBO. It's not about appealing to 250,000 hardcore boxing fans. You have to appeal to a wider audience."

Gary Shaw states, "Fans don't want to see easy fights. That's not what it's about. It's about the best fighting the best."

And Russell Peltz adds, "They're not paying attention at HBO. After all these years, they still don't get it. The solution is simple. Make fights that people want to see. If only a thousand people buy tickets for a fight, that tells you right there that people don't want to see it. And stop playing favorites."

HBO's subscribers don't care if Ross Greenburg is angry at Bob Arum and Showtime. They don't care if a particular promoter or manager knows how to stroke someone's ego. They want to see good fights.

However, the problems at HBO Sports today won't be solved by simply making better fights. Bad fights started the decline, but other factors (including the fact that the economic model that sustained HBO's boxing program for years became obsolete) contributed to it.

Significant changes on many levels are necessary.

Boxing is HBO's signature sport. Everything else that HBO Sports offers to its subscribers is available elsewhere. The network should acknowledge that primacy.

Next; HBO Sports acts like it's the only game in town when it comes to boxing. But to be successful in the future, it will have to grow the brand of boxing; not just boxing on HBO.

HBO should utilize *24/7* and other programming as part of an over-all campaign to keep boxing relevant among its subscribers and the larger population of sports fans; not just as a marketing tool to engender buys for one pay-per-view show at a time.

One of the best things about boxing coverage on ESPN2 and ESPN.com is that ESPN acknowledges fights that are telecast on other networks. That's common sense if a network is trying to appeal to boxing fans. During the college football season, dozens of networks televise college football. They report scores and show video highlights of games on competing networks. That's how a sport is grown for the benefit of every-one involved.

HBO should tell its subscribers what's happening in boxing; not just in boxing on HBO. It should take viewers behind the scenes with a low-budget magazine show that probes, investigates, and addresses serious issues in the sport. In that regard, Jim Lampley is the network's most under-utilized asset. He should be used in production; not just as a blow-by-blow commentator.

There's no debate in boxing over who the "champions" are. That's because there are so many of them that the public no longer cares. But boxing fans will care about who's #1 in key weight divisions if the issue is presented to them in a credible way.

To repeat what I've written before, "Forget about champions. The world sanctioning organizations have made a mockery of the term. HBO should identify the most credible rankings possible. That might mean con-vening its own panel of experts. Then it can tell viewers, 'This fight is between #1 and #2. This fight is between #3 and #5.' When feasible, it should match the #1 fighter in a given weight class against the top-ranked available challenger. 'WHO'S #1' works for college football and college basketball. It works for tennis and golf. It can work for boxing."

There's enormous waste in the HBO Sports budget today. As a first step, HBO has to bring the license fees that it pays for fights in line with an intelligent economic model and address unnecessary overhead costs. On a lesser scale, there are expense account abuses in the sports depart-ment that are a running industry joke.

HBO should consider licensing the HBO Sports logo for T-shirts, jackets, caps, and other apparel that would be available for sale to the public. The income from this venture would be relatively small. But every piece of clothing that a person wears would turn that person into a walking billboard for HBO Sports.

Earlier this year, HBO announced that it was bringing Roy Jones back as an expert analyst on *Boxing After Dark*. Overtures should also be made to George Foreman and Sugar Ray Leonard, who are viewer-friendly links to the glory days of HBO Sports. They would be enormously effective on pre-fight panels or participating in some other capacity in conjunction with major pay-per-view shows.

If HBO wants another compelling personality on the air, it should find a way to expose boxing fans to Chris Arreola outside the ring.

One can make the case that Arreola is the equivalent of a Hispanic John Madden. He has a larger-than-life personality. One is compelled to look when his face is on-camera. Instead of marketing Chris as a great fighter (which he isn't), HBO should market him as a great personality.

Don't give subscribers a slickly packaged segment about Arreola. Hand him a microphone and let him rip. How can you not love a guy who acknowledges the need for improved defense with the observation, ""I'm ugly, and I don't want to get any more uglier."

Some other "Arreolaisms": "I'm not big-headed. I'm one of the guys, a regular Joe Schmo. But it makes me angry when people think I'm dumb, when they talk down to me, when they think I'm a meathead because I'm a fighter . . . The best thing about being a fighter is fighting. It's two guys in the ring who hardly know each other and they beat the crap out of each other. And when it's over, they shake hands and hug each other. Go figure . . . You're so caught up in the moment that you don't feel the punches. The crowd oohs and aahs, and I want to get my oohs and aahs in."

And let's not forget Arreola in the ring after his loss to Tomasz Adamek on HBO: "He beat my ass. I look like fucking Shrek right now."

And last; as I wrote two years ago, "Instead of pretending that nothing has changed, HBO should relaunch its boxing program. It should tell the boxing community, the boxing media, and boxing fans (most notably, its subscribers) that this isn't just a paint job or new graphics over the same old product. It should declare loud and clear, 'We've listened to you and, like a good fighter, we've made adjustments.'"

One of the issues that the leadership of HBO and HBO Sports will face in the months ahead is how to approach the possibility of the proposed mega-fight between Manny Pacquiao and Floyd Mayweather Jr.

If Mayweather wants it, the fight will happen. The question then will be, "Does it go to HBO or another network?"

HBO should think big and be creative from a business point of view. It shouldn't offer TBS or TNT as a promotional partner for Pacquiao-Mayweather. It should offer TBS and TNT as promotional partners (plural). Perhaps, during the pre-fight promotional build-up, TBS could be the network of Manny Pacquiao; TNT could feature Mayweather; and HBO could give equal time to both fighters.

Would TBS and TNT do it? I assume that Bill Nelson and Richard Plepler will explore some permutation of the idea with David Levy (president of Turner Sports).

Most likely, involving Turner Sports and other components of the Time Warner empire (such as *Sports Illustrated*) in the marketing of Pacquiao-Mayweather will also require the intervention of Time Warner CEO Jeff Bewkes. But let's not forget; Bewkes was once the CEO of HBO.

That said; HBO should remember that one fight won't save boxing, and one fight won't save boxing at HBO Sports. Bob Arum promoted 39 of Oscar De La Hoya's first 42 pro fights and 35 of Mayweather's first 37. But when Oscar and Floyd met in the ring in the largest-grossing fight of all time, Arum was on the sidelines.

"Are we saddened because we're not promoting it?," Arum said at the time. "Sure; we'd have loved to promote the fight, but you can't have everything."

Since then, Arum has rebounded quite nicely. So will boxing at HBO.

The problems that HBO Sports faces won't be resolved overnight. They've been a long time in the making, and finding solutions will take time. It will take a while for HBO Sports to regain the trust of the boxing community and the trust of its own subscribers.

Also, HBO is no longer the only game in town. Showtime and CBS can compete with HBO on a level playing field for any fight they want. If events unfold a certain way, more networks will enter the fray as big-fight alternatives to HBO. That means HBO can no longer prevail based on money muscle alone. It will have to think more creatively in the future.

When there's competition, the consumer wins. It's likely that this competition will result in HBO Sports raising its performance to a higher level.

As noted in Part One of this article, this is a crucial time. Every month that goes by is a month that HBO risks falling further behind in the race for the future. There's a need to chart that future sooner rather than later. And there's a growing feeling, both within HBO and throughout the boxing community, that it's time for a change in leadership at HBO Sports.

Meanwhile, HBO should understand that boxing needs what Bob Arum is doing now. Arum's move to Showtime and CBS is sparking new corporate interest in the sweet science. It's a first step toward bringing boxing back into the mainstream. If the leadership at HBO Sports acts with foresight and imagination, it can ride the coattails of Pacquiao-Mosley and use recent events to their advantage.

HBO Sports has the HBO brand, which despite its recent devaluation, is still the best brand in boxing.

Pacquiao-Mosley held out the possibility of marking a sea change in the business of boxing.

Pacquiao-Mosley: The Stakes Involved

On June 22, 1979, Larry Holmes successfully defended the heavyweight championship of the world by knocking out Mike Weaver in the twelfth round at Madison Square Garden. Two days later, an article by Pulitzer Prize–winning sports columnist Red Smith appeared in the *New York Times*.

The article was entitled "The One That Got Away," and recounted how a fledging premium-cable network called Home Box Office had outwitted "the big brains of television's major networks" to snare Holmes-Weaver. Smith began his appraisal of the situation with the words, "It was Home Box Office's finest hour."

HBO Sports had come of age.

Thirty-two years later, the May 7, 2011, fight between Manny Pacquiao and Shane Mosley is "The One That Got Away." Pacquiao-Mosley will be televised by Showtime PPV, not HBO. Depending on how events unfold, boxing might be on the verge of another significant shift in power.

Pacquiao-Mosley is boxing's first mega-event of 2011. If Pacquiao wins, one expects that he will go on to more super-fights. If Mosley wins, a rematch would be in order.

But the stakes involved with Pacquiao-Mosley go far beyond who wins or loses this one fight. The success or failure from a business point of view of the joint effort between Top Rank, Showtime, and CBS will have a significant impact on the future of boxing.

Top Rank CEO Bob Arum has been in boxing since 1966. Over the past forty-five years, he has promoted dozens of superstars and more than five hundred world title fights.

In recent years (in part, because of the energy that Top Rank president Todd DuBoef has brought to the company), Arum seems to have been reborn. If anything, he has become even more outspoken and independent than he was before. His attitude is, "I'm old enough and have enough money to say and do what I want."

"I've had some great experiences in boxing," Arum notes. "I was with Muhammad Ali when he was young; Marvin Hagler, Roberto Duran, Ray Leonard, George Foreman, you name them. And what I'm doing with Manny is the most fun I've ever had."

What Arum is doing with Pacquiao now is keyed to "the CBS factor." As I wrote earlier this year, "The move to Showtime [from HBO] isn't simply about choosing one pay-per-view platform over another. It's about getting the broadest possible exposure for Pacquiao, Pacquiao-Mosley, and boxing. Manny is Top Rank's vehicle for breaking down some of the barriers that have separated boxing from large segments of the American public for the past thirty years. The target that Arum is pursuing here is the general sports fan and the public at large."

In choosing Mosley as Pacquiao's next inquisitor, Arum declared, "I don't worry about who the bloggers think is the best opponent. I really don't care what the writers say or even what the hardcore boxing followers say. We need to pick the opponent who is the most familiar to the casual sports fan, to the casual boxing fan, who cannot name all the fighters."

Later, Arum built on that theme, saying, "Shane Mosley will galvanize the black community in a way that nobody else except Floyd Mayweather could have done. Manny already appeals to Asian, Hispanic, and white boxing fans. With CBS and Showtime working together, we'll reach casual sports fans and the public at large. This fight has the potential to do numbers that are humongous. I have no idea what those numbers will be, but I have a very strong feeling that things will be very different for boxing when this fight is over."

Top Rank has been hands-on with regard to the marketing of Pacquiao-Mosley; more so than it was with Pacquiao's earlier fights on HBO-PPV. And Showtime is a good partner.

The network doesn't always get things right. The number of dates it has given over the years to promoter Gary Shaw mystifies many in boxing. And its super-middleweight championship tournament has moved back and forth between compelling programming and a drop-out festival. But the "Super-Six" tournament is indicative of Showtime's willingness to be creative and try new things.

Speaking of Pacquiao-Mosley, Ken Hershman (executive vice president and general manager of Showtime Sports) says, "It's now in our court. We have to execute, and we have to execute at a very high level. This is a process. We can get boxing exposed to more people, whether it's through actual fights on network television or through all the support CBS is lending us on this promotion. It's going to be great for the sport and great for Showtime."

If Pacquiao-Mosley is successful, Showtime and CBS can fine tune their business model afterward. Meanwhile, the CBS promotional platform is the potential needle-changer in all of this.

Promotional spots supporting Pacquiao-Mosley ran on CBS throughout the NCAA Men's Championship Basketball Tournament. That began the process of piercing the barrier between boxing and other sports that has risen in recent years.

On Saturday, April 2nd, the first Pacquiao-Mosley *Fight Camp 360* episode aired on CBS. With one exception, all of the commercial spots were promos for the pay-per-view telecast and other CBS programming. The exception, ironically, was an ad for a Time-Life CD collection (HBO is a subsidiary of Time-Warner). The third episode of Pacquiao-Mosley *Fight Camp 360* aired on CBS four weeks later.

As fight night approaches, CBS viewers can expect to see fighters on network talk shows and programming related to Pacquiao-Mosley live from Las Vegas during fight week.

The impact that all of this has on the future of boxing will be determined in significant measure by the number of Pacquiao-Mosley pay-per-buys.

Pacquiao's last five fights were on HBO-PPV and generated roughly 5,100,000 buys. That breaks down by opponent as follows: Oscar De La Hoya (1,250,000), Ricky Hatton (800,000), Miguel Cotto (1,200,000), Joshua Clottey (700,000), and Antonio Margarito 1,150,000.

The assumption is that, had Pacquiao-Mosley been on HBO-PPV, it would have generated in the neighborhood of 1,100,000 buys.

If buys on May 7th fall below 1,000,000, it will disappoint everyone involved with the promotion. If they exceed 1,250,000 (Pacquiao-De La Hoya), it would be a coup for those involved. If they top 1,400,000 (the total for Mayweather-Mosley), the landscape of boxing will change.

The business of boxing is like a battle royal with everyone trying to throw everyone else out of the ring. Within that milieu, HBO has been the biggest of the boys for decades. But HBO got complacent.

A strong pay-per-view showing for Pacquiao-Mosley would destroy the notion that there's a magic formula to marketing a pay-per-view fight that only HBO knows. It would encourage other terrestrial and basic cable networks (such as ESPN) to find partners for pay-per-view marketing. That would further undercut HBO's dominance in the field.

Meanwhile, Pacquiao-Mosley is introducing a whole new audience to Showtime Boxing and *Fight Camp 360*. If things break right for the network, it will elevate Showtime's entire sports franchise and lead to *360* shows for other events in the same way that *24/7* has expanded on HBO.

Just as significantly, if Pacquiao-Mosley is covered extensively by major media and CBS gets good ratings for fight-related programming, it would increase the chance of live boxing returning to network television.

The last time that live boxing aired on a major broadcast television network in the United States was on NBC at the close of *The Contender* in 2005. CBS hasn't televised a fight since 1997.

Broadcast television and basic cable networks aren't fueled by pay-per-view buys. They're fueled by the willingness of corporate America to put dollars behind programming in the form of advertising. That willingness comes from ratings (which translate into how many viewers see an ad) and a desire to be affiliated with the programming (i.e., a particular fighter, a specific fight, or boxing in general).

"You cannot have a major sport limited to a universe of thirty million homes [the number of HBO subscribers]," Bob Arum said recently. "It can't be done. Something has to change. I would want nothing more than for my legacy to be that I brought boxing back to network television."

Pacquiao-Mosley might be the wedge that opens the door.

Next point. And this is a big one.

Top Rank recently announced that Pacquiao-Mosley will be available online (i.e., on the Internet) in the United States for $54.95.

Under the prevailing business model for pay-per-view fights (championed by HBO), the promotion receives less than 50 percent of all pay-per-view revenue. The rest goes to cable-system operators (e.g., Time Warner Cable), In Demand (which clears channels and is owned in part by Time Warner), and a few other corporate entities. That's one reason why, over the years, HBO's license agreements for fights have precluded the Internet transmission of these fights. The network bargains for Internet rights and then buries them. Remember; HBO is a subsidiary of Time Warner.

The traditional economic model will still be in use for people who watch Pacquiao-Mosley on television.

However, Top Rank will be marketing the fight on college campuses (where students might not have access to pay-per-view on cable but certainly have computers); to travelers (who are stuck in hotel rooms with their computers and nothing to do for the night); and others. A three-camera shoot will allow Internet viewers to choose their own viewing experience as the fight unfolds.

Top Rank won't have to pay cable system operators or hire an entity to clear channels where Internet revenue from Pacquiao-Mosley is concerned. On Internet buys, after minor deductions, the promotion will keep the entire $54.95.

The Internet pay-per-view model will make pay-per-view more attractive to promoters in the future. That could be a minus for fight fans. But the genie is squeezing out of the bottle. Once it's out, it won't go back in. Look for corporate entities that are involved with boxing to build up their websites as a platform for future pay-per-view telecasts (as ESPN has been doing). For the moment, HBO is on the outside, looking in.

Meanwhile, recent events have made everyone in the sweet science who has a brain think about how to grow the sport. If the alliance between Top Rank, Showtime, and CBS works for Pacquiao-Mosley, what will it mean for other fighters, other fights, and the brand of boxing?

Pacquiao has aroused people's interest. But there's only one Manny Pacquiao. Can this confluence of events be replicated for fighters other than Manny?

Bart Barry frames the issue as follows: "A rising tide lifts all boats. But is Pacquiao-Mosley a rising tide or merely a rising boat?"

The purest sport in the world might also be the most tarnished.

Boxing: Pure vs. Phony

At its core, boxing is the purest of all sports. Two combatants, half-naked, square off in a one-on-one competition that tests their skill, courage, and resolve. Sadly, over the years, the essence of boxing has been undermined by greedy, incompetent, corrupt officials. Much of what one needs to know in order to understand why boxing is now a niche sport in the United States was on display on Saturday, June 25, 2011.

The cornerstones of any successful professional sport are (1) recognized champions and (2) public confidence that the competition will be fairly conducted.

Boxing today meets neither of these criteria. The sport is plagued by phony belts. The four world sanctioning organizations exist in large part to support the lifestyles of their controlling parties. The ranking of fighters, the sanctioning of title bouts (and sometimes even their scoring) are based in significant measure on the sanctioning fees that particular fighters generate.

It's significant that the Word Boxing Council refers to its championship strap as "the green belt." Green is the color of money. Anyone can go online and buy an "authentic WBC championship belt" from a WBC merchandise site for $3,867.

Would Wimbledon put "authentic" championship trophies on sale? Would the Olympics sell "authentic" gold medals to the public? No organization that oversees a sport and respects its participants should sell its symbols of athletic supremacy to the public. Championship belts should be won in the ring, not bought.

By any credible accounting, Sergio Martinez is the middleweight champion of the world. He won the title by decisioning Kelly Pavlik and successfully defended it with dramatic knockout victories over Paul Williams and Sergiy Dzinziruk.

But the WBC middleweight "champion" is Julio Cesar Chavez Jr. His road to the title was paved by WBC president-for-life Jose Sulaiman (who oversaw the process by which Martinez was stripped of his title).

Dmitry Pirog is the World Boxing Organization middleweight "champion." That wasn't expected to happen. Like the WBC, the WBO stripped Martinez of his belt to make way for a favored fighter (in this case, Danny Jacobs). But Jacobs couldn't hold up his end of the bargain and lost to Pirog.

Daniel Geale of Australia pays middleweight "championship-fight" sanctioning fees to the International Boxing Federation.

The World Boxing Association has three middleweight "champions." There's "super champion" Felix Sturm, "world champion" Gennady Golovkin, and "interim champion" Hassan N'Dam N'Jikam.

Except for Martinez, all of the above are phony champions. Just how phony was evident on June 25th.

Sturm fought Matthew Macklin in the "champion's" hometown of Cologne, Germany. The bout was televised in the United States live on Epix. It was understood going in that, if there was an outrageous decision, it would be in Sturm's favor. Felix might be a better boxer than Matthew. But on Saturday, Macklin fought a better fight. He clearly won eight of the twelve rounds. Two more were close.

I scored the fight 117–111 for Macklin. Judge Levi Martinez scored it 115–113 for Matthew, which was a bit of a stretch in Sturm's favor.

Then came the obscenity. Judges Roberto Ramirez and Jose Ignacio Martinez each scored the bout for Sturm by a 116–112 margin.

The decision was unfair to Macklin, who has made every sacrifice necessary to get to the point in his career where he was positioned to win a belt. The only consolation he has is that, had he won, he wouldn't have been a real world champion. That distinction, insofar as the middleweight division is concerned, still belongs to Sergio Martinez.

Meanwhile, Sturm is no longer a phony champion. He has been downgraded to the status of a phony phony champion. The outrageous scoring wasn't his fault; he didn't judge the fight. But he didn't win it either.

Look for Roberto Ramirez and Jose Ignacio Martinez to get more lucrative assignments from the WBA in recognition of their judging talents.

The tarnishing of the sweet science continued on Saturday night with a three-fight offering on HBO Boxing After Dark from St. Charles, Missouri (a suburb of St. Louis).

The HBO telecast began with forty-year-old journeyman Ray Austin vs. Bermane Stiverne for the WBC's phony "silver heavyweight championship." To put matters in perspective; Stiverne has been knocked out by Demetrice King, which is like losing a beauty contest to Roseanne Barr. Then, to prove that the loss to King was no fluke, Bermane fought to a draw against Charles Davis (another forty-year-old heavyweight, who has won 19 of 44 fights; scored a total of four knockouts in his career; and emerged victorious (drumroll, please) in none of his last six fights.

Austin-Stiverne was beyond horrible. Austin came into the fight out of shape, lumbered around the ring like his feet hurt, and exposed Stiverne as a club-level fighter. The primary drama attached to the bout was whether or not Ray's trunks (which kept sliding beneath his protective cup) would fall off. Leading on points, he was knocked out in the tenth round.

The WBC collected a sanctioning fee for Austin-Stiverne. Bermane is now the mandatory challenger for its phony heavyweight championship belt.

Next on the HBO telecast, Tavoris Cloud predictably knocked out Yusef Mack.

Then came Devon Alexander vs. Lucas Matthysse. Matthysse landed more punches than Alexander. Matthysse landed harder punches than Alexander. He also scored a knockdown in round four.

Alexander-Matthysse was not a championship fight. The judges were appointed by the Missouri State Athletic Commission. Did I mention that Alexander is from St. Louis?

Like Sturm, Alexander was awarded a gift decision. It wasn't as bad as the decision in Sturm-Macklin, but it was pretty bad.

Brett Miller scored the bout 96–93 for Matthysse. But he was overruled by Carlos Colon (96–93) and Denny Nelson (95–94), both of whom favored the house fighter. Fight fans might remember that Denny Nelson cast a 116–112 vote in favor of Alexander in his dubious win last year over Andriy Kotelnik.

In most professional sports, bad calls by officials are assumed to be good-faith errors in judgment. In boxing, particularly when it comes to the judging of fights, there's ample evidence to support the view that bad calls are often the result of something worse.

I can't reach into the hearts and minds of the judges who scored Sturm-Macklin and Alexander-Matthysse. I will say that their scoring speaks for itself.

Meanwhile, phony champions and mediocre officiating continue to undermine boxing.

Each year, a number of good books augment boxing's literary tradition.

Literary Notes

Gene Tunney had four children. One of them, Jay Tunney, has written an intriguing book.

The Prizefighter and the Playwright details the relationship between the former heavyweight champion and the Nobel Prize–winning playwright George Bernard Shaw. It would be more accurately titled *The Prizefighter, the Heiress, and the Playwright,* since Tunney's courtship of and marriage to Polly Lauder is given equal play.

Tunney was born in 1897 and turned pro at age eighteen. The only loss in his seventy-seven-bout career came at the hands of Harry Greb. Thereafter, he defeated Greb twice and emerged victorious over Jack Dempsey in two of the most-storied heavyweight championship fights of all time. He retired from ring in 1928 and stayed retired; the first man to achieve that dual distinction.

"What is boxing?" Tunney once asked before answering his own question: "The ability to coordinate mind and muscle at a critical moment; that is all." But in a more reflective vein, he added, "The prize ring is a terrifying place. You're on a platform glaring with bright light. All around, you see the dim expanse of the crowd. Faces nearby are clearly lighted by the glare. You see expressions of frantic excitement, emotions produced by sympathetic reaction, fear, the lust for battle, rage, gloating, savagery, mouths open and yelling. You hear the roar. It's the howl of the mob for blood."

Tunney never graduated from high school. But he read prolifically to pass the boredom of training camp and as a road to self-improvement. His tastes leaned toward the classical. That became fodder for the sporting press prior to his 1926 challenge of Dempsey.

A reporter named Brian Bell was assigned by the Associated Press to interview Tunney at his training camp in Speculator, New York. Instead of writing the typical pre-fight piece, he crafted an in-depth feature story about a fighter who read classical works.

Bell's article ran in newspapers across the country. But rather than lift opinions of the challenger, it subjected him to derision.

Paul Gallico of the *New York Daily News* opined, "I think Tunney has hurt his own game with his cultural nonsense. It is a fine thing that he has educated himself to the point where he no longer says 'dese' and 'dem' and 'dose' and where he can tell one book from another and indicate some familiarity with their contents. But the man who steps into the ring with Dempsey with nothing but his hands as weapons needs to be a fighter and nothing but. He will have to have a natural viciousness and nastiness well up in him that will transcend rules and reason, that will make him want to commit murder with his two hands. I don't think that Master Tunney, who likes first editions and works of art, has it in him."

Writers were sent to quiz Tunney on his knowledge of the classics in the hope of tripping him up.

A Chicago policeman named Mike Trant, who hung out with Dempsey, famously told the champion, "The fight's in the bag, Jack. The [expletive lost in the haze of history] is up there reading a book."

Jay Tunney writes, "Once he realized he was being made a laughing-stock, Gene agonized over it, worrying that he was too sensitive, yet unable to put it behind him. In telling the truth, in trying to be himself, he had been held up to ridicule."

Later, the fighter himself noted, "It never occurred to me that a habit of reading could be seen as a stunt or a joke. Wasn't reading something we wanted to champion?"

But to a degree, Tunney poured fuel on the fire. He maintained that he spent the day after winning the title from Dempsey studying *Meditations* by the Roman Emperor Marcus Aurelius. And according to his son, the fighter claimed he was late leaving the rented house that he lived in prior to the second Dempsey bout because he was re-reading the last two chapters of *Of Human Bondage* by Somerset Maugham.

"Sorry," Gene reportedly said. "I lost track of time. Had to finish Maugham, you know; the last few pages. It's his best."

Whatever he did or didn't read, Tunney faced his greatest ring challenge later that night. He was knocked down in the seventh round and climbed off the canvas to prevail in boxing's historic "long count" fight.

"A knockdown is a fighter's ultimate crisis," Jay Tunney writes; "the instant in battle when he has to prove he's a general in the ring. Whether a boxer can physically and mentally handle those seconds on the canvas determines not only who wins the fight but often marks the rest of his career."

Tunney began actively courting Polly Lauder after beating Dempsey for the second time. He was thirty years old, one of seven children born into a poor Irish-Catholic family in New York. She was ten years younger and had grown up in Greenwich, Connecticut, surrounded by maids, butlers, cooks, gardeners, chauffeurs, and governesses.

Lauder was a society girl, an heiress. Percy Rockefeller lived on the estate next door. Tunney's mother was of a class that would have been hired to scrub the floors in the Lauder home. When Mary Tunney first saw the mansion that Polly lived in, she told her son that she was glad she didn't have to clean it.

Tunney's engagement to Polly Lauder was announced on August 8, 1928, two weeks after his last fight and one week after he officially retired from boxing. They were married in Rome on October 3rd of that year.

"His old friends thought he was a snob for marrying rich and moving uptown with the Protestant Yankees," Jay Tunney notes. "Some of the uptown crowd felt he should go back to the docks. He was near the golden circle of America's power establishment, but also outside of it; a man between two worlds and part of neither one."

Be that as it may; the marriage lasted until Tunney's death in 1978 and appears to have been a happy one. Polly lived till the remarkable age of one hundred.

After Tunney retired from boxing, he lived what his son calls "a lifetime of grappling with balancing his past ring celebrity against his personal interests of reading, music, the arts, and, later, business. Boxing was his key to meeting the people he wanted to meet."

George Bernard Shaw was interested in boxing and had sparred a bit as a young man. "There is no sport," he wrote, "which brings out the difference in character more dramatically than boxing." Indeed, Shaw's first published novel—*Cashel Byron's Profession* (published in 1886)—centered on a boxer who wins a championship and courts a young aristocratic woman.

Furthering the coincidental parallels between Cashel Byron and Tunney, Shaw had written in that book, "The prizefighter is no more what the spectators imagine him to be than the lady with the wand and the star in the pantomime is really a fairy queen."

Tunney had approached Shaw through the playwright's agent in October 1926 to inquire about playing the lead in a proposed stage version of *Cashel Byron's Profession*. Shaw declined to pursue the project. They met for the first time in December 1928 at a luncheon hosted by Shaw at his London home. A vacation in Brioni (a cluster of Islands in the Adriatic Sea) the following year solidified their friendship, although the vacation was tinged with unwanted drama. An infected abscess on Polly's appendix turned gangrenous and brought her to the edge of death.

The former champion and the playwright enjoyed their relationship. For Tunney, it also validated his self-image and intellectual view of himself.

"I think of Shaw as the most considerate person I have ever known," he said years later. "He was helpful, directing me on questions of literature, music, art, thought. He was patient with me. No period of my life was more valuable than the long walks we took together on Brioni. It was like a matriculation in a cosmic school. He was the teacher; I was the pupil."

Shaw, for his part, fondly recalled a film of the second Tunney-Dempsey fight that he had watched and noted. "I never saw anything so wonderful as Tunney's dance round the ring when he got up with Dempsey rushing after him and slogging wildly until Gene suddenly stopped and countered with a biff that made poor Jack believe he was going to die."

Yet Shaw's fondness for Tunney stopped short of uncritical admiration. In 1932, the former champion authored his autobiography (*A Man Must Fight*) and proudly presented a copy to his intellectual mentor. Shaw read the book and responded with a letter that read in part, "Just as one prayer meeting is very like another, one fight is very like another. At a certain point, I wanted to skip to Dempsey."

Jay Tunney writes nicely and he understands boxing (which he calls "the most punishing and individual of all sporting contests"). He's on solid ground when he highlights the courage that the public demands of fighters and "the conditioned grace of an athlete." In his hands, the Tunney-Lauder courtship and marriage are lovingly re-created. And the book offers an interesting portrait of George Bernard Shaw, although too much of the Tunney-Shaw material is tedious social-diary trivia.

The book draws heavily on interviews, letters, photographs, and other documentation within the Tunney family; material that has been unavailable to other writers. That's a strength, but it also raises questions of credibility.

The Prizefighter and the Playwright is a son's homage to his parents. It gives the impression that Gene and Polly Tunney lived a fairy-tale life.

As previously noted, the Tunneys had four children (the eldest of whom served as a United States Senator from 1965 to 1977). There is no mention in the book of their daughter, Joan Tunney Wilkinson, who was committed to a facility for the criminally insane after murdering her husband in 1970. Depending on which contemporaneous newspaper account one reads, the victim's head was shattered by a club or severed by a meat cleaver.

It would appear as though some demons lurked in the happy Tunney home.

That said; it's fitting to close on a positive note.

After Tunney's death, Jim Murray wrote, "He was the best advertisement his sport ever had. He could outbox, outthink, outspeed any fighter of his day. "

And summing up, Jay Tunney says of his father, "He was fighting for a life beyond the ring. He was fighting to be a respectable gentleman. He had grown up believing in his imagination and aspiring to be someone more than what was expected for him."

★　★　★

Soulville by Mike Spector is the latest in a long line of novels to explore the world of boxing. The book is set in the 1970s, when Bennie Briscoe, Willie Monroe, Cyclone Hart, Kitten Hayward, and Bobby "Boogaloo" Watts were carving their names into boxing lore. Spector calls it "the golden age of Philadelphia middleweights."

Nick Ceratto (Spector's narrator) is a young photographer for the *Philadelphia Journal*. A chance assignment takes him to Champs Gym. The street maps say that the gym in located in North Philly. The regulars say that it's in Soulville.

"Soulville's not a neighborhood," Spector writes. "At least not the kind of neighborhood you know. Soulville is wherever a Philly fighter steps in the ring at the gym on an ordinary afternoon and fights like a world title is on the line, whenever you and a pretty girl slow dance to

Smokey Robinson. It's the guys on the corner, standing around a fire on a cold night, sharing a bottle of Thunderbird. Soulville's an attitude. It's a state of mind."

Boxing, like Soulville, is a world where, in Spector's words, the extremes of life come together, break apart, and re-connect in a continuous pattern of survival. A place where hopes and dreams collide regularly with nightmares and disappointment.

Spector re-creates that world well. His characters are nicely drawn with good back stories. The atmosphere, camaraderie, and work ethic of a boxing gym are realistically portrayed. The fight scenes are terrific.

A Greek chorus of characters offers insights throughout the book:

★ "Boxing evens things out. Once you're in that ring, it's just you and the other guy. Don't matter what his color or religion is. Ain't no bullshit. It either is or it ain't. Most of life ain't that simple."

★ "The pros is a whole lot different than the amateurs. When you're in that ring and some animal is right on top of you, slobberin' and blowin' snot and throwin' elbows, you're gonna wonder what the hell you're doin' there. The basics are gonna be the last thing you'll be thinkin' about. But the basics are the only thing that you got; the only thing that can save you."

★ "The crowd? It's like they ain't even there. You hear them when you first in the ring, but it's kinda like the ocean in Atlantic City. When you first step out on the boardwalk, you hear them waves hittin' the shore. But after a while, you stop hearin' them. You know they there; you just don't hear them no more."

★ "Some say a man's life ain't nothing more than a 'cumulation of all his days, from the time he born to the time he die. I say that ain't how it is. A man's life, most time, come down to a moment—one single moment—a moment where everything come together and give him a chance to find out exactly who he is. What he do in that moment define him for the rest of his life."

Where boxing is concerned, Spector gets it. *Soulville* has both soul and heart.

★　★　★

There's a growing belief among those who seriously study boxing that Sugar Ray Leonard is the best fighter of the past fifty years. Leonard really would fight anyone. His inquisitors were men like Marvin Hagler, Roberto Duran, Wilfred Benitez, and Thomas Hearns. Take away the four ill-considered fights at the end of his career, and his ring record would have been 35-and-1 with 25 knockouts. As it was, he lost three times and still "agonizes" over each defeat.

Leonard is in the news these days because of his recently published autobiography, *The Big Fight,* authored with Michael Arkush. The book's headline-grabbing revelation is Ray's account of being sexually abused in the early-1970s by an unnamed "prominent Olympic boxing coach."

Two themes run throughout *The Big Fight.* The first centers on Leonard's illustrious ring exploits. The second details a life spiraling out of control in a haze of fame, alcohol, and drugs.

Let's start with the boxing.

One of the notable things about Leonard's ring career is that he accomplished so much so young. At age twenty, he won a gold medal and was the darling of the 1976 United States Olympic boxing team in Montreal. He turned pro and, at age twenty-three, defeated Wilfredo Benitez to claim the WBC welterweight crown.

"I loved to hit other men," Leonard writes in *The Big Fight.* "I loved to see them crumble. I was not one to hold back when my opponent was in trouble, no matter what chance there was of inflicting permanent damage. Fights can turn in a matter of seconds. The next thing you know, you're the one getting beaten up and the guy doing it will not show you any mercy."

The counterpoint to that thought is a scene in which Leonard recounts visiting Benitez in an assisted living facility in Puerto Rico two decades after their ring encounter. "I was devastated," Ray writes of the hellish dementia that confronted him. He then describes his former foe: "His face and stomach bloated, his eyes staring blankly into space, his mind essentially gone."

After dethroning Benitez, Leonard knocked out Dave Green. Then, still only twenty-four, he returned to Montreal for the first of two back-to-back bouts against Roberto Duran.

Duran had won 71 of 72 previous fights. He was a master craftsman inside the ring and a master of psychology outside it. In the months leading up to his battle against Leonard, he got inside Ray's head.

"I fought Duran toe-to-toe instead of exploiting my superior boxing skills," Leonard admits. "Why was I so stupid? Because I wanted to hurt Duran the way he hurt me with his constant insults. My desire was there. Unfortunately, my power was not. Roberto Duran, at least on that night, was the better man. He cut off the ring and used his expertise to outmuscle and outwit me. His heart was every bit as impressive as his hands. When the bell [ending the fight] rang, I walked toward him to touch gloves. He would have no part of it. Instead, he shouted at me in one final act of defiance, 'Fuck you! I show you.'"

The fight had been close. Duran won a 146–144, 145–144, 144–144 majority decision.

"The first few days after losing to Duran were perhaps the worst days of my life," Leonard writes. "I felt a deep sense of loss, as if a part of me had been taken away for good. I was certain I would defeat every opponent until there was none left and then retire on top like Marciano, invincible forever. I was not invincible. Equally disappointing was finding out that, contrary to the image I constantly tried to convey, I was not a model of composure who saved his best for the sport's grandest stages."

Five months later, Leonard and Duran fought again. "I was desperate for a real victory; not a moral one," Ray recalls. Employing speed and guile, he won four of the first seven rounds on each of the judges' scorecards. In round eight, a frustrated Duran said "no mas."

The victory was bittersweet.

"From that moment on," Leonard recounts, "the evening ceased to be about me and regaining my title. I took on a supporting role in a more complicated drama in which an icon to an entire continent became, in one sudden unfortunate act, an object of derision for the rest of his life. I was given more credit for losing courageously in Montreal than for winning cleverly in New Orleans."

By the time Leonard beat Duran, the balance of power in sports journalism had irrevocably shifted from the printed word to television. That was a plus for Ray in that he was remarkably telegenic. The downside, he says, was that many boxing writers resented the fact that the launching pad for his success had been television rather than their reporting. They were slow to give him full credit for his accomplishments.

"A number of veteran boxing writers," he says, "still saw me as a fighter created by television who had yet to defeat a star opponent. In their view, Benitez was not in that class. Duran was, but they argued that the outcome in New Orleans was more about him surrendering that my causing him to surrender."

That changed on September 16, 1981, at Caesars Palace in Las Vegas, when Leonard fought back from the brink of defeat to knock out Thomas Hearns in the fourteenth round. Their encounter is widely regarded as one of the greatest fights of all time.

"The fight with Tommy was my greatest achievement in the ring," Ray writes. "Thirty years later, it remains my defining moment as a fighter."

When Leonard vanquished Hearns, he was twenty-five years old. "I was at the peak of my abilities," he says. "And so was Tommy. I was nowhere near my best ever again."

That assessment is correct.

The rest of Leonard's ring career consisted of eight fights contested over the course of sixteen years. All told, he retired from boxing five times, coming back on four occasions. The one glorious moment during that stretch was a split-decision victory over Marvin Hagler on April 6, 1987.

Hagler had twelve successful middleweight championship defenses to his credit and hadn't lost in eleven years. When he and Leonard met in the ring, Ray, despite being thirty years old, had fought only once in the preceding five years.

Leonard and Arkush nicely reconstruct the action in Ray's biggest fights. They also offer an inside look at the endless infighting between Dave Jacobs, Janks Morton, Pepe Correa, and Angelo Dundee.

"Angelo was my official trainer," Leonard writes. "But he didn't train me the way people thought. I'd been trained already by Pepe Correa, Dave Jacobs, and Janks Morton. I used to laugh at stories in the paper that gave the credit to Angelo for swooping in a week or two before every fight with the magical formula to get me ready. No disrespect to him; but if I did not have a strategy by that point, I wasn't going to find one in a few days. His true value was in the corner during the battle and as a matchmaker. In those roles, there was no one else who could have served me better."

Dundee was also at odds from time to time with Mike Trainer (Leonard's attorney). According to Ray, the lawyer initially thought that

Angelo would fulfill many of the traditional managerial duties in addition to his trainer's role for a 15 percent fee. But Dundee, Ray says, didn't live up to his end of the bargain. Thus, his contract was rewritten to cap the 15 percent fee at $75,000 for non-title fights and $150,000 for championship outings.

"The new arrangement would wind up costing Angelo millions," Leonard notes. "In the Hearns fight, for instance, he would have received $1,800,000 of my $12,000,000 take instead of $150,000."

Then Ray acknowledges that residual hard feelings exist, saying, "Angelo complained in his book several years ago that he wished I had stood up for him in the contract dispute with Mike. With all due respect, he is totally off base. Working for me from my debut in 1977 through the Hagler fight ten years later afforded Angelo the chance to stay in the spotlight long after his first meal ticket [Muhammad Ali] retired and make a ton of money. The truth is, he has no one to blame but himself. He failed to do what he was hired to do."

"In this corrupt business," Leonard adds, "I had to pick one person to trust. That was Mike Trainer. He never let me down."

Leonard's ring accomplishments are a matter of record. Over the years, much of his personal life has been shrouded in secrecy and rumor. That leads to the second theme in *The Big Fight;* Ray's tumultuous personal life.

Leonard grew up in a violent home. His parent drank and often quarreled about Cicero Leonard's profligate womanizing. Once, when Ray was six or seven years old, Gerta Leonard stuck a knife in her husband's back. "Forty years later," Leonard writes, "I still can't cope with any yelling and screaming, though I was unable to avoid it during my own doomed marriage."

Ray met Juanita Wilkinson when he was sixteen. It took a while for them to start dating. Then—"In no time, Juanita and I were having sex on a regular basis. We never used a rubber or any other method of birth control. We did it everywhere. In the car. In my house. In the woods lying down on my jacket. Everywhere. The inevitable came next. Juanita was pregnant."

On November 22, 1973, Ray Jr was born.

Over the next six years, Leonard admits, "I was neither a boyfriend to Juanita nor a father to Ray Jr. I made what I would describe as cameo appearances, showing up in their lives for brief stretches before disappearing again for days or weeks at a time. Either I hung out in the gym in pursuit of my next victory or I hung out with friends in pursuit of my next piece of ass. No matter what financial responsibilities I assumed for Juanita and little Ray, I saw myself as a free man in every sense of the word. After the three of us started to live together in the summer of 1977, I rented a separate apartment that I kept secret from Juanita. Little Ray didn't complain, though no amount of bribery could make up for my failings as a father. The gift he wanted most, my time, was the one gift I didn't give him. I rarely attended any of his sporting events. If he needed something, I handed a few bucks to my personal assistant to pick it up."

Years later, in 1984, a second son, Jarrel, was born. Meanwhile, Ray and Juanita were married on January 19, 1980 (her twenty-third birthday).

"We should never have been married," Leonard says. "That was entirely because of me, not her. I wasn't ready to commit. I chose to spend my last evening as a single man with another woman at a bachelor party. I didn't know the girl and I never saw her again. Marriage was not about to change my life. I promised myself I would still go to the coolest clubs and sleep with the hottest girls. I was Sugar Ray Leonard."

During the course of his career, Leonard earned six purses in excess of $10,000,000. Ten million dollars in 1980 adjusted for inflation would be the equivalent of $27,300,000 today. Ray fought Roberto Duran twice in 1980.

Then, in 1981, he beat Thomas Hearns.

"I thought I knew what fame was before the fight with Tommy," Leonard writes. "It was nothing compared to how I was treated after the fight. I used to walk into Odell's, a black nightclub in downtown Baltimore, and the girls would scream as if I were a rock star. I'd take the hottest ones I could find to the local Holiday Inn, sharing them with the rest of the boys. Once I beat Tommy, the amount of women we met and the caliber of those women rose to a whole new level. They were faster, looser, better dressed. I didn't know their names. I didn't care. We weren't there to make friends. The first choice was mine. 'The one in the red dress,' I'd say. And presto; the woman and I would retreat to my bedroom, leaving the boys to fight over the rest. It wasn't a matter of money; these women weren't getting paid. They just wanted to be with the champ."

Leonard was flying out of control.

"Wherever I went, whether in public appearances or intimate gatherings, Sugar Ray was the main event," he says. "I wanted to hear how special I was all the time, and I surrounded myself with people I knew would tell me just that."

Then alcohol and cocaine took over his life.

Leonard began using cocaine in the summer of 1982 after eye surgery for a detached retina.

"If I could handle Benitez, Duran, and Hearns," he recalls, "I could certainly handle a little white powder. Besides, during my trips to California, the people I did coke with lived in mansions with swimming pools. They were some of the most high-profile stars in music and movies, people of stature. If they thought cocaine was cool, who was I to argue. The high I got from cocaine was incredible. Coke made me feel like I did in the ring, in complete control. I became funny, engaging, articulate. Coke made the anxieties go away. I was Sugar Ray again. Except [the anxieties] kept coming back. Which meant I needed more coke. Lots more. The high rollers I hung with were thrilled to share with the champ, coke being another symbol of their vast wealth and power. As time went on and my appetite grew, I couldn't wait for the next party in Bel Air or the next visit to a swanky club in West Hollywood. I paid for the stuff myself, doling out one thousand dollars here, two thousand dollars there. Those dollars began adding up in a hurry. One friend I used as a supplier estimates that I spent a quarter of a million dollars per year on coke."

Leonard recalls that, once during his tenure as an expert analyst for HBO, Ross Greenburg (then HBO's executive producer) was conducting a production meeting. Ray reached for a vial of cocaine and took a hit in full view of everyone. Greenburg, Leonard recalls, "kept talking as if nothing happened."

The 1980s, Ray says, were characterized by "one sad shameful incident leading to another." One time, he woke up in his room at a Las Vegas hotel-casino after spending the night with a woman he'd met in a club and discovered that his cash and $35,000 worth of jewelry were missing.

The lesson he learned?

"From then on, whenever I had a girl, I stashed valuables in the hotel safe or under the mattress."

In late 1987, Juanita decided that enough was enough.

"The night that ended our marriage fit the pattern perfectly," Leonard remembers. "Me wasted, her ranting. I demanded she hand over her wedding ring, which I then placed on my finger. As the argument got more heated, I gave her a shove, accidently scraping Juanita on the forehead with the ring's large diamond. Blood trickled down the bridge of her nose. I was horrified."

Juanita left that night with Ray Jr and Jarrel.

"I hate you," three-year-old Jarrel shouted at his father.

The divorce became final in 1990.

"Looking back," Ray says, "I can offer no defense for my conduct. Juanita gave me more chances than I deserved. I was wrong, and I have to live with these sins every single day. They cost me my first marriage and deeply harmed the relationship with my two older sons."

Leonard says that he's in a better place today. He has since remarried. He and Bernadette Robi have a son and daughter (Daniel and Camille).

More importantly, in 2006, Ray confronted his substance abuse problems and began attending meetings at Alcoholics Anonymous. Recalling the pivotal first meeting, he writes, "I stayed in the back row, my hat and shades on, head down, trying not to be noticed. Suddenly, it was my turn to introduce myself. 'I'm Ray Leonard,' I said. 'Your first name is enough,' I was told. I started over. 'I'm Ray.' Everyone laughed."

Leonard says that he has been clean for the past five years. One hopes that it continues; for his sake and the sake of his family.

In assessing the merits of *The Big Fight*, the first things to note are that the story flows nicely and Arkush captures Leonard's voice. At times, the treatment of issues is a bit superficial. There are a few more layers of varnish over Ray's feelings that he might strip away. But he's honest about his shortcomings as a father and husband in his first marriage.

He also deserves credit for acknowledging that Thomas Hearns should have been declared the winner of their second fight, contested long after both men had passed their prime.

"When the fight was over," Leonard admits, "the only uncertainty left was the margin of defeat. I braced myself for the announcement. The judges must have been watching a different fight. It was ruled a draw."

The most troubling issue surrounding *The Big Fight* concerns the aforementioned revelation that Ray was sexually abused in the early-1970s by an unnamed "prominent Olympic boxing coach."

Three men were involved in coaching the 1976 United States Olympic boxing team. Speculation has centered on them, and one of them in particular. All three are deceased.

I don't condone sexual harassment in any form, and the crime is worse when the victim is underage. But Leonard had the platform to address this issue long before it became a factor in the sale of his book. To raise it now in a manner that casts suspicion on at least two coaches (and possibly others) who by definition are innocent seems unfair.

That said; *The Big Fight* is an interesting passageway into the mind of a great fighter, who describes boxing as an escape from places in his psyche that he otherwise dared not enter.

Before one of Leonard's fights, a camp assistant asked, 'Boss, where are you?" Ray answered, "Somewhere you'll never go. Somewhere you don't want to go."

Writing of the seconds before the bell rang for round one of his fight against Wilfred Benitez, Leonard recalls, "I never felt more alive and more authentic. It was as if I entered a room where no one else was permitted to go, where there was no confusion and no fear, where I felt happy and at peace despite taking part in a sport that required merciless brutality."

And speaking of the ritual ending to a long hard-fought battle, Leonard explains, "Some might wonder how two men who for forty-five minutes tried to destroy each other can embrace so soon after their battle is over. But as most of us who fight for a living come to recognize, the opponent is a partner on the same journey."

★   ★   ★

Greg Page of Louisville, Kentucky, knocked out Gerrie Coetzee in 1984 to become the WBA heavyweight champion. Who was the first heavyweight champion from Louisville?

Wrong.

Muhammad Ali was the second. The first was Marvin Hart. That bears mention because of a book by Adam Pollack entitled *In the Ring with Marvin Hart*.

Pollack is an Iowa attorney who is illuminating an era by writing biographies about boxing's early gloved champions. Books about John L. Sullivan, James J. Corbett, Bob Fitzsimmons, and James J Jeffries preceded his work on Hart. In each instance, Pollack draws heavily on contemporaneous newspaper and magazine accounts of fights. At times, the writing seems repetitive with fight report after fight report. But Pollack's world comes to life when he focuses on the big fights contested by his subjects.

Hart is the least known of boxing's gloved heavyweight champions. When James J. Jeffries retired undefeated in 1905, Marvelous Marvin (yes; that was his nickname) was matched against Jack Root in a bout that was refereed by Jeffries and promoted as a contest for the "championship" of the world. Hart was given the honor of competing for the title because, ten weeks earlier in San Francisco, he'd been awarded a twenty-round decision over Jack Johnson. Root was the designated opponent because, three years earlier, he'd bested Hart.

Hart-Root was contested in Reno, Nevada, on July 3, 1905. By contract, it was a "fight to the finish." That is, the fight would continue until one of the combatants was knocked out. The two men battled in 120-degree heat with an edge to Root until one punch ended matters in the twelfth round.

As recounted by Pollack, Root missed with a left hook to the jaw. Then— "Hart stepped in close and ripped a terrific right uppercut that landed under and a little to the left of Root's heart, near the short ribs, possibly in the solar plexus. The sound of the punch could be heard in every part of the arena. Root dropped to the ground and began writhing. His face wore an expression of extreme pain. Jack rolled over and grasped the lower rope. He tried to pull himself up but was too feeble. He sank back to the floor and was counted out. A new world champion was proclaimed."

Hart was never fully accepted as champion by the public because Jeffries had retired undefeated and Hart hadn't beaten The Man to become The Man. His place in boxing history was further diminished when he lost in his first championship defense to Tommy Burns.

But in Pollack's words, "Hart was a very entertaining fighter who was never in a dull fight. He could be hit and hurt, but he always came forward, always hit hard, and he could keep it up. He was a fan's delight, deserving of more recognition than history has given him."

One might add that, in a quirk of fate, Hart's signature is now more valuable than the known existing signature of any other fighter. Once, it was of minimal value. But noted boxing memorabilia dealer Craig

Hamilton says that, because of its scarcity, a well-documented Marvin Hart signature in good condition is now worth between $10,000 and $12,000.

★   ★   ★

The press release that came in the mail with *An Accidental Sportswriter* by Robert Lipsyte (Ecco) begins with the thought, "Lipsyte is not a sports fan. He never was." It then references him as "one of the most important and provocative sportswriters of our time."

I've known Lipsyte and enjoyed his writing for decades. The second part of his publisher's declaration sounds accurate to me.

As a young reporter, Lipsyte covered sports for the *New York Times*. Later, he authored *SportsWorld: An American Dreamland;* one of the first books to seriously examine the role of sports in contemporary American culture.

I won't tell you that *An Accidental Sportswriter* is a boxing book, because it isn't. It's a memoir that has two chapters on Muhammad Ali, who Lipsyte calls "the single most important sporting lens through which I learned about politics, religion, race, and hero worship. The Ali story," Lipsyte writes, "was a magic carpet, although the ride was not always smooth."

But the Ali material is just part of an overall narrative that chronicles the likes of Billie Jean King, Mickey Mantle, and Howard Cosell, and explores issues as diverse as the use of performance enhancing drugs in sports and the plight of gay athletes in what Lipsyte calls America's "jock culture."

"In some ways," he writes, "sports have replaced westerns and jocks have replaced gunslingers in our national imagination, not necessarily to our advantage."

Lipsyte has a gift for putting sports in their social, political, and economic context. But my favorite passage in *An Accidental Sportswriter* is free of that weight. It recounts a chance meeting in 1967 between the author and the legendary Joe DiMaggio.

DiMaggio had been known throughout his career with the New York Yankees for "gliding effortlessly" in the outfield and "drifting" to just the right place at just the right time to catch fly balls.

"That's an outfielder's sky," DiMaggio told Lipsyte as the two men looked upward.

"And then," Lipsyte recounts, "as if he were Michelangelo describing the ceiling of the Sistine Chapel, he talked about the roof of his world; about the danger of losing balls in the clouds as easily as in the sun, about smog and shadows and smoke, about the line of the ball, rising or looping, about the spin. I was mesmerized. I barely breathed, afraid to break the spell. I suddenly understood that he hadn't just 'drifted' after all; that he was a scholar, that he had prepared for every kind of sky, patch of blue, burst of sun. He always knew where he was going to meet the ball."

Poetry like that leads me to the conclusion that, despite his protestations, Lipsyte is a sports fan after all.

As a contrast to "Fistic Nuggets," these "Notes" were on the serious side.

Fistic Notes

It's time to revisit that region of purgatory known as boxing's heavy-weight division.

A critic might say that Wladimir Klitschko vs. David Haye on July 2, 2011, set the sweet science back forty years. But that would place boxing in the halcyon days of Muhammad Ali vs. Joe Frazier. Better to say that Klitschko-Haye did nothing to lift the sport's flagship division out of the doldrums that it has been in since Lennox Lewis retired seven years ago.

Klitschko-Haye was built on Haye's mouth; not his boxing skills. But once the bell for round one rings, it's impossible for a fighter to bullshit his way through a prizefight. Either a fighter is there to fight or he's there to run. Haye was there to run. When the moment of truth came, his resolve faded. He was elusive and not much more.

Putting the best face on things, David's fans could say during the early going that he was fighting a cautious tactical fight. But by the fourth round, the horrible realization set in that this would be twelve rounds of boredom.

There was no way that Haye could beat Klitschko from the outside, but he was content to stay there for the entire fight. He fought like a man who simply wanted to make it through the fight without taking much punishment, collect his paycheck, and go home. Over the course of twelve rounds, he landed a meager six punches per stanza.

Meanwhile, Klitschko fought like Klitschko. He landed (count them) zero body punches during the entire fight and an average of 2 ½ "power" punches per round. A viewer who didn't know that this had been adver-tised as a fight between two of the three best heavyweights in the world and watched with the sound off could have been forgiven for thinking that he'd tuned into an encounter between inartistic club fighters.

Klitschko prevailed on a lopsided unanimous decision. Afterward, Haye complained that he'd broken a toe on his right foot three weeks before the bout and couldn't push off properly on his punches.

Vitali Klitschko will defend his version of the heavyweight title against Tomasz Adamek in Poland on September 10th. That fight will have more action than this one but be just as one-sided. People are fond of saying these days that the American heavyweights suck. Except for the Klitschkos, the European heavyweights aren't very good either.

Meanwhile, Klitschko-Haye was reminder that, in boxing, a good jab and a straight right hand beat a big mouth.

And let's acknowledge the fact that, while Wladimir has flaws as a fighter (including, possibly, a cruiserweight chin), there are things that he does very well. If boxing fans are going to praise Floyd Mayweather Jr for his defensive skills, Klitschko deserves credit too.

★ ★ ★

The contentious on-camera exchange between Floyd Mayweather Jr and Larry Merchant in the aftermath of Mayweather's victory over Victor Ortiz is now part of boxing lore.

Floyd told Merchant, "HBO needs to fire you. You don't know shit about boxing. You ain't shit." Merchant responded, "I wish I was fifty years younger. I'd kick your ass."

That raises the question of how other interviewers might have handled a similar verbal assault by Mayweather.

"I'm not sure," says Showtime's Jim Gray. "I really don't know. With several weeks' hindsight, I'd probably say, 'Floyd; I'm glad you're not my boss.'"

Teddy Atlas of ESPN is a bit more expansive.

"It was a difficult moment," Atlas says. "Both sides have to take responsibility for what happened. Larry had his mind made up and was going somewhere with his questions. There was a mean spirit in what Floyd said, but Floyd felt that there was a mean spirit in the questions that he was being asked."

"I'm not a Floyd-hater," Atlas continues. "I don't condone what Floyd said. I disagree with a lot of the things that he says and does. But I try to see Floyd's side on issues too. And I've always liked Larry. He's a substantial guy with a lot of pride."

So . . . To repeat the question: "How would Atlas have reacted to a similar verbal assault by Mayweather?

"I don't want to go into that," Teddy answers. "I have an idea, but I don't want to go there. Maybe my initial approach would have brought a different response from Floyd. If not, and if he said the same things to me that he said to Larry, I would have been upset too. I'm not going to let someone disrespect me, and we are what we are. I know I would have reacted strongly."

★   ★   ★

The conventional wisdom is that there are no credible challengers to Sergio Martinez in the middleweight ranks. The conventional wisdom might be wrong.

Forget Dmitry Pirog's bogus belt. Martinez was stripped of the WBO title in 2010 so Danny Jacobs could fight (and beat) Pirog for the WBO crown. Dmitry upset the applecart by knocking out Jacobs in the fifth round. But consider the fact that Pirog has successfully defended his title twice since then. The twenty-nine-year-old Russian is 19-and-0 with 15 KOs. He has a good chin, power in both hands, and the ability to change styles from fight to fight. He's also intelligent, thoughtful, and dedicated to his craft.

Given the opportunity to define himself, Pirog offered the following thoughts during a recent sitdown:

★ "A happy man is someone who loves what he does and makes money doing it. I'm not just boxing for the money. I'm also doing it because I like it."

★ "For me, the best thing about being a fighter is that it has helped me to learn what is in me and to better understand myself."

★ "I don't have heroes. I don't like to idolize any one person. It is more that I respect a type of person who has gone through great trials and found a way to succeed."

★ "If I could go back in time, the two people I would most like to meet are Pyotr Velikiy [Peter the Great] and Ivan Grozni [Ivan the Terrible]. I have always been interested in the Tsars. I have read a lot about them in history books. Pyotr and Ivan were so important to the history of my country. I would like to find out for myself what they were like."

★ "When the Soviet Union broke apart into many countries [in 1991], I was young but I understood what was happening. We didn't worry at the time because we felt that it would bring more prosperity and democracy. But capitalism and democracy have moved more slowly than we thought they would."

★ "When I was young, I watched tapes of Sugar Ray Leonard. I would have loved to fight him, to match my skills against the best. In my head, I had a plan to beat him. I knew that, after beating him, I'd be one of the best fighters in history, at least in my head."

★ "When I fought Danny Jacobs, I could not leave the outcome of the fight to the judges. I understood that people with influence wanted him to win. When I knocked him out, wave after wave of emotion went through me until it was like a tornado of emotion. The same people who disrespected me before the fight continued to disrespect me afterward. But I respect myself and what I accomplished. That is the most important thing to me. Whether people liked the outcome of the fight or not, everybody saw what happened."

★ "During a fight, I don't feel the punches. After the fight, I feel all of them."

★   ★   ★

Brandon Rios vs. John Murray at Madison Square Garden on December 3, 2011, was a good action fight.

Rios (who was required to make 135 pounds in defense of his WBA title) tipped the scales at 136.4 on his first try at the Friday weigh-in. Moments later, the same scale registered 135.6. Seconds after that, it was 136.4 again. That seemed odd until it was suggested that, on the second try, Robert Garcia had his finger under Rios's right elbow and was pushing up. Whatever the truth, Brandon was unable to make weight and forfeited his 135-pound crown.

Rios is easy to hit. The problem for opponents is that he hits back. When Brandon gets hit, he smiles like Freddy Krueger. When he hits his opponent, he smiles like Freddie Krueger. The harder the punches, the broader the smile. One doesn't stand in the pocket and trade with Rios unless one knows something that the rest of us don't. But that's what Murray did.

It was trench warfare all night, with Rios throwing 1002 punches to Murray's 921. John had his moments; but over time, Brandon beat him down. It was entertaining while it lasted, which was until 2:06 of round eleven. Rios will have an exciting and successful career, but probably not a long one.

* * *

Too often, it seems as though common sense is unwelcome in boxing. Here are three common sense suggestions to improve the sport:

(1) Forty people in the ring before a fight is absurd. That's three-and-a-half tons of mostly waste material piled high on the ring canvas. In a worst-case scenario, it can damage the canvas. Under the best of circumstances, it keeps the fighters from circling the ring and testing for dead spots. Don't let anyone but the fighters, their chief seconds, the referee, and ring announcer in the ring before a fight.

(2) Sooner or later, a fighter will have eye trouble during a fight because a sequin that came off someone's trunks will find its way into his eye. Ban sequined trunks before that happens.

(3) Intelligently-run sports (like baseball, football, and basketball) require opposing teams to wear different color uniforms so spectators can tell them apart. Make different color trunks mandatory in boxing. Put the requirement in bout contracts with a monetary penalty assessable against the promoter of whichever fighter violates the color code. Faced with the prospect of losing money, promoters will make sure that the provision is enforced.

* * *

Cameron Dunkin has become one of boxing's most successful managers. Recently, he reminisced about the first professional fight he ever saw:

"I was in the first grade, nine years old," Dunkin recalled. "My father was a truck driver and not a nice man. He was physically abusive more often than I care to remember, so I spend a lot of time out of the house. I had a friend named Brian Johnson who lived down the street. His father took him to pro wrestling from time to time. This time, he took Brian to the fights, and they asked me if I wanted to come along."

"I didn't know what to expect," Dunkin continued. "The fights were at the Olympic Auditorium [in Los Angeles], which is a small place but it looked very big to me then. I remember walking into the arena, seeing the ring, and thinking this was going to be special. We had good seats, about six rows back. Some of the fighters were very young but they showed no fear at all. I thought it was incredible that they had the guts to get in the ring and do what they did with everybody watching. It was a thrill for me. My heart was pounding the whole time. I didn't want it to end; and it hasn't. I've been hooked on boxing ever since."

★   ★   ★

Muhammad Ali went on the college lecture circuit to make ends meet in the late-1960s during his exile from boxing. Gene Tunney once lectured on Shakespeare at Yale. And Mike Tyson was a commencement speaker at Central State University in Wilberforce, Ohio (where he accepted an honorary doctorate degree with the declaration, "I don't know what kind of doctor I am. But watching all these beautiful sisters here, I'm debating whether I should be a gynecologist").

Vitali Klitschko is cut from a different cloth. The reigning WBC heavyweight champion ran for mayor of Kiev in 2006 and 2008, finishing second both times but winning election to the Kiev City Council on each occasion. Thereafter, he was appointed to the Ukrainian delegation to the Congress of the Council of Europe. In April 2010, he became chairman of the Ukrainian Democratic Alliance for Reform (a political party dedicated to challenging the status quo).

On October 13, 2011, the forty-year-old Klitschko lectured before a standing-room-only crowd at Columbia University. His appearance had nothing to do with boxing. He was invited to speak under the auspices of the school's Ukrainian studies program in his capacity as chairman of UDAR.

Vitali spoke in English (his fourth language) for twenty minutes; then answered questions for an hour more. On occasion, he asked a translator to assist him. "Politics is a dirty game," he told his audience. "I came into politics six years ago with rosy glasses. The glasses fell off fast."

One of the hot-button social issues in Ukraine today is whether Ukrainian should be designated as the official state language. Roughly half of Ukraine's citizens speak Ukrainian. The other half speak Russian or a smattering of different languages. Klitschko elicited applause when he stated, "I'm a Ukrainian who speaks Russian. I started studying Ukrainian ten years ago. The state language in Ukraine must be Ukrainian."

During his lecture, Klitschko called for more free speech in Ukraine, election laws that do more than safeguard the ruling party's hold on power, gender equality in all aspects of Ukrainian life, and equal economic opportunity to replace what he called "a closed oligarchical economic system."

"Twenty years ago," Vitali declared, "Ukraine became independent. Since that time, our hopes for democracy have not been realized. We need to recognize the potential in what we have. People must get involved. We have millions of armchair experts. They sit at home; they watch television; they complain. And they change nothing. The will to change must come from the people. The government today is there for the power; not for the people. Politics for the people who control the government is simply a business. The main value for them isn't people; it's money. It's a corrupt system. We want to change that."

Is Vitali Klitschko a modern-day version of Don Quixote tilting at windmills?

Time will tell. But he's fighting the good fight outside the ring.

In recent decades, boxing in the United States has been slow to adapt to changing times. That doesn't mean Bob Arum hasn't been trying.

Top Rank, Innovation, and Boxing

The kick-off media tour for the November 12, 2011, mega-fight between Manny Pacquiao and Juan Manuel Marquez highlighted the international scope of the promotion.

It began in the Philippines with a September 3rd news conference at the Manila Hotel. Later that day, the fighters appeared at the Quirino Grandstand for a public rally that was attended by 70,000 people and televised live nationally by GMA 7. After stops in New York and Beverly Hills, the tour proceeded to Mexico City, where the fighters were greeted by an estimated 50,000 fans.

One day before the fight, the weigh-in was televised live on HBO. A "Fight Day" telecast modeled on ESPN's college football "Game Day" was hosted by Jim Lampley in the lobby of the MGM Grand Hotel and Casino. When the fighters entered the ring, their every move was seen on a giant cylindrical LED video screen suspended above the canvas. From beginning to end, the evening unfolded in carefully calibrated light amidst a cacophony of sound.

None of the above could have been foreseen when Bob Arum entered the boxing business forty-five years ago.

Arum got into boxing in 1966 as one of the participants in Main Bout, a company formed to promote Muhammad Ali's fights. The other equity owners were Herbert Muhammad (Ali's manager), John Ali (chief aide to Nation of Islam leader Elijah Muhammad), Mike Malitz (an expert in the area of closed-circuit telecasts), and football great Jim Brown (who put Arum together with the Ali camp). Their first promotion was Ali vs. George Chuvalo on March 29, 1966.

Top Rank (Arum's current promotional company) was incorporated in the early 1970s. Since then, it has featured the likes of Ali, Joe Frazier, George Foreman, Larry Holmes, Sugar Ray Leonard, Marvin Hagler, Roberto Duran, Thomas Hearns, Oscar De La Hoya, Floyd Mayweather Jr, Carlos Monzon, and Pacquiao.

Statistics are in the lifeblood of sports. Arum's numbers are staggering. As 2011 draws to a close, he has promoted 1,829 fight cards (approximately 11,500 fights) in twenty-three countries around the world. There have been 574 world title bouts and 104 pay-per-view shows. Domestically, he has promoted in more than 200 cities and forty-one of the fifty states.

Throughout his career, Arum has applied solid business principles to the chaos of boxing. But equally important, he has been open to new ideas and new business models.

For more than four decades, Arum has been on the cutting edge of innovation in boxing. Some of his innovations were implemented out of necessity; others as a matter of choice. Here, in rough chronological order, is this writer's list of the ten top innovations that Bob Arum and Top Rank have brought to boxing.

(1) BOXING ON ESPN

When ESPN was launched in 1979, the Entertainment and Sports Programming Network was far from the colossus that it is today. "The programming was awful," Arum recalls. "Replays of Australian rules football and nonsense like that."

Then Barry Frank (an executive at IMG) suggested to ESPN president Chet Simmons that the network meet with Arum to discuss a weekly boxing series. *Top Rank Boxing* on ESPN began its run on April 10, 1980, and continued through 1995. Top Rank has promoted 759 shows on ESPN to date.

Arum regards the ESPN series as his greatest accomplishment. It was hugely important to boxing because it offered the sport an anchor to hold onto a fan base that had been dwindling since the demise of the *Gillette Friday Night Fight*s and guaranteed regularly scheduled programming, fifty-two weeks a year in a specific time slot. With its introduction, basic cable became a significant new tier for boxing.

(2) MARVELOUS MARVIN HAGLER TO HBO

Seth Abraham (former president of Time Warner Sports and the architect of HBO's boxing program) says, "There's no question in my mind that Bob is the most advanced thinker ever in the marriage of tele-vision and boxing."

Abraham dealt with Arum for years. The cornerstone of their relation-ship was a 1981 contract that called for Hagler to appear three times on HBO. Those fights were contested against Fulgencio Obelmejias, Vito Antoufermo, and Mustafa Hamsho for a total license fee of $1,100,000. It was the first multi-fight contract ever for an elite fighter to appear on HBO.

Before that, Hagler had been primarily an afternoon fighter on ABC's *Wide World of Sports*. The conventional wisdom was that moving him to a premium cable network would diminish his marketability. But HBO's offer was so far above the prevailing market rate that Arum took the plunge. Moving Hagler to prime time on HBO also allowed Top Rank to raise tickets prices in the arena for Hagler's fights.

Six years later, Arum brought Showtime into the boxing business when he sold rights to Hagler vs. John Mugabi to HBO's chief premium cable rival.

"We wanted to do Hagler-Mugabi on closed-circuit," Arum recalls. "But [HBO CEO] Michael Fuchs said no. So I made a deal for Showtime to do the closed-circuit production, and then Showtime showed the tape-delay a week later."

The rest is history. As 2011 draws to a close, Top Rank has promoted ninety-six nights of boxing on HBO.

(3) CHAMPIONING THE LIGHTER WEIGHT CLASSES

Legendary matchmaker Teddy Brenner once observed, "There's heavyweight boxing, and then there's everything else." But by the early 1980s, the number of good heavyweights was dwindling, and Don King had a stranglehold on the division. In response, Arum began to concen-trate on developing major attractions in the lighter weight classes.

One can argue that it was a no-brainer to build around Sugar Ray Leonard, Marvin Hagler, Roberto Duran, and Thomas Hearns. Ditto for Aaron Pryor and Alexis Arguello. But Arum took 108-pound Michael Carbajal out of the 1988 Olympics and promoted him to a million-dollar purse in a 1994 match-up against Umberto Gonzalez.

The legacy of those fights is clear. Boxing's two biggest stars today (Manny Pacquiao and Floyd Mayweather Jr) are "small" fighters.

(4) TARGETING THE HISPANIC MARKET

"I began to realize the potential in the Hispanic market in 1983," Arum recalls. "That's when we promoted Roberto Duran against Davey Moore at Madison Square Garden. We sold out and the place was a mad-house. But the Hispanic market in New York was mostly Puerto Rican and Caribbean-based. I didn't understand its full potential until I moved to Las Vegas in 1986. Then I saw the power of the Mexican-American market; particularly on the west coast."

Oscar De La Hoya was Arum's wedge for breaking open the Hispanic-American market. When Oscar came out of the 1992 Olympics, he wasn't embraced by Mexican-Americans as one of their own. Savvy marketing changed that. Next, Erik Morales became the first Mexican national signed by Top Rank to a long-term promotional contract. Then, in 1995, ESPN cancelled *Top Rank Boxing* and Arum reconstituted the series on Univision. Later, he established a beachhead in the Puerto Rican community with Miguel Cotto as his flagship fighter from the island.

(5) THE "CURIOSITY" FIGHTER

Arum knows how to tell a story. In the late-1990s, he took an obese white guy from Jasper, Alabama, and anointed him "King of the Four-Rounders." Eric Esch (better known as "Butterbean") subsequently knocked out Peter McNeeley in one round and went the distance with fifty-two-year-old Larry Holmes. He's still fighting at age forty-five (albeit not for Arum) and weighed in for his last fight at 405 pounds.

Arum brought the world Mia St. John in boxing gloves and Muhammad Ali vs. Antonio Inoki (his imagination got the better of him on that one). He also sold the world on the possibilities inherent in a comeback by a "washed-up" overweight hamburger-eating heavyweight who hadn't fought in ten years.

When George Foreman re-entered the ring in 1987, he was thought of in the same vein as Butterbean would be a decade later. His early opponents (Steve Zouski, Charles Hostetter, Bobby Crabtree, Tim Anderson, Rocky Sekorski, Tom Trimm, Guido Trane, et al.) did little to dispel that notion. In 1991, Big George lost a unanimous decision to Evander Holyfield. That was supposed to be the end of the line. Except Foreman kept fighting and, in 1994, knocked out Michael Moorer to regain the heavyweight championship of the world.

(6) CLOSED-CIRCUIT TELEVISION

Lester Malitz pioneered closed-circuit television in the 1940s. Arum brought closed-circuit to a new level with the help of Lester's son, Mike Malitz.

"I can't take credit for the advances in technology," Arum acknowledges. "That was crucial everything we did. In the old days—or the very old days, if you want to call them that—closed circuit was an iffy proposition. You had to transmit everything on telephone lines. The projectors in the theaters broke down. You could only show a fight in a limited number of locations because there wasn't enough equipment. Then satellite transmission came in and everything changed."

Top Rank was one of the first promoters to take full advantage of the advances in satellite transmission. Also, closed-circuit marketing was largely regional when Arum entered the business. He forged the idea of national tours, national advertising, and a unified whole.

(7) PAY-PER-VIEW

The 1991 fight between Evander Holyfield and George Foreman (co-promoted by Top Rank and Main Events) was the first fight ever on TVKO, which would evolve into HBO-PPV. Just as significantly, Arum has used pay-per-view niche marketing to build and control the destiny of his own fighters.

Rather than let his fighters sit on the sidelines due to a lack of available premium cable television dates, Arum promoted fights like Miguel Cotto vs. Paulie Malignaggi and Cotto against Gary Jennings as independent pay-per-view shows. Before that, he'd utilized small PPV shows to build fighters like Erik Morales.

The best example of Top Rank using niche pay-per-view to maintain its independence and build a fighter is the case of Julio Cesar Chavez Jr. HBO and Showtime didn't want Chavez. ESPN couldn't have cared less. Arum never said that Julio Jr was an elite fighter. But he thought that enough boxing fans wanted to see him in action to make him a substantial attraction. The results speak for themselves.

(8) "BACK TO THE FUTURE" WITH STADIUM SITES

When Arum started in boxing decades ago, big fights were held in big city settings. Then site fees took over and casinos became the favored host for big fights.

In recent years, Top Rank has made an effort to bring boxing back to its roots by promoting big fights at sites like Yankee Stadium and Cowboys Stadium. In doing so, it has made venue a key marketing point in the storyline for the fight and encouraged the on-site presence of a broader fan demographic.

(9) THE NEW MEDIA

Top Rank was among the first major boxing promoters to understand the power of the Internet and treat Internet writers with the same respect as the print media. In recent years, it has embraced social media platforms like Twitter and Facebook and developed its own iPhone application.

Manny Pacquiao vs. Shane Mosley was the first mega-fight to be streamed live on the Internet. In the not-too-distant future, Internet transmission of pay-per-view fights will revolutionize the economics of boxing.

(10) THE NEW BUSINESS MODEL

For decades, Top Rank was a boxing promotional company that promoted one fight at a time, one deal at a time. Arum's staff consisted of a matchmaker, publicist, closed-circuit adviser, and secretary.

Now Top Rank is a media company with in-house production facilities and a fulltime staff of two dozen employees. When it promotes an independent pay-per-view show, an additional fifty people are on the payroll. This is part and parcel of a business built in significant part on long-term output deals with television networks around the globe.

Arum understands that the tribal nature of boxing is still important. He has taken the idea of Irish and Italian boxers fighting at Madison Square Garden in the 1940s and developed that theme on an international stage.

It's a changing world and Top Rank has changed with it. But some things remain the same.

"I can do all the planning in the world," Arum says. "We can come up with brilliant idea after brilliant idea at Top Rank. But it doesn't mean a thing unless our fighters can fight."

As 2011 drew to a close, the New York State Athletic Commission
seemed like an agency in drift.

Cotto–Margarito II and the New York State Athletic Commission

There's something about a Miguel Cotto fight that brings chaos to the New York State Athletic Commission.

Cotto fought at Yankee Stadium against Yuri Foreman on June 5, 2010. Early in round seven, Foreman's right knee gave way and he fell to the canvas. He rose in obvious pain, hobbling when he tried to walk. Later in the round, his knee buckled again and he fell to the canvas for the second time without being hit.

In round eight, the inspector assigned to Foreman's corner advised referee Arthur Mercante Jr that Joe Grier (Yuri's trainer) wanted to stop the fight. Mercante refused and Grier threw a white towel of surrender into the ring. The referee then consulted with New York State Athletic Commission chairperson Melvina Lathan, who declined to stop the fight. The bout continued into the ninth round before it ended.

It's impossible to know the extent to which Foreman's injury was aggravated by the authorities allowing the fight to continue for two rounds after Yuri was injured. What is known is that, afterward, Foreman underwent reconstructive surgery for a torn ACL and a significant meniscus injury. Nine months later, he returned to the ring. But his mobility was diminished and he lost every round en route to a sixth-round stoppage at the hands of Pawel Wolak. His career as a fighter is now on hold.

Medical contretemps were also part of the storyline for Cotto's December 3rd fight at Madison Square Garden against Antonio Margarito. Only this time, the controversy was before the fight, not afterward. And it centered on an eye, not a knee.

Dr. Barry Jordon (chief medical officer for the New York State Athletic Commission), Dr. Anthony Curreri (its ocular specialist), and the commission's medical advisory board (including retinal specialist Dr. Vincent Giovinazzo) recommended that Margarito not be licensed to box in New York. In making their determination, they considered five problems that Margarito faced after his 2010 fight against Manny Pacquiao: (1) a retinal detachment; (2) a large retinal tear necessitating the use of silicone oil as part of the repair process; (3) a fractured orbital bone; (4) a vitreous rupture; and (5) the removal of a cataract followed by the implant of an artificial lens. Taken together, these factors led to further concern regarding the total construction of Margarito's right eye.

Thereafter, the NYSAC was on the receiving end of some unfair commentary. For example, considerable attention was paid to the fact that Ms. Lathan enjoyed a "free lunch" at the September 20th kick-off press conference for Cotto-Margarito II without indicating that licensing Margarito might be a problem.

References to Ms. Lathan's lunch skewed the debate. The writers in attendance at the press conference (including this one) ate lunch too. But there was more valid criticism with regard to the substantive issue of how Ms. Lathan had overseen the licensing process.

With the fight in jeopardy as the clock ticked down, Bob Arum declared, "Can you believe this? We're two thousand tickets away from a complete sellout, and the New York State Athletic Commission wants to pull this nonsense. It's a complete kangaroo commission up there. This woman, who knows nothing, says that two leading ophthalmologists [retained by the promotion in support of Margarito's application] are lying. I don't understand her. She knew he had eye surgery before we even had a first press conference. The government should throw them all out of office. In all the years I've been in boxing, this is the most incredible experience I've had."

Arum, of course, had a vested interest in the process. He was promoting the fight. But Dan Rafael of ESPN.com (a more impartial observer) had a comparable view.

"The NYSAC has handled this whole sorry episode like a bunch of amateurs who have no idea what they are doing," Rafael wrote. "What is wrong, and what stinks here, is that the NYSAC waited until the eleventh hour to make a decision that should have been made months ago. Now thousands of people are in limbo and tens of millions of dollars are at stake when it never should have come to this. It was up to the commission to give Top Rank a firm deadline by which any paperwork or exams were due so that it would leave enough time to make a decision;

not risk forcing the fight out of town less than two weeks before and with the Garden already nearly sold out."

"This whole thing is a mess," Rafael continued. "And it's because of how irresponsibly the NYSAC has behaved. The fight was agreed to in July. The site was selected not long after that. Then there was a news conference in New York to formally announce the fight in late September; a news conference that Lathan attended, where she was one of the speakers. She lauded the fighters and Top Rank. At that point, there wasn't a hint of a licensing issue. Do you think for one second that Arum would have spent so significantly on the promotion and made a deal with the Garden and HBO-PPV if he hadn't been given assurances from New York that Margarito's license was in the bag? And it's not as though Margarito's eye injury and surgery were a secret."

"I have no quarrel with the NYSAC wanting to make sure Margarito is healthy enough to fight," Rafael concluded. "But if the commission was so concerned, why didn't it have Margarito submit to an eye exam when he was in New York in September rather than wait until the last minute for this dog and pony show? How do you tell thousands of people who have bought tickets, booked flights and hotel rooms, and planned their lives around the week of the fight that it's being kicked out of town on less than two weeks' notice? Do you think this mess is going to make any promoter want to bring a big fight to New York in the future?"

Thereafter, medical testimony from outside physicians at odds with the thoughts of the NYSAC medical staff was introduced into evidence at an eleventh-hour hearing. After considerable maneuvering behind closed doors, the commission relented. In legal-medical terms, it was determined that licensing Margarito was "contra-indicated but not prohibited."

Looking back on it all, Dr. Curreri says, "Our medical guidelines are written for doctors, not lawyers. Now I'm a bit concerned about what happens in the future. A fighter with multiple pathologies passed through the licensing process. After allowing this fight, we must review our guidelines and change some of the terminology so that the intent of the guidelines—which is to protect the safety of the fighter—is enforced. What I believe will happen next is that the medical staff will work with others to develop proper terminology that satisfies all legal requirements as well as medical considerations. What I can also tell you with great certainty is that the doctors in the commission medical department were looking out for the safety of Mr. Margarito. And we continued to perform our duties even after the commission decided not to follow our advice with regard to licensing him. The commission medical staff will continue to put fighter safety first in New York."

Meanwhile, neither Ms. Lathan nor anyone else from the NYSAC attended the final main-event press conference at Madison Square Garden on November 30th. That notable departure from custom was repeated when the undercard press conference was held at B. B. King's a day later.

Then things got even more strange.

Media coverage was particularly important to Cotto-Margarito II because of the issues involved (from Margarito's handwraps to the condition of his eye). But there were times when Lathan seemed more concerned with controlling the media than efficiently administering the fight.

The NYSAC continued to follow its ridiculous practice of refusing to allow HBO to weigh the fighters on "the unofficial HBO scale" in the dressing room prior to the fight. Then a more serious issue arose when the commission wouldn't let Naazim Richardson supervise the wrapping of Margarito's hands on behalf of the Cotto camp.

HBO analyst Max Kellerman was dispatched to the dressing room. NYSAC officials sought to preclude him from interviewing Richardson, but were unsuccessful in their attempt.

HBO commentator Emanuel Steward expressed sympathy for the situation that Lathan and other commission members found themselves in. Jim Lampley and Kellerman were less sympathetic.

"It's amazing how these commissions behave sometimes," Kellerman told the viewing audience. "Naazim Richardson didn't think they had done anything wrong. But just by [my] asking the question about what he thought about it, the commission members who were in the room wanted to immediately stop the interview.

"Really?" Lamply inquired. "Is there a media blackout on the subject?"

"Which is absurd," Kellerman responded. "No one is accusing them of any wrongdoing, although it does seem that they're not allowing him in on a technicality. This happened not long ago in California. There was an issue with the commission. The commission stopped answering questions and behaved defensively and it makes them look very bad. They're accountable to boxing fans and the media as the outlet for boxing fans; or maybe they don't think they are."

Then the situation got crazier. As the handwrap debacle stretched on, Robert Garcia (Margarito's trainer) and the fighter himself said that they had no problem with Richardson overseeing the handwrapping process. "Bring him in," Garcia urged.

"That answers the question you might have had about the Naazim Richardson situation," Lampley told HBO's viewers. "Obviously, it was no problem for anybody in Margarito's camp. It was entirely the New York State Athletic Commission's issue."

"It's like a bouncer at a club door who flexes some muscle simply because he can," Kellerman added. "The New York State Athletic Commission."

Problem resolved . . . Not.

"And now, here's another change," Lampley reported. "Hold the phone because I've just been told there's another shift in gears. Naazim Richardson won't be allowed into Margarito's dressing room to watch the handwraps."

Two of the best ring inspectors in the country—chief inspector Felix Figueroa (who was assigned to Cotto's dressing room) and George Ward (who was assigned to Margarito's) were caught in the middle of it all.

Ultimately, Pedro Luis Diaz (Cotto's trainer) watched Margarito's hands being wrapped. No one from the commission was able to explain why Richardson (a widely-respected trainer) wasn't allowed in Margarito's dressing room, but actors Tony Sirico (*The Sopranos*) and Chuck Zito (*Oz*) were allowed into Cotto's.

Some memories of 2011 are tinged with sadness.

In Memoriam

February 18, 2011, would have been Artie Curry's fifty-first birthday. In honor of the occasion, Artie's mother and some of his friends got together at Portobello's pizzeria in Manhattan to share memories.

Artie's family and friends have established the Arthur Curry Scholarship Fund at St. Francis College in Brooklyn. In the words of the charter, scholarships will be awarded to "students of high academic achievement and outstanding character who are entering their senior year of college and, by word and deed, have shown the ability to bring people together."

HBO (where Artie worked throughout his adult life) was particularly generous in funding the scholarship program.

The scholarship program was formally announced on February 18, 2010 (on what would have been Artie's fiftieth birthday). That morning, Jim Lampley served as master of ceremonies at St. Francis College for a celebration of Artie's life. Over the course of an hour, friends and co-workers shared memories of Artie with the St. Francis student body. Among the thoughts offered were:

★ Jon Crystal: "There are very few one-of-a-kind people who you meet in your life. Professionally, they say that everyone is replaceable. But not Artie. He had a gift for making people feel good. He loved them and they loved him back."

★ Seth Abraham: "No matter what was going on in his life, Artie took great joy in helping others."

★ Curt Viebranz: "The sorrow I feel is joined with the joy I feel at having known Artie."

Roy Jones Jr was among the speakers who sought to infuse Artie's spirit within the St. Francis College community. His remarks were particularly moving.

"I thank God for giving me the opportunity to know Artie Curry," Roy said. "He came through a lot of things that most people wouldn't be able to make it through; times when he wasn't sure he'd see tomorrow. And he came through it with that beautiful smile of his that would melt your heart. There were a lot of years of suffering behind that smile; it didn't come about easy. But the smile was so big because he overcame all those years of suffering. He was a beautiful person. And he became somebody much bigger than he knew he was."

"There will never be another person who touches my life like Artie did," Jones continued. "In our hearts, we were like twins. Nothing he ever did bothered me. The only that bothered me was, I couldn't be standing there right next to him when he left us. Having a friend is one thing. Having a true friend who's always there for you, and therefore you must be there for him; those are hard to find. When you find them, hang onto them and don't be afraid to tell them how you feel about them, because you never know what tomorrow holds. If you talk to your loved ones, let them know that you love them and how you feel about them. If you love somebody and you talk to them, make sure that conversation is always the note you want to end on, because you never know when that song might end."

★   ★   ★

I met Gil Clancy in 1984 when I was researching a book about the sport and business of boxing. Gil had already earned acclaim as a hall-of-fame trainer, manager, and matchmaker. At the time, he was providing expert commentary for CBS's boxing telecasts and also had considerable input into which fights the network bought.

Gil viewed me with a healthy dose of skepticism. I was chronicling the exploits of WBC super-lightweight champion Billy Costello and manager Mike Jones. Gil was suspicious of outsiders who appeared on the scene to write about his beloved sport.

"Jesus, Mike," he demanded at one negotiating session. "Do you have to keep bringing this guy with you all the time?"

"Yes," Mike told him.

After a while, Gil got used to having me around and a friendship was forged. As the years passed, he became one of my "go to" guys whenever I needed to educate myself on a particular facet of boxing.

Boxing is a shady business. The warning "protect yourself at all times" applies to action outside the ring as well as in it. Trainer Jimmy Glenn once famously said, "Everybody in boxing wants to screw somebody. They don't feel comfortable, they think they're doing something wrong, if they're not screwing somebody."

Gil was the antithesis of that. His word was his bond. He was a straight shooter and voice of reason in an often-irrational duplicitous sport. Over the years, he won countless awards for his contributions to the sweet science. He was part of that wonderful group of people who truly understand and love boxing. He died on March 31, 2011, after a long illness at age eighty-eight. Boxing will miss him.

★ ★ ★

The boxing world lost a treasure on June 30th with the death of English "Bouie" Fisher.

Bouie was best known for taking a twenty-five-year-old ex-con with an 0-and-1 record and molding him into the middleweight champion of the world. His relationship with Bernard Hopkins soured when the mega-dollars started rolling in and Bernard decided to cut his longtime trainer's end of the purse. They split bitterly, reunited, then split again.

During good times, Fisher said of Hopkins, "When it comes to boxing, Bernard isn't old; he's old school. Bernard is a throwback fighter when it comes to dedication in and out of the ring. Boxing never leaves his thoughts. He lives, eats, and dreams boxing. He puts in the work that's necessary to be great. I know a thing or two about growing old. And I can tell you that no one grows old overnight. As long as a fighter is properly conditioned, his age won't show all at once. You can see a lot of things with old eyes if you've been around boxing a while. Young eyes aren't always as good."

Then came the split, and Bouie noted, "Bernard is a very difficult person to deal with. He wants all the glory. He wants all the credit. He wants all the money. It's all about him, him, him. At one time, Bernard was like family to me. But my family has been raised and taught to be respectful and kind to other people; and Bernard just isn't that way. Bernard thinks money is everything. Money is good to have; you need it. But it's not everything. Right and wrong matter. I believe that, if you do right, everything will be fine. When you do wrong to other people and then try to justify what you've done, you wind up lying because the truth won't help you."

Yet in the end, Fisher said reflectively, "I had a nice run with Bernard. It could have been better here and there. But I'm proud to have been with Bernard. I think he's one of the best middleweights since Sugar Ray Robinson."

Bouie was a gentleman. He adhered to the view, "In boxing, there's always people saying bad things about other people. So I say, 'Protect yourself at all times and mind your own business.'"

Some other thoughts that he shared with this writer over the years follow:

★ "Boxing is a great sport. It will always be a great sport. It's not easy; that's for sure. There's nothing easy about boxing. There's plenty of heartache. A lot of tears have been shed in this business. But I'm proud to have been part of boxing history."

★ "Too many times, when you try to tell young men something today, they become resentful and don't want to listen. They say, 'What's this old gray-haired guy talking about!' And I tell them, 'You know, I didn't just dye my hair gray. I earned my gray hair. You should go out and earn yourself some gray hair too.' But what makes me want to pull my gray hair out sometimes is when a young man with all the talent in the world doesn't want to do the work and make the sacrifices that are necessary to reap the rewards that his talent can bring him."

★ "Becoming a great trainer takes years of knowledge and experience. Some of the trainers who people call 'great' today aren't even good. They were just placed in great situations. I'm still in school with boxing. No one ever learns everything there is to know about boxing."

★ "I've had my glory. I've seen my children grow to be good men and women. I raised eight children in the middle of the ghetto and didn't have two hours of trouble with any of them. All my children finished high school and have good jobs. Four of them graduated from college. One of my daughters has been voted 'outstanding teacher of the year' two times at her high school. Another works with retarded children. Now I'm sending my grandchildren to college. Right now, I'm sitting in my home, looking out the window at the sun melting the snow. This afternoon, I'll be in the gym teaching some young kids how to slip a jab. Everyone should be as happy as I am now."

★　★　★

George Kimball was diagnosed with inoperable esophageal cancer in the summer of 2005.

Many people engage in a flurry of activity when they're in their sixties to make up for time lost when they were young. George was determined to make up for time that he knew he would lose at the end.

Over the next six years, George was living, not dying. He was as content and productive as most people are at any time in their lives.

He added to his legacy as a writer by authoring *Four Kings* (the definitive work on the round-robin fights among Sugar Ray Leonard, Marvin Hagler, Thomas Hearns, and Roberto Duran). That was followed by *Manly Art* (a collection of George's own columns about the sweet science). He also edited two anthologies with John Schulian (*At the Fights: American Writers on Boxing* and *The Fighter Still Remains: A Celebration of Boxing in Poetry and Song*).

On a more personal level, George's wife and soulmate wife, Marge Marash, was a source of strength, comfort, and joy to him throughout these difficult years.

George confronted his illness with candor and courage, adding a measure of humor to the mix. Earlier this year, he asked me if I'd be available, if necessary, to cover for him at a reading of his work.

"I agreed to do an April 7th event," George wrote to me on January 9th. "But I start a pretty heavy-duty chemo regimen on Monday [January 17th]. I've had all three drugs they'll be using before, though not in this particular combination. None of them were much fun. They'll do another PET scan in early March to see if it had any effect. If it hasn't, I imagine they'll discontinue treatment and just try to make me comfortable for as long as I last. In other words, there is a possibility that I won't last until April, in which case you might have to do my share of the reading. I have every intention of being there on April 7th. But if I'm not, I'll have the best of all excuses. Cheers, GK"

George made it to the reading, as well as other readings including a celebration of his work at the New York Athletic Club. By that time, he was fortified by the knowledge that he would never go back to the hospital again regardless of how his illness progressed. He died at home last night (July 6, 2011).

George took pride in his writing. He was more than a chronicler of the boxing scene; he was part of it. He was one of the people who I knew would always be at ringside when I went to the fights. It's sad that he'll no longer be there.

★   ★   ★

I've written at length about Joe Frazier in the past and will do so again in the future. For now, a few words on his passing.

Frazier fought with an intensity, determination, and pride seldom seen in the sometimes glorious, sometimes ignominious, history of boxing.

Some fighters try hard until they get hit. Then they stop trying. Joe always kept trying.

As a young man, Eddie Futch sparred with Joe Louis. Later, he trained Frazier. "Anywhere they hit you, you felt it," Futch said. "When they hit you, it hurt for days."

Naazim Richardson (like Frazier, a fixture on the Philadelphia boxing scene) later observed, "The body is different from the mind. Your body would rather lose a fight to Muhammad Ali than win a fight against Joe Frazier."

On March 8, 1971, Frazier entered the ring at Madison Square Garden for the first of three historic fights against Ali

"You don't win fights by talking," Joe said. "You win fights by fighting."

Ali's record was 31-and-0 when he entered the ring, and 31-and-1 when he left it. That night, Frazier became immortal.

"If God ever calls me to a holy war," Ali said years later, "I want Joe Frazier fighting beside me."

Joe Frazier ennobled the sport of boxing. He was pure fighter.

★   ★   ★

*Author's Note: Several weeks after the above tribute to Joe Frazier was written, I
was asked to provide a brief look at Joe's relationship with Madison Square
Garden for the Cotto-Margarito II fight program.*

Joe Frazier was born in South Carolina. He was a "Philadelphia
fighter." But Madison Square Garden was his home.

Frazier fought at The Garden ten times. On March 4, 1966, he scored
a fifth-round knockout of Dick Wipperman at "the old Garden" on
Eighth Avenue and 50th Street. It was Joe's first fight as a pro outside of
Philadelphia. He was 5-and-0 at the time. Later that year, he climbed off
the MSG canvas twice in the second round to win a narrow majority-
decision over Oscar Bonavena. A 1967 stoppage of George Chuvalo
followed.

On March 4, 1968, with Muhammad Ali in exile, Frazier fought on
the first fight card in the current Garden. He shared the spotlight that
night with Nino Benvenuti, who decisioned Emile Griffith in the rubber
match of their three-bout trilogy. Joe knocked out Buster Mathis in the
co-feature to win the New York State heavyweight crown.

Knockout victories at MSG over Manuel Ramos and Jerry Quarry
followed. Then, on February 16, 1970, Frazier notched his biggest victory
up until that time by annihilating Jimmy Ellis in five rounds to consoli-
date the WBC, WBA, and New York State titles.

That set the stage for "The Fight of the Century."

It takes two fighters to make a great fight. On March 8, 1971, Frazier
and Ali obliged. Joe, Muhammad, Madison Square Garden, and boxing
history were forever united on that historic night.

"I don't care how much lateral movement a guy has," Eddie Futch
(who assisted Yank Durham in training Joe) noted. "In order to punch, he
must come to you. And when he comes, he's got to bring that head and
body."

The one-minute rest periods between rounds were painfully short for
Ali that night. Slowly, inexorably, Joe wore him down.

A handful of punches have earned a special place in boxing lore. The
devastating right hand that flattened Jersey Joe Walcott and made Rocky
Marciano heavyweight champion of the world is on the short list. So is
Sugar Ray Robinson's one-punch left-hook knockout of Gene Fullmer.

In the fifteenth round of Ali-Frazier I, Joe flattened Muhammad with a left hook that sent shockwaves around the world. Later, Frazier reminisced, "That night, when I put Ali down, a fight like that; I stood where no one else ever stood."

Ali rose from the canvas. That's the measure of the man he was. But he was a beaten fighter. Frazier prevailed 11–4, 9–6, 8–6–1 on the judges' scorecards.

As Thomas Paine observed, "The harder the conflict, the more glorious the triumph."

There's a fraternity of great fighters. The brotherhood is smaller when limited to great heavyweights, and smaller still with the requirement that the fighters be linked to key moments in history. Joe Frazier is part of that elite group. Long after his career was over, he was always welcome at Madison Square Garden. He respected the sport, and everyone in boxing respected him.

As the crowd roars tonight, listen closely and you might hear the ghostly thud of Joe Frazier's punches echoing through the arena.

My career as a boxing writer began with Billy Costello. He was the foundation for everything that came afterward.

Billy Costello
(1956–2011)

I met Billy Costello in the summer of 1984 when I visited the Concord Hotel in the Catskill Mountains. I was researching a book about the sport and business of professional boxing with the intention of building the narrative around a fighter who was preparing for a championship fight. Over time, I interviewed close to a hundred people for the project. Gerry Cooney and Mike Jones (Cooney's co-manager) were on the list. Mike invited me to visit Gerry in the Catskills, where he was training for an upcoming fight against Phil Brown.

Billy was Gerry's stablemate. Earlier in the year, he'd knocked out Bruce Curry to win the WBC 140-pound title. Several weeks after we met, he defended his championship with a unanimous-decision victory over Ronnie Shields.

I liked Billy. We hit it off. I decided to build my book around his next title defense; a November 3, 1984, fight against Saoul Mamby.

"Lots of fighters have articles written about them," Billy told me after *The Black Lights* was published. "I've got a whole book."

Billy lost his title to Lonnie Smith in 1985. The only other blemish on his record was a 1986 defeat at the hands of Alexis Arguello. Whatever happened, he told it like it was. In 1999, he made an ill-advised return to the ring at age forty-three to fight forty-year-old Juan LaPorte on a "legends" card in North Carolina.

Billy won a split decision in a bout that many thought should have been scored the other way. "To be honest with you," he told the media afterward, "I think a draw would have been fairer."

His final record was 40 wins against 2 losses, with a 4-and-1 mark in world championship fights. After he retired as an active fighter, he stayed in boxing as a ring judge. He knew what he was watching and scored fights the way they unfolded without favoring the house fighter.

In spring 2010, Billy learned that he was suffering from adenocarcinoma. That's a particularly deadly form of lung cancer that afflicts nonsmokers.

"For a long time, I thought it was just a pulled muscle in my chest or something like that," Billy told me. "But it didn't get better and then I started having trouble breathing, so I went to the doctor. Who the hell knows where this came from. I'm not a smoker. Shit happens. This time, it happened to me."

By the time Billy sought treatment, the cancer was inoperable and had metastasized to his bones. After initial consultations at a hospital near his home in Kingston, New York, he sought help at Memorial Sloan-Kettering in Manhattan (one of the leading cancer-treatment centers in the world). The doctors there told him that he should continue treatment at the hospital where he'd started.

Reading between the lines, that could have meant Memorial Sloan-Kettering didn't want to tarnish its statistics with a hopeless case. Or maybe Billy's insurance wasn't up to par.

Fighters are used to enduring physical abuse. Cancer imposes physical suffering of a different kind. The chemotherapy added to Billy's suffering. He began having excruciating headaches. In mid-August, he made an appointment with a doctor named Gil Lederman.

Lederman has a checkered past. His defenders say that he's brilliant, creative, and willing to treat patients whom other doctors turn away because of the hopeless nature of their condition. His detractors take a different view.

In May 2010, a New York jury found Lederman liable for malpractice in the treatment of a cancer patient named Giuseppa Bono. According to the *New York Times,* Lederman was part of a group that recruited patients in Italy for specialized targeted-radiation treatment at Staten Island University Hospital in New York. The *Times* further reported, "About two hundred Italian cancer patients paid $17,500 for the treatment, lured by promotional materials that promoted 'success' and 'cure' rates above ninety percent. None of the patients were cured."

Bono died after being treated by Lederman for pancreatic cancer. The lawyers for her estate argued that she had actually been suffering from pancreatitis and that Lederman had failed to perform medically appropriate tests (such as a biopsy) to determine the nature of her illness before conducting radiation treatment.

Prior to that, Lederman had been sued by the estate of George Harrison, whose wife accused the doctor of forcing Harrison (who was dying of cancer) to autograph a guitar and of violating doctor-patient confidentiality.

As reported in *New York Magazine*, "When the rock star died, Lederman gave touching anecdotes to *Good Morning America*, CNN, NBC, Fox News, *Us Weekly*, *Newsweek*, the *New York Post*, *Daily News*, a variety of British tabloids, and the *National Enquirer*, which somehow got the erroneous impression that Harrison had been convalescing in Lederman's own home. He even allowed the *Enquirer* into his home to take a photo of his son, Ariel, playing the guitar that George had signed for him. Olivia Harrison [Harrison's widow] filed a complaint with the State Board of Professional Medical Conduct, which fined and censured Lederman. To prevent the autographed guitar from potentially ending up on eBay, she slapped him with a $10 million lawsuit. As part of the settlement, Lederman relinquished the guitar [which was subsequently destroyed] and agreed not to speak further about Harrison or the case. The same week the case was filed, Staten Island University Hospital announced that Lederman would be replaced as director of radiation oncology."

Lederman's past troubled me. I suggested to Billy that he discuss the doctor with a medical professional whom he trusted before starting treatment with him. Billy did that. Then, on Labor Day (September 6, 2010), he told me, "I got nothing to lose. I've decided to give it a shot."

Eight weeks later, Billy reported, "There are four tumors in my chest. One big one and three little ones. Lederman says he can shrink them and then maybe get rid of them by taking them out with a laser. He says it will take fifteen treatments or something like that. But there have been all kinds of delays about starting with the treatments."

Eventually, the treatments started. By late-November, Billy was seeing Lederman twice a week. Six days before Christmas, we spoke again.

"This thing with Lederman is working," Billy said. "There are two more nodules they got to get rid of, but the treatment is working. Lederman says, once they're gone, they won't come back."

Five weeks later, on January 23, 2011, reality intervened.

"I got rid of Lederman," Billy told me. "I got the feeling that he was starting to play games with me. I can't trust what he's telling me, and he wasn't communicating with my other doctors."

The last five months were a sad end game.

"I get headaches all the time now from the stress. The pain pills they're giving me to take the headaches away make me shaky . . . I don't know how much time I've got left . . . I'm feeling positive. I gotta think that way . . . One way or the other, I'll be all right."

The last time we spoke, Billy was in a reflective mood.

"I got two good kids . . . I've had a good life . . . I'm blessed with the people I've known and the things I've done . . . I want to thank you for everything you've done for me."

"No, thank you. Whatever happens, you'll always be my champion."

I meant it.

Billy died at Benedictine Hospital at 10:38 this morning (June 29, 2011). He was my friend. I'll miss him.

This one came from the heart.

Elvis (and Ali)

I saw Elvis Presley perform in 1971.

One month earlier, I'd finished a stint as a law clerk for a United States district judge. Five years as a litigator at a large Wall Street law firm would follow. I was taking three months off between jobs to travel cross-country and explore America.

I stopped in great cities and small towns; staying with friends, camping out at night, checking into cheap motels, and spending several days at a commune in Wolf Creek, Oregon. I visited steel mills, Disneyland, and the Grand Canyon. I passed through cornfields in Iowa, wheat in Nebraska, and potatoes in Idaho. There were times when I drove too fast because I was young and foolish and didn't consider what the consequences of an unseen pothole along the open highway might be. I walked the streets of Selma, Alabama, at a time when the term "nigger" was commonly used, and retraced the route that John Kennedy traveled in Dallas on November 22, 1963.

On the night of August 14th, I was at The International Hilton in Las Vegas.

Two years earlier, Presley had signed a five-year contract that called for him to perform at the International for eight weeks each year. During his run, there were two shows nightly, at 8:00 PM and midnight. The ballroom seated 2,200. Elvis was Las Vegas's signature act. All 826 of his shows, which continued until his death in 1977, sold out.

I arrived at the Hilton at 7:45 PM, knowing that no tickets were available. I just wanted to feel the mood. Hundreds of people were standing in line outside the ballroom. They had tickets for the midnight show and were queuing up because they wanted to sit as close to the stage as possible. The audience for the 8:00 PM performance had long since been seated.

As unlikely as it sounds, there was only one security man at the main door and he was looking away. I simply walked in.

The ballroom was jammed, but I found an open seat at a table with a group of women. The show began with a set from Elvis's back-up group, the Sweet Inspirations. A comedian was up next.

Then the sound of *Thus Spake Zarathustra* (popularly referenced as the theme from Stanley Kubrick's *2001*) pulsated through the ballroom. Elvis strode onto the stage wearing a white fringed suit accessorized with a purple scarf. The audience roared its approval.

It was an off night for Elvis. By mid-performance, he was letting the orchestra carry the tune while he wandered around the stage, mopping his brow. There were flashes of greatness but not much more. I didn't appreciate what I was seeing then as much as I do now.

Thirty one years later, when I was in Memphis to cover the heavy-weight championship fight between Lennox Lewis and Mike Tyson, I visited Graceland.

Elvis lived there from 1957 until his death at age forty-two. The mansion reflected his tastes. Some of the décor is garish. Many of the furnishings are what one might find in a typical middle-class home. There are the obligatory Elvis artifacts: gold records, movie posters, outfits that Elvis wore onstage. And a "jungle room" with an indoor waterfall.

After I returned home, I found myself listening to Elvis's music more than before.

I met Muhammad Ali in 1967. I was a senior at Columbia University, hosting a weekly radio show called *Personalities In Sports* for the student-run station. Ali was in his prime, preparing to fight Zora Folley at Madison Square Garden. It would be his seventh championship defense in less than a year.

Ali told me to turn on my tape recorder. We talked about Nation of Islam doctrine, with some questions about the military draft and boxing thrown in. Ten minutes after we began, Muhammad announced, "That's all I'm gonna do," and the interview was over.

In 1988, through a twist of fate, I became Ali's biographer. Over the course of a decade, we spent countless hours together in his home and mine. I experienced the joy of traveling around the world with him.

I've been thinking a lot lately about the parallels between Elvis and Ali. They grew out of the same soil, the segregated American south; one black and one white. Each had a magnetic personality. They were remarkably good-looking, albeit in different ways; instinctive showmen with an energy about them. They weren't deep thinkers; they did what they did.

Ali fought intuitively. Elvis sang intuitively. It was genius on each man's part. They were craftsman with remarkable natural gifts who honed their gifts in marvelous ways.

Elvis and Ali were curiosities, human-interest stories for a slow day in the newsroom, before they evolved into something more.

Then they became counterculture symbols; feared as Pied Pipers, who would lead their followers (young people for Elvis, black people for Ali) in rebellion against the establishment and the status quo.

They weren't trying to change the culture. They were simply doing what they wanted to do.

Over time, they became "safe"—benevolent monarchs in all their glory, sharing the bond of almost incomprehensible fame. Elvis was a global superstar unlike any who had come before him. Ali followed suit, rising to iconic status in his lifetime.

Finally, they got old and their dissolution made them even safer. Neither let his disability keep him out of the public eye.

I'm recognized as an authority on Muhammad Ali. I'm not an Elvis Presley scholar. But I lived through Elvis's rise and fall and grew up in a culture that was shaped in part by his music and persona. I decided recently that I wanted to write about Elvis.

Here goes.

I

Elvis Aaron Presley was born in Tupelo, Mississippi, on January 8, 1935. Franklin Roosevelt's "New Deal" was just coming into being. Social Security had not yet been enacted.

Elvis was an only child. His twin brother was stillborn. The family often found it difficult to make ends meet. "Poor we were," Vernon Presley (Elvis's father) acknowledged years later. "I'll never deny that. But trash, we weren't. We always had compassion for people. We never had any prejudice. We never put anybody down. Neither did Elvis."

Elvis's first love was gospel music. At age ten, he entered a singing contest at the Mississippi-Alabama Fair and Dairy Show. At twelve, he performed on a local radio show.

In 1948, the Presleys moved to Memphis, Tennessee. Elvis graduated from Humes High School in 1953. Classmates later described him as a loner. He wasn't about fitting in. He dressed and styled his hair differently from the other students. He was obsessed with music.

After graduation, Elvis took a job driving a truck and began studying to be an electrician. In August 1953, he went to a Memphis recording studio and, for four dollars, cut a two-sided record of *My Happiness* and *That's When Your Heartaches Begin* as a birthday present for his mother. The only accompaniment was his own primitive acoustic-guitar playing. He returned in January 1954 to cut another record. This time, Sam Phillips (owner of the studio and a record producer) was there.

In some ways, America's airwaves in 1954 were as segregated as other closed institutions. Mainstream radio stations wouldn't play "race music" by black recording artists. Phillips had once said, "If I could find a white man who had the Negro sound and the Negro feel, I could make a billion dollars."

Now he had found him.

Six months later, Phillips called Presley back to the studio and matched him with guitarist Scotty Moore and bass player Bill Black. Soon, Elvis's records were being played locally. Then they rippled through the south.

In the mid-1950s, the youth market in the United States was exploding as a separate economic entity. Families no longer sat around the living room listening to the radio together. Adolescents had their own radio in their own room and their own money to spend on records. Music was a common denominator among the young and a primary lifeline for the new youth culture.

Before long, the spirit of Elvis Presley was wafting through America.

In November 1955, Sam Phillips sold Presley's contract to RCA for the then-generous sum of $40,000. RCA released *Heartbreak Hotel* in January 1956. It was Elvis's first number 1 hit. That was followed by an LP album entitled *Elvis Presley*. Soon after, a record that paired "Don't Be Cruel" and "Hound Dog" rose to the top of the charts and stayed there for eleven weeks; a mark that would not be surpassed for thirty-six years.

At the same time, Elvis began performing outside the South; most notably, on a fifteen-city Midwest tour. More significantly, he was discovered by the exploding medium of television.

Elvis's first national TV exposure came on CBS's *Stage Show* in early 1956. That was followed by two appearances on *The Milton Berle Show* and one with Steve Allen. By mid-1956, he was receiving ten thousand fan letters a week.

Elvis had soulful eyes and a sensual voice. He wore his hair in a pompadour style that looked as though it had been made for him. At times, he curled his lip into a sneer, but always with a twinkle in his eye. The sneer was akin a secret smile; good-natured, not mean, part sexual come-on, part flaunting of authority.

There had been popular music stars before Elvis; most notably Rudy Vallee, Bing Crosby, and Frank Sinatra. But their performances had been highly stylized and controlled. Yes; women screamed when the young Sinatra sang. But he'd been cloaked in the elegance and glamour of the Tommy Dorsey band.

Popular music wasn't sexy before Elvis.

Elvis put sex (not love, sex) in the music. Sinatra whispered in your ear in the wee small hours of the morning. Elvis grabbed at your body with the lights on.

Before Elvis, singers were heard. Elvis was heard and seen. Gyrating, thrusting his hips. If he'd come along a decade later, his long hair and gyrations might have seemed unremarkable. But audiences in 1955 were accustomed to seeing some guy wearing a suit and tie sing, "M-o-o-o-n over Miami . . ."

Elvis onstage was like a force of nature. He was spontaneous. He let it all hang out. His music resonated. He never explained intellectually what he did or why. He just did it.

"You have to put on a show for the people," he said of his performing style. "People can buy your records and hear you sing. They don't have to come out and hear you. If I just stood out there and sang and never moved a muscle, the people would say, 'My goodness; I can stay home and listen to his records.'"

But it was more than that.

"I don't know where I picked up my style," Elvis acknowledged. "I just started out doing what I'm doing now. I do whatever I feel onstage. It's like a surge of electricity going through me. It's almost like making love, but it's even stronger than that. Sometimes I think my heart is going to explode."

The message in Elvis's music was simple. Express your emotions; do what you want; feel good about yourself; the world is yours.

"Presley, more than anyone else," it was later written, "gave the young a belief in themselves as a distinct and unified generation."

Adolescence is a time when boys and girls are developing their own artistic tastes and finding new dimensions within themselves. Before Elvis, there had been a hint of teen rebellion in the culture, personified by James Dean in *Rebel Without a Cause*. To young men and women who came of age in the mid-1950s, Elvis was something more.

At a certain age, liking the music is about being part of a group. Elvis was the group leader, brimming with promise and doing things that simply weren't allowed.

Sex is the most mysterious and exciting of unknowns for adolescent girls. Elvis was an adolescent girl's fantasy machine. He was a bad boy with an innocence about him; handsome, exciting, and safe at the same time. When the powers that be refused to show him from the waist down on television, the imagination kicked in. There's nothing more enticing to a girl entering puberty than forbidden fruit that her parents don't want her to see.

Girls dreamed about Elvis, literally. Boys thought he was cool. And identifying with Elvis was a good way for them to impress girls. They grew sideburns and let their hair grow long.

The first article about Elvis in a national magazine ran in April 1956 in *Life* (the premier general-interest magazine in the country at the time). It referenced him as a "howling hillbilly" and likened his gyrations to burlesque. That was in keeping with the view that his music was vulgar and had the potential to lead young people into sexually wanton conduct.

In May 1956, after Elvis performed in La Crosse, Wisconsin, the local Catholic diocese newspaper sent an "urgent" letter FBI director J. Edgar Hoover, warning, "Presley is a definite danger to the security of the United States. His actions and motions were such as to rouse the sexual passions of teenaged youth."

Three months later, when Elvis performed in Florida, Reverend Robert Gray told the congregation at Trinity Baptist Church in Jacksonville, "Elvis Presley has achieved a new low in spiritual degeneracy."

A local judge ordered Elvis to tone down his act. He responded by forsaking gyrations during the show but wiggling his little finger suggestively throughout.

However, sex wasn't the only perceived threat that Elvis posed. There was another theme, more ominous to some, lurking in the background.

Elvis was becoming the dominant symbol of a new form of music: rock and roll. Rock and roll, especially the way he sang it, played into issues of race.

There were no black entertainment icons in America in the mid-1950s. Elvis fused black and white music in his art; blending country music, gospel, and rhythm-and-blues. He was a white man who "sang black," creating his own form of expression and bringing it into the mainstream of American culture.

He was blurring the lines between the races, and also opening a door that would allow black men and women to become crossover stars.

"Elvis was a blessing," Richard Penniman (better known as "Little Richard") said years later. "They wouldn't let black music through. He opened the door for black music."

Then Elvis got bigger.

Within the entertainment industry, *The Ed Sullivan Show* was the most influential television program in America. Sullivan was stung by the fact that, for the first time ever, rival Steve Allen had drawn a higher rating than he had. Allen's featured attraction that night had been Elvis Presley.

In response, Sullivan booked Presley for three appearances. The first, on September 9, 1956, was seen by sixty million viewers; a mind-boggling 82.6 percent of the television-viewing audience. Performances on October 28, 1956, and January 21, 1957, drew comparable numbers.

Millions of Americans who were young at the time still remember where they were when Elvis appeared on *The Ed Sullivan Show*. It had been decreed that camera angles would be such that the most provocative of his gyrations would not be shown. He also toned his act down for the shows. At the close of his third appearance, Sullivan assured the country that this was "a real decent fine boy."

Elvis's appearances on *The Ed Sullivan Show* boosted his celebrity status to unprecedented proportions. He was a tidal wave washing over American culture. There had never been a phenomenon like him. Then he added Hollywood to his credits, appearing in a feature film entitled *Love Me Tender*.

Ironically, in many ways, Elvis represented conservative American values. He revered his mother. He was a Southern Baptist. All he wanted to do, really, was sing, buy a car, and make money.

Press conferences were awkward affairs. Off-stage, Elvis was polite and a bit shy. When called upon to speak publicly, he struggled with his words and never knew quite what to say apart from platitudes about loving whatever city he was in and appreciating the opportunity to perform before a live audience.

"I don't like to be called 'Elvis, the Pelvis,'" he told a radio interviewer in Florida. "It's one of the most childish expressions I've ever heard coming from an adult. But if they want to call me that, there's nothing I can do about it."

Asked about rock and roll, he replied, "Rock and roll has been in for about five years. I'm not going to say that it's gonna last, because I don't know. All I can say is, it's good; the people like it; it's selling; and I enjoy doing it."

Then Elvis's world was turned upside down. He was drafted and, on March 24, 1958, inducted into the United States Army. The haircut he received at the start of basic training was as symbolic as any shearing ever. The old culture had asserted itself.

A more debilitating blow followed. In August 1958, Elvis's mother fell gravely ill. He was granted an emergency leave to visit her. Two days after he arrived in Memphis, Gladys Presley died. She was forty-six years old.

Elvis lost his center when his mother died. As she lay in an open coffin at Graceland, he stroked her face again and again, saying, "Wake up, mama. Wake up, baby, and talk to Elvis." He had to be restrained from climbing on top of her coffin when she was laid in the grave. He came close to a complete emotional breakdown. There was inconsolable extended grieving.

"He changed completely," Lillian Mann Smith (Elvis's aunt) said years later. "He didn't seem like Elvis ever again."

For most of his time in the military, Presley was stationed with the Third Armored Division in West Germany. He was honorably discharged on March 5, 1960. Two months later, he was on a television variety show again; this time as the featured guest on *The Frank Sinatra Timex Special*.

Several years earlier, Sinatra had belittled Elvis as utterly lacking in talent. Now the two men, each wearing a tuxedo, stood side by side. Sinatra (looking uncomfortable) sang *Love Me Tender.* Elvis (without sideburns) sang *Witchcraft,* one of his host's signature songs.

Two-thirds of Americans watching television that night watched *The Frank Sinatra Timex Special.* Elvis was back. But the rebellious rock-and-roll figure had died.

II

On January 17, 1942, six years before the Presleys moved to Memphis, Cassius Marcellus Clay Jr was born in Louisville, Kentucky.

Kentucky was a Jim Crow state. Segregated facilities were mandated by law. In parts of the country at that time, blacks were denied the right to vote and it was a crime punishable by ten years in prison for a black and white to intermarry. Major league baseball ("America's national pastime") had yet to open its doors to Jackie Robinson.

In some respects, Cassius Clay was very much like Elvis. He adored his mother. He was a Southern Baptist, who said "yes, sir" and "no, sir." He wanted to make money and own a red Cadillac convertible. He was remarkably telegenic, photogenic, and charismatic. One can argue that he and Elvis had two of the prettiest smiles ever.

Elvis's art was singing. Clay's was fighting. Each was an entertainer. Elvis's performances were scripted and safe. Clay's world was more brutal. He put his physical well-being on the line every time he entered the ring.

Like Elvis, Cassius was obsessed with his art when he was young and had a rhythm all his own.

Older generations had condemned Elvis, saying, "He wouldn't have to jump around and shake his hips like that if he could sing." Older generations condemned Clay's ring style, saying, "He wouldn't have to dance around like that if he could fight."

On November 22, 1963, John Kennedy was assassinated in Dallas. On February 9, 1964, the Beatles made their American television debut on *The Ed Sullivan Show* (drawing 73,000,000 viewers). Sixteen days after that, Cassius Clay knocked out Sonny Liston to claim the most coveted title in sports, the heavyweight championship of the world.

"The Sixties" had begun.

Two days after defeating Liston, Clay announced that he had accepted the teachings of a black separatist religion known as the Nation of Islam.

On March 6, 1964, he took the name "Muhammad Ali," which was given to him by his spiritual mentor, Elijah Muhammad. On February 17, 1966, he was reclassified 1-A (eligible for the military draft) by the Selective Service System and uttered the now immortal words, "I ain't got no quarrel with them Vietcong."

Elvis's followers had expected him to go into the military. He would have lost their love and respect if he hadn't.

The Nation of Islam had different expectations with regard to Ali. On April 28, 1967, citing his religious beliefs, he refused induction into the United States Army.

Elvis had set music free in America and fit into the spirit of, "What would it be like to be free of my parents' rules?"

Like Elvis, Ali was about personal freedom. But he was meeting issues of racism head-on and asking, "What would it be like to be free of society's rules?"

Ali was perceived by the establishment as being even more dangerous than Elvis had been.

Meanwhile, popular culture was passing Elvis by. By the time he was discharged from the Army, rock and roll was in full bloom and evolving at the speed of sound. By 1964, the Beatles were dominating pop culture the way that Elvis had a mere eight years earlier. Mick Jagger did everything onstage that Elvis had done (and more). Bob Dylan freed music with lyrics that were as different and daring as Elvis's gyrations had been. Elvis's music, which had been socially relevant in the 1950s, wasn't anymore.

Elvis's manager, Colonel Tom Parker (as he liked to be called), contributed to the decline. Parker (who had been born in Holland and whose real name was Andreas Cornelis Van Kuijk) had an overbearing manner and managed to extract an exorbitant percent of Elvis's earnings for himself.

As soon as Elvis was discharged from the Army, Parker locked him into a series of Hollywood movie contracts that lasted for the better part of a decade. During that time, Elvis starred in twenty-seven films in which the character he played was always a thinly veiled version of himself regardless of the role.

James Dean had been one of Elvis's boyhood heroes. Elvis wanted to be a serious actor. With good training and better roles, he might have become one. Instead, he was mired in a string of low-budget musicals that were profitable but critically panned. The soundtracks had a formulaic assembly-line quality. The Beatles were conquering the world, and he was in films like *Tickle Me* and *Harum Scarum*.

Ali would lose three years of his ring career because of his refusal to accept induction into the United States Army. Elvis wasted a decade his life making bad Hollywood movies.

"I'd like to make better films than the films I made before," he said ruefully when the run was over. "I didn't have final approval of the script, which means I couldn't say, 'This is not good for me.' I don't think anyone was consciously trying to harm me. It was just, Hollywood's image of me was wrong, and I knew it and I couldn't do anything about it. The pictures got very similar. Something was successful and they'd try to recreate it the next time around. I'd read the first four or five pages, and I'd know it was just a different name with twelve new songs in it. It worried me sick. I didn't know what to do. I was obligated a lot of times very heavily to things I didn't believe in and it was very difficult. I had thought they would get a property for me and give me a chance show some acting ability, but it did not change. I became very discouraged. I would have liked to have something more challenging instead of Hollywood's image of what they thought I was."

Then Elvis's world turned again; this time for the better.

In 1968, America was in turmoil. Martin Luther King Jr and Robert Kennedy were assassinated. The anti-war movement was in full bloom. Mayor Daley's police rioted at the Democratic National Convention in Chicago. A new drug culture was sweeping the country.

On December 3, 1968, NBC aired its highest-rated show of the year. It's now known as "The Comeback Special." At the time, it was titled *Elvis*.

The show mixed a handful of elaborately produced studio numbers with songs performed in an intimate setting before a small live audience. Elvis wore black leather, looked good, and sang well. It was his first "live" performance since 1961. A whole new generation took notice and said, "Hey! This guy is pretty cool." And for those who had been young in the 1950s, Elvis was back.

Five months after Elvis's comeback special, the International Hotel (soon to be acquired by Hilton) announced that it had signed him to perform fifty-seven shows over a four-week period in Las Vegas for the then-astronomical sum of $500,000.

Thirteen years earlier, in April 1956, a young Elvis Presley had unsuccessfully played the New Frontier Hotel in Las Vegas. The audience had been unimpressed. A reviewer for the *Las Vegas Sun* wrote at the time, "For the teen-agers, the long tall Memphis lad is a whiz. For the average Vegas spender or showgoer, a bore. His musical sound with a combo of three is uncouth, matching to a great extent the lyric content of his nonsensical songs."

Times change.

Elvis opened at The International on July 31, 1969. The next day, the hotel extended his contract to provide for eight weeks of performances annually (in February and August) over a five-year period. His salary would be one million dollars a year.

Elvis and Ali met twice in Las Vegas. The first time, Muhammad saw him onstage and they chatted briefly afterward. "All my life, I admired Elvis," Ali said years later. "It was a thrill to meet him."

Their second meeting, in February 1973, was more consequential.

Ali was less threatening to the establishment by then. He'd been stripped of his championship and denied a license to box after refusing induction into the United States Army. After three years in exile, he was allowed by court order to fight again, but had lost to Joe Frazier in "The Fight of the Century." His rematches with Frazier and triumphant battle against George Foreman in Zaire to reclaim the heavyweight crown were yet to come. Ali's adversaries had exploited his vulnerabilities and seemed to have beaten him down.

From time to time, Elvis's life had intersected with the sweet science. He tried out for his high school boxing team, but quit the first day after suffering a bloody nose. Later, in the 1962 movie *Kid Galahad,* he'd played a professional fighter.

On February 14, 1973, Ali fought Joe Bugner at the Las Vegas Convention Center. Prior to the bout, he and Elvis met in a hotel suite and Elvis presented him with a faux-jewel-studded robe emblazoned with the words "The People's Champion." Ali wore the robe that night and beat Bugner.

The Las Vegas years are an important part of Elvis's legacy. The city's dream machine revived him and gave him new life as a superstar. Soon, he was performing around the country again.

"The most important thing is the inspiration I get from a live audience," Elvis said in Houston before a 1970 engagement at The Astrodome. "I was missing that."

Time and again, he elaborated on that theme: "A live concert to me is exciting because of all the electricity that's generated in the crowd and onstage. It's my favorite part of the business . . . I missed the closeness of a live audience. So as soon as I got out of the movie contract, I decided to play live concerts again . . . It's a good feeling. There's a new audience each time. What's interesting about music and all the people here [his back-up musicians] is, they find new sounds and they do things differently themselves; so it's like a new experience every day."

Elvis was appearing onstage more often now than ever before. In 1973, there were 168 concert performances; the most notable of them at the Honolulu International Center in Hawaii.

Aloha Hawaii was taped in January and aired in the United States on April 4, 1973, capturing 57 percent of the viewing audience. More significantly, it was transmitted by satellite to thirty-six countries around the world.

Meanwhile, Ali was experiencing a rebirth of his own. In 1974, he dethroned George Foreman to regain the heavyweight championship of the world. Then he abandoned the separatist teachings of the Nation of Islam and, while still a devout Muslim, embraced the philosophy that hearts and souls know no color.

Ali's kingdom was now the world. And Elvis had become a symbol larger than himself; the quintessential larger-than-life celebrity rock star. He was an Elvis; the only one of its kind.

Only a select few people have ever experienced what Elvis and Ali came to experience in the mid-1970s. They were icons of the highest order, universal royalty, instantly recognizable around the globe.

Ali loved being king. But Elvis couldn't ride the wave and seemed burdened by the crown.

There are people the spotlight never turns away from. Wherever they go, they can never be anonymous. These people either give in to their fame and embrace it (in the manner of Ali); manage their fame by setting strict boundaries; or it devours them.

Ali embraced his fame, gave himself completely to the public, and mingled joyously with them. People who met Ali one-on-one loved him more afterward. If Ali was feeling low, he could walk down the street and cause a traffic jam by hugging people and signing autographs to lift his spirits.

For Elvis, that was the stuff of nightmares. Fame was a trap that he couldn't escape. He was oppressed by it. He cut himself off from the public and lived largely in seclusion.

"I felt sorry for Elvis," Ali said a decade after Presley's death. "He didn't enjoy life the way he should. He stayed indoors all the time. I told him he should go out and see people. He said he couldn't because, everywhere he went, they mobbed him. He didn't understand. No one wanted to hurt him. All they wanted was to be friendly and tell him how much they loved him."

In many ways, fame is a stronger test of character than adversity. People act obsequiously and pay homage to the famous. Ali had the fact that he was black and people were throwing punches at him to remind him of life's harsh realities. Also, Ali had something much larger than himself—his religion—to flow into.

Elvis had music, which was his means of expression. But it wasn't enough. His fantasies had come to fruition when he was twenty-one years old. After that, what was left? In his orbit, everything was about him. He was surrounded by a tight coterie of enablers who indulged his every whim, never held him to the standards of accountability that apply to most men and women, and lived off him. But he had a fragile psyche and never found a calm center. He grew older but not wiser. He lost his way.

Ali was more comfortable with who he was than Elvis was. He was at peace with himself. And he was stronger at his core.

Where Elvis's "real-life" interaction with women is concerned, one can speculate that the happiest relationship he enjoyed was with Ann-Margret (his co-star in the 1963 film *Viva Las Vegas*).

He married once.

Elvis and Priscilla Beaulieu met in 1959. Her father was a United States Air Force officer serving in Germany. Elvis was twenty-four years old; she was fourteen. They were married eight years later. On February 1, 1968, nine months to the day after their wedding, their only child (Lisa Marie) was born.

Elvis pushed Priscilla away sexually after the birth of their daughter. That and his profligate womanizing led to an affair on her part. Soon after Christmas 1971, she told him that she wanted a divorce. Their marriage was formally dissolved on October 9, 1973.

One can speculate based on anecdotal evidence that Elvis was an unsophisticated lover. He was more comfortable cuddling and kissing than he was making love. After Priscilla left him, the women who stayed in his life for any length of time moved quickly from sexual object to caretaker.

As the 1970s progressed, things got worse. Elvis had looked like he was having so much fun when he was young, particularly onstage. Then the fun came to an end and it seemed as though life was an ordeal.

After the *Aloha Hawaii* special, his weight burgeoned out of control. Worse, he became increasingly dependent on prescription drugs.

Elvis had begun self-medicating heavily long before his marriage ended. The drug use increased after he and Priscilla separated. He took pills and overate because he was depressed. He took pills and overate because he was bored. He took pills and overate because he was nervous. He took pills to help him sleep at night, to start his day (which often began in mid-afternoon), to raise his energy level to perform, and to calm down afterward.

In October 1973, Elvis was hospitalized in semicomatose condition after receiving excessive injections of Demerol. He was nursed back to health, then relapsed. In 1974, he added cocaine to his drug habits.

It had always been hard to imagine Elvis Presley doing anything normally. During the last few years of his life, his mood swings became more and more pronounced and he was increasingly out of control.

He was reclusive but, at the same time, afraid to be left completely alone.

He acted petulantly toward those around him; then sought to regain their affection by lavishing gifts upon them. On a single day (July 27, 1975), he bought and gave away thirteen Cadillacs.

The drugs interfered with his sex life, which was reduced at times to having women wearing white panties parade in front of him.

He shot at television sets and fired his gun into ceilings and walls.

There were times when he fell asleep with his mouth full of food.

He was still surrounded by enablers, who gave him whatever was necessary to maintain their favored position. But like Humpty-Dumpty,

Elvis had suffered a great fall. There was no way that all the king's horses and all the king's men could put him back together again.

He had lost his dignity and self-respect. He was dangerously depressed. Each day when he woke up and looked in the mirror, he was reminded of what he'd become. His famous hair had begun to thin. He underwent cosmetic surgery around his eyes in an effort to conceal the ravages of drug abuse. There was an emptiness inside that he couldn't fill. He needed an emotional center to stabilize his life, and it wasn't there.

Yet through it all, Elvis kept performing. He needed the adulation that he received from his adoring fans. He wanted to give of himself and make them happy. And he still loved music. It was the only anchor that he had in his life. Without music, he was nothing.

For the most part, the reviewers were kind. But a few of them incorporated hard truths in their critiques.

After Elvis returned to the International Hilton in August 1973, the *Hollywood Reporter* declared, "It's Elvis at his most indifferent, uninterested, and unappealing. He's not just a little out of shape, not just a little chubbier than usual. The Living Legend is fat and ludicrously aping his former self. His voiced was thin, uncertain, and strained. His personality was lost in one of the most ill-prepared, unsteady, most disheartening performances of his Las Vegas career. It is a tragedy and absolutely depressing to see Elvis in such diminishing stature."

That was followed by a two-week engagement in Lake Tahoe. A review in *Variety* noted that Elvis was "thirty pounds overweight" (a kind estimate) and observed, "He's puffy, white-faced, and blinking against the light. The voice sounds weak; delivery is flabby. Attempts to perpetuate his mystique of sex and power end in weak self-parody."

The last four days of the Lake Tahoe engagement were cancelled.

Elvis onstage in the 1950s had been uninhibited. Elvis onstage in the 1970s was increasingly out of control. There were times when he seemed like an Elvis impersonator; lumbering around, engaging in rambling monologues that were all but impossible to understand. Sometimes he forgot the words to songs he'd sung a thousand times. There were moments when he seemed perilously close to having a psychiatric breakdown in front his audience. Or maybe he was having one.

Yet he remained a viable ticket-seller, performing before overflow crowds in huge arenas until the end. He was obese and drugged out. He was a heart attack waiting to happen. But he was still Elvis Presley, and still capable of isolated moments of extraordinary performance art.

Elvis had a beautiful voice and had learned to use it well. In some respects, his celebrity status overshadowed his talent. Throughout his career, he captured the emotional import of his songs. He understood intuitively what worked musically and what didn't. He was passionate about his music and sang from the heart.

When he was young, his music was characterized by sexual energy and excitement. As he aged, it was more about showing off the range of his voice and how long he could hold a note. But his singing also became more powerful. He could sell a ballad. He began to tell stories—often about sadness and regret—and give deeper meaning to the lyrics. He could sing anything.

But by June 1977, when his final tour began, Elvis could barely perform. There was nothing left in him anymore. He died at Graceland on August 16, 1977. Fourteen drugs were found in his system; ten of them in significant quantities. The assumption is that "polypharmacy" was the primary cause of death.

He was an old forty-two when he died.

As Elvis was sliding toward the precipice, Ali was also in decline. Like Elvis, he was in a profession where it's hard to age gracefully. But if Ali had a bad night, he paid for it with a beating.

The damage to Elvis's health had been self-administered. The damage to Ali was inflicted by others. The punishment he took began to mount. Against Joe Frazier in Manila in 1975; at Madison Square Garden against Earnie Shavers seven weeks after Elvis died; in Las Vegas in 1980 at the hands of Larry Holmes.

Elvis had paid an emotional price for his greatness. For Ali, the cost was physical. The ravages of Parkinsonism turned his face into a mask and restricted his movements as surely as Elvis had been diminished.

Time goes by. Thirty-four years have passed since Elvis died. He's still a cultural force. His music remains popular. Thousands of entertainers around the globe dress up as Elvis impersonators and groom themselves in a certain way in an effort to imitate his performances. No other star, past or present, has that sort of following.

The entertainment conglomerate CKX now controls Elvis's name, likeness, and image for commercial purposes. It also manages Graceland.

Six hundred thousand fans make the pilgrimage to the mansion on Elvis Presley Boulevard in Memphis each year.

CKX has also acquired a controlling interest in Ali's name, likeness, and image for commercial purposes. But to date, Elvis has been a more profitable marketing venture.

Elvis and Ali were passionate men who inspired passion in others. They grew up in humble surroundings and dreamed of being more than it was thought they could possibly be.

Each man impacted most significantly on society when he was young. Elvis, before he went in the Army; Ali, before his exile from boxing.

Elvis in the Las Vegas years gave pleasure to the people who saw him sing, but he was no longer an important social force. The acceptance of Ali as a beloved monarch marked an important turn for American society. But he was no longer setting the world ablaze.

Neither man set out to be the leader of a movement. They were just doing their thing. But each was an agent of change.

Elvis was a precursor of the sexual revolution and a transitional figure who brought black music into the mainstream of American culture. He was the standard-bearer for, and one of the founding fathers of, rock and roll. Like Frank Sinatra, he defined his genre.

Elvis's legacy is as an entertainer. He was about the music. He shied away from political issues. When asked to comment on anti-war protests at the height of the war in Vietnam, he responded, "I'd just as soon keep my own personal views about that to myself. I'm just an entertainer."

"Do you think other entertainers should keep their views to themselves too?" the questioner pressed.

"No; I can't say that," Elvis answered.

By contrast, Ali has two legacies; as an athlete and as a moral force. Elvis was a superstar. Ali was a superstar and a hero, who fit into the two great moral crusades of the 1960s (the civil rights and anti-war movements). For most of his adult life, he sought to use his fame to make the world a better place. He wanted to advance the cause of racial justice and world peace. His work had social, political, and religious implications.

The day after beating Sonny Liston, Cassius Clay told the media (and by extension, the American power structure), "I don't have to be what you want me to be. I'm free to be what I want."

Elvis exploded on the national scene in the same manner. But while Ali stayed true to that creed, Elvis didn't. Ali's greatness in and out of the ring sprang from personal courage. That quality was less evident in Elvis's life. In the end, he seemed intent on trying to be what his fans wanted him to be.

That said; singing is no less real than fighting. Ali earned universal recognition as a great fighter. Elvis was an amazing talent who brought joy to a lot of people and, like Ali, changed the way his art was practiced. They didn't just mirror the culture they lived in. They helped shape it.

And they were so good when they were young.